Perpetual Motion

An Autobiography Of Relative History

D. A. Pitts

Introduction by Dave Brosha

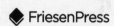

FriesenPress

One Printers Way
Altona, MB R0G 0B0
Canada

www.friesenpress.com

Copyright © 2024 by D. A. Pitts
First Edition — 2024

All rights reserved.

No part of this publication may be reproduced in any form, or by any means, electronic or mechanical, including photocopying, recording, or any information browsing, storage, or retrieval system, without permission in writing from FriesenPress.

Photo acknowledgments:
Front and back cover: D.A. Pitts, Author
Author Image: Ian Proctor Photography

ISBN
978-1-03-830658-6 (Hardcover)
978-1-03-830657-9 (Paperback)
978-1-03-830659-3 (eBook)

1. BIOGRAPHY & AUTOBIOGRAPHY, PERSONAL MEMOIRS

Distributed to the trade by The Ingram Book Company

Carole + Verne...
Thanks for your friendship... always!
Dana

Perpetual Motion

To My Grandchildren

Whether we know it or not we have reasons to write,
History was founded on this.
For my grandchildren's lore,
My words are preserved,
The stories that no one should miss.

The teachings I've penned,
The life lessons I've learned,
Given freely—all wrapped in a wish,
Scribed in a way that comes from my heart,
All bound and sealed with a kiss.

Leena Catherine-Anne, Noelle Mary-Anne, Lochlan Shaun, Mila Yasmin, and Sloane Mara, you are my inspiration and guiding light each and every day. I wish you love and bliss.

Forever,

Papa

Introduction

Heirlooms we don't have in our family.
But stories we've got. —Rose Cherin

We humans are given a gift that the many bountiful creatures we share this planet with don't get—we have the ability to pass down stories—to record events—to document—to snap photographs, and to put words to paper. We have the ability to pass down family histories, legends, lies, and folklore. We can record what has happened—or at least our various interpretations of those moments. We can do it in a very no-nonsense, clinical way—or we can do it with flair, pizzazz, and pop.

We have that gift.

For centuries upon centuries, we have used that gift. Dates etched in dust-covered notebooks. Old and yellowed photographs with curled edges, tucked into albums that are then tucked into shelves or boxes—often forgotten about but occasionally pulled out and shared over smiles and a splash of a treasured fiery liquid. Scrolls, tablets, and Word documents. Stories shared around campfires, and kitchen tables. History, passed from one person to another—one generation to another.

Proof of our existence.

What is shared, in whatever form it is shared, has importance. The ability to know where we, collectively, come from—is paramount. It gives meaning to a life—a series of seemingly endless and scattered moments. It can help string these moments together and give a person a sense of collective identity. It can help us know who we are and where we came from.

One of the problems with lives lived however, is that they happen in but a flash. Time is a pool with endless depths, and the ripples we make as individual humans barely make a tremor in the infinite mass. Many tremors occur, slowly dissipate into smaller and smaller vibrations, and eventually fade—with little proof that the event ever happened.

The thought of a life passing without some degree of recording who that person was—what they liked, where and how they lived, what they were proud of, and what made them laugh—has always bothered me. There are too many entries in my own family tree that are nothing more than two simple dates. X was born on this date. X died on this date.

Start and finish.

But what about the in-between? Isn't that the most important? Isn't that the delicious bit of our existence? The apple pie filling?

Fortunately, we have people in this world who understand the importance of capturing story, presence, and life—people that understand words and memories matter. Dana Pitts is one of them, walking the world with a sparkle in his eye, and a passion for the beautiful nuances of experience that time and place offer each and every one of us. I've known Dana for the better part of two decades, and as much as I thought I knew who Dana was, I, of course, didn't know his fuller story. His collection of happenstances. The bits and pieces that give way to personality, and the external-facing presentation of who he is. I've known him as a fun-loving, kind, and helpful man. A friend. Although I knew, of course, that he must have endured struggle, as all humans do, he doesn't present himself with any degree of "poor me." Rather, he presents himself as a lover of life, with a mischievous glint, and a passion for his many hobbies, friends, and family. There's something special, for me, in piecing together the fragments that have made Dana who he is. There's something special in learning about someone's story.

Dana writes with an eye for detail and an obvious zest for life. He embraces his own narrative and is unapologetic in the telling of it. He tells of his follies and his life lessons. Moments of sadness, moments of regret, and moments of magic.

This book stands as a testament to the power of stories. Dana realizes the importance of capturing moments—both big and small—in figuring out not only his own history but the greater timeline of those family and friends around him. He has researched dates, sought out the missing gaps in his own (incredible) memory, and added colour and polish to the existence of his loved ones—all carefully documented through this autobiography. This is the work of a self-described "history buff," and *Perpetual Motion* will take a proud place on, not only the shelves of his own very large family, but on the shelves of those who have been blessed with a copy. It's a personal record, and it's the whole apple pie.

His memories recount everything from relatable and regrettable youth (freezing his tongue to schoolyard steel), the contradictory lightness and weight of young romance, his love of music, tales of petty theft, and eventual redemption as a firefighter, bravely putting himself in danger where many others would walk away. He recounts, with obvious love, stories of his children and grandchildren. How he navigated career and loss. A sometimes nomadic existence. Retirement and hobbies. In short, this is a tapestry—with many fine threads.

I have a memory of Dana that I love—one that speaks to his tenacity. I know Dana most intimately from his relatively new rediscovery of photography. A workshop that he took with me in Cape Breton sparked an eventual friendship. This workshop led to others, and in time, I found myself in Scotland with Dana, wandering around the idyllic beauty of the Isle of Skye. We had a group hike planned to a famous attraction called The Old Man of Storr—a towering pinnacle of imposing basalt rock up a steady and strenuous incline.

Dana wasn't the best physically, that day. He was coming off injury and the long road of recovery, but he was determined to complete the hike. After a collective effort to ascend the large hill leading up to the "Old Man," I wandered around checking in on the various workshop participants. Eventually, I happened upon Dana sitting on a rock. Despite his obvious pain—which I had witnessed throughout the hike, he was sitting there with a smile and a faraway look in his eyes. "I did it," he said. I was the only one in the vicinity—but he wasn't talking to me. He was celebrating, for himself.

Yes, Dana, you did. Just as you did this—this beautiful retelling of your life. You should be proud, not only of these words, but knowing you might inspire others to do the same—so they may capture and document their own story.

We are more than dates of creation and expiration. We live lives full of good and bad, joy and pain, triumphs and setbacks, laughter, tears, and beauty—even in the struggles. Knowing more about the lives that are important to us—whether it be a friend, a family member, or a stranger—can only make us richer. Stories make us richer. I know you'll enjoy this one.

Dave

Preface

It was in the early days of winter, that January of 2018. A cold blast of Arctic air enveloped me like an invisible tsunami. I was still in the Great White North, just over the Canada/USA border, house-sitting for some friends while they suffered through another extended heat wave at their vacation home in South Florida. The winter before, I had experienced the same, spending six months in the southern sunshine, so I knew of what hardships they would endure. I also knew it was time. I had been procrastinating the fulfillment of a dream for several months, and now having the time and the space to scratch that itch, I pressed the power button on my laptop. Given the convergence of my current living arrangements, no urge to leave the den, and bathed in the warmth of the glowing fire, it seemed like the right moment to begin my story.

So, how did I get here? Truth be known, I have contemplated many times in the past few years about the way seemingly ordinary events—big and small—shape the eventual path we travel, and how those twists and turns create a legacy, defining one's existence. Throughout this book, you will be introduced to many of those incidents and events—seemingly random at first, but in the end uniting to define a life only I had the privilege to live—a journey only I had the privilege to take, and memories only I had the privilege to make.

During many conversations with my siblings, we talked about wishing our grandparents—and for that matter our parents—had written down snippets of their lives so we could better understand the history of our clan. Yes, we talked to them about it, and yes, some of it was haphazardly recorded, but if I really thought about it, did I ever ask them what their favourite song was? And if they did tell me, why couldn't I remember the reasons it was so special to them. Get the picture?

So, before we go any further, my favourite song is "Time of the Season" by the British rock band, The Zombies—released in 1968. It just brings back great memories of youthful experiences.

Being a history buff, and knowing how important the yesteryear record is to future generations, the reason for penning my biography became clear. My friends and family—especially my grandchildren—would not be denied the chronicles of my time spent on this planet. I knew I had a story to tell, and if what I had to say truly was to become my legacy, then something needed to be done about it now. I was definitely going to scratch that itch.

As I wrote, I realized I had so much more to say. It soon became a labour of love. I have included—among many other things—intimate details of how local influences, coupled with world events, shaped me while growing up in the last half of the twentieth century and beyond. All of this was carefully written with a smattering of the history behind the words, and the many lessons I've learned included for good measure. The end result—you will witness—is a time capsule of my life in perpetual motion.

So, for all of you about to embark on this journey with me, welcome! If you didn't know me before, you certainly will soon understand why my book title is so apropos. For those who think they know me, there is much to be learned. Either way, you're in for a ride!

And now—being so fortunate to have completed my passion project, I want you to sit back and enjoy the shenanigans as described herein. Who knows, some of you just might see your name in print!

I know our leisure time is precious, and I hope each of you reading my story finds value in the time you have committed to discovering a little about me. I certainly value the effort it took to pen this book. I derived so much enjoyment writing it for you by keeping it all as real as my memory serves. Where questions become inevitable, it will be up to you—if interested—to delve into further research.

Dana
Currently–Milford, Nova Scotia

PART 1

1. Off to a Shaky Start: A Premature Departure Averted

Neil Alden Armstrong was born in Wapakoneta, OH on August 5th, 1930. He would celebrate his twenty-sixth birthday on the day I was born. Mr. Armstrong would go on to become the very first human to set foot on another planetary body—the moon—in July of 1969. He was, at that time, thirty-eight years old, and the most famous person born on that date. I believe he still is.

I, on the other hand—Dana Augustine Pitts—came into this world on a cloudless Sunday morning, August 5th, 1956, the fourth child of my parents, Helen Marie Boyle and Maurice Bernard Pitts. It was at Saint Martha's Hospital in Antigonish, Nova Scotia at about 9:30 a.m. that Mom and Dad's family of five grew by one more. My older siblings, Barbara Lorraine, Karen Ann, and my big brother, Brian Gregory were just toddlers at the time. My grand entrance gave Mom and Dad four children under the age of five. Little did anyone know at the time, there would be many more mouths to feed by the time their childbearing days were over! Later chapters will attest to that.

By all accounts and according to my family, I was a happy child. Certainly for me, it was a carefree time living with my siblings in Tracadie, NS in a little white house overlooking Tracadie Harbour. Dad's Place—as it has become known—was constructed solely by his tireless hands, high on a hill adjacent to his parents' homestead. Often, he would tell us he picked this spot for the beautiful vistas which surrounded the property. At the time of my arrival, the house was not yet complete—there was no running water and no washroom in our little mansion on the hill. The outhouse would serve its one and only purpose for several months to come, as the space intended for the indoor facilities was being utilized as a small bedroom for me.

Dad's mother and father were Rose and Martin Pitts. We called them Nanny and Gampy. They lived a stone's throw from us, just across the meadow. My grandparents, so active in their youth, seemed to be always on the go. Stories of them tap dancing the night away, or enjoying some ten-pin bowling, showed us their enthusiasm for life. I remember in later years they were always dressed in their finest—Nanny in a floral, three-quarter-length dress, and Gampy in his dark suit and tie, his black dress shoes shining so bright we could use them as a mirror.

I have no recollection of those early times, being just a baby, but in the years that followed, I have many memories of staying at their house over the course of different summers—the wild blueberry patches up the hill and the cherry trees in the orchard out front of the house, both fruits turned into delicious pies. The fish/meat monger pulling into the driveway every Saturday morning—a selection of fresh seafood or chunks of beef at the ready—we ate well.

Nanny was as fine a baker as there ever was—making bread, buttermilk biscuits, and many delicious desserts every day. She would stand at the kitchen counter, open the giant built-in flour bin, scoop the freshly milled flour onto her work surface, and get to work on so many scrumptious treats. Gampy was a conductor on the railroad his whole life until he passed away from cancer at the age of sixty-three.

But I digress. It didn't take long before I was no longer the baby. A year after my arrival, and shortly after the water closet was completed, little sister Joan Marie was born in August of 1957. She added so much more love and happiness to our growing brood. This poor child—as the truth comes out—would eventually be the recipient of some rough-housing by yours truly. I'm so sorry, Joan (this being the first of many written apologies).

As much as I'm sure there are many stories from that idyllic time that could be retold here, I, of course, was too young to remember any of them, and have had to rely on the recollections of my family, and even at times, my aunts, uncles, and cousins.

Firstly, all the verbal storytelling by my relatives over the years has informed me that I was a rambunctious kid—being active to the point of somehow developing a hernia. I needed immediate surgery and spent some time back at Saint Martha's Hospital.

Next, and the most significant of those retold tales involving me, is the widely accepted fact that my grandmother saved my life when I was just two years old. Just imagine, if things had turned out differently, this story and all my future offspring would not exist. As the story goes, as told by Nanny several times and reiterated by Mom, I was nestled in my high chair eating an orange and somehow got hold of a piece of the rind. Into my mouth it went. I attempted to swallow it but unfortunately the sizeable chunk didn't make it all the way down—somehow getting lodged in my windpipe. I commenced choking. My dad's first cousin, Catherine Ann, was babysitting the gang. In a panic, she first attempted to remove the orange peel from my throat, to no avail. I was starting to turn blue. Leaving the other kids alone, she grabbed me and ran like the wind across the field in search of some help.

Nanny heard the commotion, and after trying to understand my hysterical cousin's explanation, came to the rescue. Throwing caution to the wind, she literally reached her fingers down into my tiny throat and pulled the orange peel free. As we now know, that action could have had dire consequences by pushing the object further into the windpipe, but as they have stated, some divine intervention happened, so I am here today because of the heroic actions of my grandmother. Thank you, Nanny!

2. Sarnia: Where's That?

If I could have formed the thought this early on, I would have lamented that not much else of significance could possibly go awry—as it turned out, I was wrong. Due to lack of work, Dad had to travel afar, eventually to a place called Sarnia in the province of Ontario, to find meaningful employment. His trade as a finish carpenter was just not providing enough to feed his growing family. He had chosen this beautiful town on the shores of Lake Huron because his brother, Tony, had moved there the previous year after finding work as an electrician. Dad arrived a few months later and, after a few false starts, finally landed a job with a flooring company. Joe Meneghin, the proprietor of Hutchison's Quality Floors, must have seen something special in this young East Coaster, and hired him on as an apprentice. Having no previous experience but being a hands-on, talented guy, Dad quickly got the hang of it. Within a year, he called for the family to move west.

Ironically, years later—somewhere around 2018—I ran into Joe Meneghin's daughter, Sandy, and we had a great conversation about our dad's enduring friendship over the years—I might have even shed a tear or two.

Dad made his way back to Tracadie and, after taking care of the family affairs, boarded the train at the station in Monastery with Mom and the four of us for the long ride back to Ontario. We embarked on what would be my very first travel adventure. Now of course, I was just shy of my third birthday so therefore have no recollection of the actual trip. We arrived in Mooretown, a small hamlet on the St. Clair River outside of Sarnia, the first week of April 1959. Uncle Tony and Aunt Shirley housed us for a short while until we could find a place of our own. The first memories I do have after arriving in town are of us living in the south end of Sarnia. We landed on Devine St., four houses east of Christina St. This rented home was a fenced, two-storey, wood structure with a covered veranda—just up the block from the river. For reasons I can't explain, knowing we were all very young, I have memories of playing in the snow and, after a fun-filled day outside, each of us having a bath in the kitchen sink. It was probably easier on mom's back. That house still stands today—the same two-tone siding adorning its exterior.

The area we came to know as the South End was the very oldest part of Sarnia. There were many children around—some well-behaved and others not so much. Big brother Greg and I were allowed to walk to the corner and back by ourselves. The distance was the length of three houses but to us was a brave new world. One afternoon we were confronted by—whom we would later find out, was the neighbourhood bully. I will never forget the little blond-haired boy looking at us, raising his right fist, and saying: "See my finger. See my thumb. See my fist—you better run!"

And run we did!

Greg may remember it differently. To this day, each time he and I get together, we reminisce about our youthful adventures, maybe even embellishing the stories with a bit more rhetoric each time. In the early days, with him being my big brother and protector, I always felt safe with him by my side. I haven't asked, but he may even know whatever became of that little monster. For me, it was the first real frightening and traumatic moment of my life that I do remember—vividly, to this very day.

3. Putting Down Roots

Early 1960 brought another significant change. Mom and Dad bought a single-family dwelling at 184 Campbell St., right across from the railroad tracks. It was even further south than our rental unit was—purchased for the exorbitant sum of $4300. Their first home was a sprawling old two-storey house, covered in some type of fake asphalt siding called Insulbrick, which was used extensively back in the day. We had a tree-lined backyard with a large clapboard chicken coop at the rear of the lot. Yes, we even inherited the residents of said coop! At a very young and impressionable age, I would soon learn what was meant by the phrase "a chicken with its head cut off." Oh ya, Mom was pregnant again.

The four years we resided on Campbell St. held many firsts. Dad built a homemade skating rink in the backyard, complete with sideboards and discarded Christmas trees used for windbreaks. It also brought for me the desire to learn how to skate. My brother, sisters, and I would spend hours attempting to skate on that rink—well, slipping and sliding and falling down mostly, but you get the picture. Our treat was having Mom come out with hot chocolate to warm us up because we were too afraid to go inside to get warm—knowing that our skating day would be over if we did.

I continued my rambunctious ways. I was playing in the front yard that winter with my little sister Joan—she being the brave one sitting on the snow with her arms stretched out from her sides—while I was playing some superhero, jumping over her. Murphy's Law prevailed and I missed one of the jumps—landing on my wee sister's arm, breaking it and sending her to the hospital for a cast. I didn't do it on purpose, Joan, really, I didn't!

Now, back to the mention of another baby on the way! The family was growing again. Another sibling to make six—Valerie Janine was born on

October 12th of our first year in the house. Valerie's inaugural Christmas that cold December, was the first time I remember having a real Christmas tree with presents scattered beneath. I was four at the time—some may think a late bloomer in remembering such a momentous occasion. Thinking back upon the piles of presents under a brightly lit tree, and now knowing that Mom and Dad were really dirt poor, sure shows me they loved each of us very much. They were willing to sacrifice for our happiness. To this day, I love the Christmas season, and can fully appreciate that it was Mom's very favourite holiday. She was such a fanatic for anything Christmas.

Dad was always really good with his hands, and I mentioned earlier that his career prior to moving west was that of a finish carpenter. He had worked with wood all the time, and after a very long, and physically demanding day on his knees installing flooring, would find the time to make handmade gifts for us. I kick myself to this day with the knowledge that I was given homemade wooden toys—especially my train engine, handcrafted by my father, only to be eventually—just thrown out. At that time, I definitely had no appreciation for what these items would mean to me as an adult. It makes me sad to think about that.

Around this time also, Dad came home with a Bell & Howell Super-8 movie camera and projector—from where, I have no idea. It was such a rare and expensive commodity in those days. I have vague memories of him pointing the camera our way, and of nights sitting in front of the portable screen, viewing the reels of family movies. I'm not sure where all that stuff is now but I hope it is safe. It could be a future restoration project.

Dad would come home with old bicycles, broken-down rocking chairs—anything he could find that he deemed salvageable. He would lovingly rebuild them, all repurposed for many more years of enjoyment by us. It was on one such bicycle that I learned to ride a two-wheeler. Three houses down towards Emma St. was a vacant corner lot, and I would ride along the sidewalk, very unsteadily, toward that open patch of grass. I would turn round and round in circles until I fell because the bike didn't have any brakes. I eventually mastered that skill, and my world opened up to new horizons.

Perpetual Motion

On the afternoon that I decided to run away from home, my father carved me a hobo stick from a fallen oak branch, with a little sack tied to the end of it, complete with a spare T-shirt and a pair of clean tightywhities wrapped inside. With a kiss goodbye, and a wave from the front porch, he and Mom allowed me to head out on my own. I was five.

It was a big old world out there, and I remember making it as far as that vacant lot at the end of the block. Come to think of it, that's probably as far as I had ever ventured to that date prior to my bicycle accomplishments. After pausing a moment to look into the abyss of my future, I turned around, came home, and never felt the urge to run away again for a long time.

We siblings were still very young, and even though it was a safe world around us, we were still forbidden to venture off on our own. I'm not sure what came over us this one day, but the milk wagon—yes, that was a thing—had just dropped off our daily supply of glass-bottled quarts, and Joan and I decided to follow the wagon and horse around the corner. Dad was coming home for lunch and saw us on Emma St. looking at that beautiful mare. He told us to get on home, and when we did, we were given an ass-whooping while perched across his knee. Yup, corporal punishment was also the norm back then, and yes, it hurt—but more importantly, we never made the mistake of chasing the milk wagon again. Without dwelling on the fact, I'm sure the consequences of my actions that day, and the punishment administered because of the "horse" affair, all had a positive effect on my future behavioural patterns. I learned to behave myself.

4. Miracles and Mountains

The next two years continued to hold great memories for me, but truth be known they were very dire years for Mom and Dad. Mom took sick with an undiagnosed illness in early 1961 and was hospitalized. She was rapidly losing weight and unable to figure out what was causing her debilitating symptoms. Dr. Gladdy, her friend and physician, feared for her life.

Having to continue working to support the family, and truly not having a clue how to do domestic chores, Dad summoned his mother-in-law to come and live with us for the summer. Grammy (Irene Boyle) arrived, and without hesitation took over the household chores and ownership of our well-being. Being a farmer's wife, she definitely knew how to handle those tasks with ease. To the best of my recollection, it was a normal summer for us children. We played outside when it was nice, and did some colouring and crafts at the kitchen table when it wasn't fit to venture out. I'm not sure what it was about my sister Joan, and the fact that she was accident prone, but at one such sitting, she managed to tip her high chair over backwards and took a nasty tumble down the basement stairs. Lucky for her, there were no broken bones this time.

Several months passed with Mom still in the hospital, and for much of that time there was no improvement in her health. When we could, we would talk to her briefly on the phone. We were too young to understand the severity of her illness and only wished to see her . . . which, of course, was strictly forbidden. The risk was too great. Fear of a virus or infection, passed on to her by any one of her children, would most likely cause the death of her. The doctors were taking no chances.

For months, toxins were building up inside her and it seemed, no matter what her medical team tried, nothing worked. Mom lay in bed virtually wasting away. By this time, the priest was being considered to perform last rites. It was that grave.

The summer rolled on. Finally, after several months in the hospital, a battery of tests performed, and one very miraculous incident, Mom was on the mend, and all because of her very strong faith. As heard from Mom's lips, she was lying on her deathbed and staring at a framed picture of Christ on the wall opposite the foot of her bed. In a last desperate attempt at salvation, she prayed to her Saviour and spoke the words that spared her life. Mom quietly but emphatically asked God to instruct her body to void all the toxins that had built up inside her, so she could go home to her husband and children. At that moment, she uncontrollably moved her bowels. She hadn't been able to defecate for quite some time, and the poison was literally killing her. A miracle happened that day, and from that very moment, she began to heal. Years later, as Mom was recounting this story to us—probably for the fiftieth time—she would interject some rather colourful language as she described her request to God, making us laugh until our sides hurt. Something to the effect of, "Please God, I just need to shit!" said in a not-so-loving manner, was apparently all the prayer she needed!

We were told she was coming home but it would be a long recovery. The next few months, and into the spring of '62, while Mom convalesced, we were the best-behaved children on the planet. We had loved having our grandmother at our side for all that time, but now that Mom was on the mend, Grammy needed to go home to attend the chores on the farm in Afton.

My mother and her father, Grampy (John Thompson Boyle), were very close, and it broke his heart to see his little girl so severely sick. It wasn't long before he arrived in Sarnia. I have vague memories of my grandfather's visit. One such vision of him, dressed in his pyjamas—his suit coat draped atop his shoulders, sitting at the dining-room table smoking his pipe, will always be a treasured memory. To this day, the sweet smell of pipe tobacco conjures up that unforgettable portrait.

During the next two years, my mother had two more children. Both unfortunately died at birth. There is not much to remember about this period, but I want you to know I did have a little brother named Jerome

Francis and a little sister named Rose-Marie. They are buried in the Catholic Cemetery on Colborne Rd. in Sarnia. A footnote to this fact is that in 2019, we as a family finally installed a granite headstone to honour the burial site of my two young siblings.

After Mom got home, and during that time of much needed healing for all of us, we embarked on a road trip to Nova Scotia to see our relatives. I believe it was the summer of 1962. Dad's boss, Joe, loaned us his '62 Pontiac Parisienne to make the trek. Long days in the car with my five siblings made for some uncomfortable hours. Valerie—not quite two years old—got the footwell in front with Mom, and the rest of us made due with whatever small amount of real estate we could claim. Sleeping over the hump on the floor of the back seat area was very uncomfortable. One of the coveted spots to sleep was above the backseat on the rear window ledge—unheard of today, but we survived.

We were driving after dark somewhere near Valleyfield, Que. when Dad noticed a car broken down on the side of the road. Being the good Christian man he was, he decided to stop and see if he could lend a hand. My mother was furious. Six young children in the car, a dark road in the middle of nowhere, and total strangers in need was a formula for trouble, even back then. As Dad opened the car door, he showed no fear. He just knew all would be ok—and it was. The world has changed a lot since those simpler times. I think often about my father's fearless actions that night, in the name of being a Good Samaritan. Dad, it turns out, was quickly becoming my hero and mentor.

We stayed several weeks at the homestead in Afton, the Boyle family farm. It was an idealistic time to be young and witness the goings-on of farm life. Those summer days showed us a lamb being butchered for supper by my grandfather—and the hay being taken off the fields by pitchfork and tossed into a horse-drawn wagon. We would walk through the barn to see my grandmother milking the cows—and try to avoid a quick squirt of raw milk from the cow's teat, aimed squarely in our direction. Oh, how we laughed at that! Although I didn't understand the workings of it at the time, she would also use a manual milk separator—a necessary piece of farm machinery she had sitting on the back porch. This marvel of engineering was designed to remove the heavy cream from the fresh cow's milk, brought in from the barn in galvanized buckets. Using the manual crank, Grammy would churn the separated cream into creamy butter. All this was done without pasteurization and no added chemicals for preservatives—and we didn't die! Later, we would watch her gather the eggs from the chicken coop and carry them back to the house coddled in her apron—without dropping any. All in a day's work for my grammy.

There was a very large pile of firewood out just beyond the porch, which had recently been delivered by my uncles for use in the wood-burning kitchen stove. We climbed on that pile for hours. The odd scrape or splinter embedded in the skin was a minor inconvenience. We were never once told to stop, and again we survived to tell about it.

Coming from a good Irish Catholic family, I had many cousins who all seemed to live very close to, or at the farm itself. It was wonderful having so many kids to play with and, because of the fact that Mom and Dad continued to visit Nova Scotia on a regular basis, we got to know our cousins well. To this day we are still close.

A unique feature of life on the farm in Afton was the railway tracks which ran through the property. You could set your watch to the exact times—morning and evening, when the train would pass through. We were warned time and time again to stay clear of the tracks, and we did for the most part. Unbeknownst to the elders, some of the older cousins would bring us young'uns down to the tracks just before the train would pass and let us put pennies on the rails for the train's wheels to squish. What a thrill.

I think I started, and then quickly ended my very short-lived singing career that summer. All my aunts and uncles were gathered on the back porch enjoying family time when, for some unknown reason, I was paid a whole dime to sing Hank Snow's national anthem of the province, "My Nova Scotia Home." I must have, at one point, demonstrated that I knew the lyrics, but sure cannot recall how.

Our summer came to an end, and so it was that we prepared to travel back to Sarnia for our next school year. Mom's oldest sister, Margie Prosser, who was by then an accomplished traveller, agreed to the task of getting us six siblings and Mom to Sarnia by car since my father had only stayed for ten days—needing to get back to work. We piled into her 1957 Studebaker

Golden Hawk—and with no seatbelts, GPS, or a care in the world, made the journey home.

I entered Grade 2 with Miss LeBlanc. Little did I know this would be my last year at St. Joseph's for quite some time. Due to an impending cross-city move to our new family home, St. Margaret's School on Devine St. was where I would continue my education in Grade 3 and beyond. Several years later, I would be forced to take classes once again at St. Joseph's for my 7th grade, as a result of a population surge in the city. Overcrowding at St. Margaret's School had become an issue. Fortunately, this was for one year only and we got to attend our senior year back at our regular school.

My first neighbourhood friend on Campbell St. was Mike Jolly. Mikey lived next door to us, and although I didn't know it, he had polio and walked with a limp. I don't recall it slowing him down at all. One of our proudest moments as friends was when we built a picnic table out of wood, I'm sure with my father's help. It was a great learning experience, building something with your bare hands, with lessons I still use today.

This was also the fall that I made my first communion at St. Joseph's Church on Stuart St. It was a very elaborate affair, and I believe the first time I ever wore a tie—even today, a rarity. It was also the same church that eighteen years later, I would be married in.

That fall, I received my first corporal punishment at school. I got into a fight in the schoolyard and I dropped a kid on his head. I was taken to the principal's office where I was given the strap, roughly five times on each hand. In case you need a reminder, corporal punishment—similar to that spanking from Dad—was an archaic method of discipline, allowed in the school system to deter bad behaviour. The strap is exactly what you would think it is, a piece of leather approximately eight inches long and two to three inches wide with some sort of handle on it. The principal of the school in this case, Sister Anna Catherine, yes, a Catholic nun, would make you hold your hands out, palm side up so she could smack you with that piece of leather as hard as she deemed necessary to fit the punishment deserved by the bad behaviour. Damn, it hurt enough to cry, but cry we did not for fear of being called a sissy. That would have been by far the worst part of the punishment. The world certainly has changed in its approach to discipline in the education system today.

Perpetual Motion

That winter, with constant freezing temperatures, was the first and only time I was tricked into putting my wet tongue on a cold piece of steel in the schoolyard. There was a round latch on the gate to the chain-link fence surrounding the yard. I was goaded into putting my tongue on that latch, and of course it instantly froze there. Anyone's first reaction would be to immediately pull away. That I did and proceeded to leave every taste bud I owned stuck to the frozen metal. Damn that hurt. I certainly learned a lesson that day, and hopefully each of you had more brains than I did. It was so painful!

Even with all the miracles experienced, and the mountains symbolically climbed in my short life, there were still many more lessons to be learned. I was only getting started.

5. Shaping a Young Mind

Three noteworthy events happened in 1963 that had a significant impact on me. The first was my participation in a school-wide variety show. I was part of the junior square-dancing set in which several of us actually learned how to do that particular dance, and then performed it several times. The highlight of the show was us being able to perform for an audience of family, friends, and others on the big stage in the basement of the parish hall, next door to the school. What I recall vividly is that my father was chosen (or volunteered) to be one of the curtain attendants for the evening. All the while I danced, I kept an eye on him to see if he was watching me. Like I said, he was my hero, and I wanted nothing more than to impress him, even at such a tender age. Maybe this was the beginning of my budding social life, so to speak. I was figuring out how to have fun in social situations and learned to mingle easily.

The second event, in August of that year, was the earliest I remember seeing the Sarnia Fire Department at work. St. Paul's United Church stood at the northwest corner of Devine and Emma streets. I first remember seeing the smoke rising from the building a block away. The sirens from the fire trucks were loud, even on Campbell St. We made our way to the scene, and for hours I stood on the opposite corner—leaning against a big oak tree, watching the building burn and subsequently collapse. I was fascinated with the helmets, the black rubber boots, and the shiny red fire trucks. It was fifteen years later that I walked into the Sarnia Fire Department for the first time as a firefighter. I was put on the A-1 squad, which ironically was the same squad that fought the church fire all those years before. As you can imagine, there will be several more fire-service-related stories to come.

Perpetual Motion

The third—which had a huge impact on my later years—was the assassination of President John F. Kennedy on November 22nd, 1963. It is the first significant world news event that my young self remembers. I arrived home from school to the sight of my mom sitting on the couch crying. When I asked her what was wrong, she told me the news and with such empathy tried to explain the significance of what had transpired. JFK was a new hope for a new world, and being young and ambitious, he was looked up to by many as a strong political leader. Everyone just knew he would do great things. It was not meant to be. I would go on to read well over twenty books on the subject of JFK and the very controversial circumstances surrounding his demise. I still don't know the truth but have my beliefs, and most likely will never know the full story behind the assassination.

President John F. Kennedy, and the whole aura of his presidency, still fascinates me greatly. I didn't know it at the time, but those tragic events would lead to a love of history—and especially that of the American presidents.

6. On the Move—Again

Christmas came and went, spring finally arrived, and for the first time in recent memory, there were no babies on the way! That may have been a blessing in disguise, because in the late spring of 1964, we moved from 184 Campbell St. to 884 Wellington St., as soon as school let out.

The Campbell St. property, as mentioned, had been much further south from our original rental property on Devine St.—bordered by the railroad tracks and in the shadow of a big blue municipal water tower. Beyond those barriers was the industrial machine that gave Sarnia its identity as "The Chemical Valley of Canada." This area, and the city as a whole, would eventually play a significant role in my life, and my future career.

The new house on Wellington St.—a side by side duplex—was less than a year old, and right in the middle of central Sarnia. That section of Wellington St. was so new, there were no sidewalks or street curbs yet. I don't think my parents cared much about that—they were just happy to be able to put a good roof over our heads. No more South End for the Pitts'! As TV's George Jefferson always said, "We're movin' on up!" (That tag line is a reference to a '70s sitcom—"The Jeffersons," a spin-off from "All In The Family," which saw a black family moving to a deluxe apartment on the east side of New York—and not surprisingly—the show had many racial overtones for the times.)

This home was smaller than the previous one but had three bedrooms. The four girls got one, Greg and I another, and Mom and Dad the third. There was one bathroom to share. No matter the size, Wellington St. served its purpose nobly, and for the next twenty-one years, it was where we grew to adulthood.

Perpetual Motion

Just shy of my eighth birthday, I was able to wander further than ever before. That summer of '64 was a momentous year of discovery. Three blocks away to the east of our new home was a large tract of woodland. It probably wasn't a week after we moved that Greg and I went exploring deep into that bush. To our surprise, there was a set of railroad tracks running right through the trees, and I remember wondering if those tracks were connected to the ones by the old water tower, across from our previous house. My universe certainly was expanding! It would be twenty-five years later that I found myself working at the Wellington St. firehall for the first time, realizing that it was built only metres from the spot Greg and I first laid eyes on the train tracks through the woods—now long since cleared away, and overcome by urban sprawl. We had only moved a mile away from where we previously lived, but to me, it opened up a whole new world.

The new neighbourhood was very friendly. Roy and Peggy Barnes lived in an old farmhouse across the street, and their son Bob and his wife Marg lived in a new house they had just completed next door. They would quickly become best friends with Mom and Dad and were very influential to me on many occasions in my life. Bob worked for the local gas company and did very well. He always seemed to have the latest car or lawnmower or shoes. They were also a very ambitious couple. One of the coolest things about them was their love of Volkswagens. They owned a VW Beetle, and a camper van known as the T2 Westfalia. They would travel all over the country in that van and upon return spend evenings with our family telling stories of their vacations. It's not a stretch to believe they were partially responsible for me catching the travel bug.

It was summertime and I was playing organized sports for the first time. I signed up for softball at Germain Park and rather enjoyed the experience. Up until that point, I had always been under the watchful eyes of my parents, but now I had the freedom to go distances on my own without supervision.

As will be explained with more detail in later chapters, I have suffered from anxiety and depression for most of my adult life. I often look back and wonder when and where it was that I first had those symptoms of anxiety and panic. One initial incident was when I came home from my baseball game in late August of that first summer on Wellington St. It was just before supper. I walked into the house and found nobody there. Again, this was the first time that anything like that had ever happened to me. I don't know why I panicked, but I did. I vividly recall the feeling of abandonment and didn't know what to do. I knocked on my neighbour's door and was greeted by what I would now describe as a recluse. Mr. and Mrs. McCabe were much older than Mom and Dad and were probably bothered by a snot-nosed kid pounding away on the screen door. A stale smell—something akin to a bear hibernating—accosted me as I stood on their porch, crying, because I didn't know where my family was. As I stood there in bewilderment—stammering through my tears—my parents pulled into the driveway. I was never so happy to see my family, ever. Ironically, I had actually suppressed that memory for many years, and it only came to light after I retired and was seeing a counsellor for post-traumatic stress disorder (PTSD). The unfortunate thing is that the issue described above was the first time something like that happened, and it certainly was not going to be the last.

Shortly before summer ended, I was playing at a construction site a couple of doors down from the house. There was a three-storey apartment building being erected, and they were in the bricking phase. Being a typical boy, I started climbing the stack of bricks by the building when I inadvertently pulled one off the top of the pile—said brick landing point first on my skull. When I arrived home, my mother was horrified to see all the blood streaming down my face. I must have looked like something out of a Stephen King novel. A particularly gruesome scene from *Carrie* comes to mind. It was off to the hospital for me this time, and after several stitches to my cranium, I was back home. My father told me they had given me a painkiller—Demerol I think, which provided me with my first drug-induced high that I could remember, and that too, wouldn't be the last.

September saw me attending our new school, Grade 3 at St. Margaret's on Devine St. Upon arrival on my first day, I met Paul Butler, a stalky kid with a great laugh and huge hands. I will never forget his brown cardigan and the plaster cast on his wrist, the result of a fall during the summer break. It didn't take long before we would become fast friends, and we remained so for years after, spending many weekends together enjoying our young lives.

The first and only time I ever opened Christmas presents, and then taped them back up so that no one would know, was at Paul's. His mom had hidden all the Christmas gifts in a hall closet, and Paul found them one day. I came over on a Saturday to play, and I will never forget him saying, "Do you want to see what I got for Christmas?"—knowing that it was still two weeks before the actual date. The thought of doing that never crossed my mind, and I was so panicked to think that Mrs. Butler would walk in at any time. This was enough to deter me from ever thinking about doing it again. And I never did. To this day, I love the surprise factor—the unknown of opening gifts at Christmas.

That same Christmas brought another snafu to my days. Dad, still working for the flooring company, was bringing home enough pay to just barely squeak by financially. However, every once in a while—say on a Friday night in which he got paid—he would line his children up in a row and, with much pomp and circumstance, hand each of us a one-dollar bill. Yes, there was such a thing, now long out of circulation. We could do with it what we liked. This particular Friday evening about a week before Christmas, we each received our one-dollar bill but were told it was for Christmas presents, and we were going to Kresges's Department Store in the morning to do just that. Excitement reigned supreme. I bought my mom a green glass ashtray and was so proud of my one purchase that I ended up revealing it to her when I got home. I was devastated. Christmas came, and she acted completely surprised at such a thoughtful gift. It was a hard lesson to learn, but it has stuck with me all these years. The best part is that after all these years, I inherited the green ashtray back from her after she passed away, now a treasured keepsake.

Paul's mom made Batman and Robin costumes for us one Halloween. Of course, Paul was Batman and I was Robin. I think they were the coolest costumes I have ever worn in search of free candy. In later years I rocked a Slash costume, the guitarist for the rock band Guns & Roses, and a really authentic-looking Dracula, but those efforts were more alcohol-induced than candy-crazed.

As close as Paul and I had become—I still hadn't had a sleepover at his or anyone else's house, a childhood thing we all loved to do. The simple and traumatic reason for this was because—to put it bluntly—I wet the bed uncontrollably almost every night—for years. I am not sure when it started, but by the time I was nine years old, it was as traumatic as anything a young boy could imagine. The growing embarrassment of having to say no to anyone's sleepover invitation caused me high anxiety. It was ok to have them at my house because I could cover up any accidents, but how to remedy that issue at someone else's house? It was insurmountable.

At home I had a thick covering of plastic permanently laid between the mattress and my sheets, for years. Thinking back, I'm sure my father had an endless supply of that thick plastic, which now I realize most likely came from the wrappings of the rolls of carpeting that he would install on a daily basis. To this day, if I happen to sit or lay on something covered in plastic, it brings back those very unpleasant memories. Just try and test a new mattress in a furniture store with those memories to haunt you.

With grave trepidation, and some huge pep-talks by my loving mother, I overcame the bedwetting stage of my life. I also enjoyed sleepovers, and yes—shit probably happened—but suppressed memory can also be a wonderful thing when some of the fears of a child that had been blocked out for a lifetime are finally freed. Most definitely there were accidents, but I don't recall any repercussions from my increasingly sporadic nocturnal emissions. I think Paul's mom must have just dealt with the wet sheets and saved me from the trauma of owning up to the accident. I also wonder if our moms talked about this amongst themselves. They were both such angels, and it was not beyond reason to believe they had my best interests in mind. I am also quite sure because it was never made out to be a big deal, I was able to overcome my incontinence—medically known as *Nocturnal Enuresis*—and eventually live a more normal childhood.

Grade 3 did end on a high note. I was awarded a copy of a *Hardy Boys* mystery novel—very popular back in the day—for the achievement of perfect spelling for the whole year. This was signed by my wonderful teacher, Mrs. Murphy, with a note handwritten on the inside of the hardcover, congratulating me on the achievement. Most likely, besides the influence of my mother, that achievement is one of the main reasons why I enjoy wordsmithing to this day. It is also a perfect example of why children should be praised and congratulated when they do something of significance and not just for waking up before noon. It is that affirmation that sticks in the minds of the young and impressionable, and as it did for me, propels them to higher achievement.

My early days at St. Margaret's School went off without a hitch for the most part. Several new friendships were formed, and I continued to learn the subtle art of becoming a social being. The news came out that Mom was pregnant again, and it took us a bit by surprise. This was both a blessing and a very scary time for all. We had lost two siblings in the last couple of years and didn't want to think of the possibility of it happening again. We said the Rosary around the table every night and prayed that all would be well. I don't remember Mom or Dad showing any worry during this time but I'm sure they were stressed at the possibility of what could happen—again.

Grade 4 held some interesting moments. Richard Boucher, a heavy-set kid with a big heart, breaking Rod Chartrand's leg with a misplaced attempt at kicking a soccer ball, was huge. Rod was quite the athlete, and prior to that day was the fastest runner at the school. I had never seen the likes of that before, and poor Richard—well, he took it so hard, I still don't know if he's over the trauma it caused him. Meanwhile, sticking with the soccer theme, I attempted to score a goal on John Stewart one day at recess. The only problem was that the ball was very muddy. My well-placed shot hit John square in the chest, lacing him with the mud. John was upset, and embarrassed. He took after me immediately. I happened to be the second-fastest runner at the school, and try as he may, he couldn't catch me. After chasing me around the school yard for the rest of recess, he vowed that he would get me eventually.

Things quieted down for a little while, and it seemed John was over his embarrassment. One day, upon my return to school after lunch, John approached me in a kindly manner and, when he got close enough, punched me squarely in the nose, knocking me off my bike. I surely didn't see that one coming. Upset, and with a bloody nose, I turned right around and went home for the afternoon. We were now even, our friendship remaining intact for several more years.

7. External Influences and Growing Pains

The highlight of the year—it was still early on—was the addition of a healthy little brother. Christopher Martin was born in March of 1966. He was our miracle baby because Mom was told after the loss of Jerome and Rose that she would most likely never be able to conceive again. This little guy made everything right with the world. Our family was growing, and we loved it.

That summer, the family travelled to Nova Scotia once more for a family wedding. My mom's brother, Eugene, was marrying his sweetheart, Jeanie Bowie, at Tracadie Church, and we were not going to miss such an occasion. Given the fact our growing family was getting too large to travel together in one car, it was decided that Lorraine and Greg would ride east with the soon-to-be newlyweds. They had been staying with us for the past few months while Eugene worked in the area.

Around this time, music—or at least songs on the radio—started to creep into my life at an accelerated pace, one rock and roll song after another. The musically inspired British invasion of North America which included artists such as The Beatles, The Rolling Stones, The Dave Clark Five, The Kinks, Gary Lewis & the Playboys, and many other formidable groups had singles on the AM stations. I knew this genre of music was something special but still wasn't old enough to grasp the meaning or the future historical significance of it all. A good friend of mine, Keith Toohey, and I would pretend we were John Lennon and Paul McCartney. I was left-handed, so I was automatically Paul. We would take two tennis rackets and pretend we were live in concert playing "I Want to Hold Your Hand" or "Please Mr. Postman" or any number of other great tunes that we knew every word to.

The Beatles' famous album *Revolver* was released on my birthday in 1966. Keith bought a copy of that vinyl for $2.99, and we played it hours on end. Songs such as "Eleanor Rigby," "Yellow Submarine," "Good Day Sunshine," "Got to Get You into My Life" and "Here, There, and Everywhere" fast became the soundtrack of my life.

Grade 5 would start in the fall of 1966. We as a family were settled into our school and home life, and friends were plentiful. The highlight of that school year was a speech I wrote the following spring, as a part of the English curriculum. The theme I chose was Charles Darwin's theory of evolution. It must have been ok because I won the Outstanding Male entry for my school and was entered to compete at the city-wide finals held on the big stage at St. Patrick's High School, my future Alma Mater. I know I didn't win that contest, but it did have a profound impact on my future as I have never again been hesitant to speak in public, to this day. I remember enjoying Grade 5.

In the spring of 1967, Mom and Dad announced they were expecting yet again, and we all prayed that this little baby would be as healthy as Martin was. There was never any knowing the gender of the baby back then, so we just waited in anticipation of a healthy delivery.

The summer of that year was cause for celebration in Canada. It was the country's one-hundredth birthday and there were many activities scheduled nationwide. Each city or town tried in some way to honour this momentous occasion. Montréal for instance, hosted EXPO '67, one of the most successful world exhibitions ever. I wanted so badly to go but was a wee bit young for such an adventure.

On a much smaller scale, our local newspaper, the *Sarnia Observer*, included one maple tree sapling in the fold of each newspaper to be delivered to each household so we could plant the trees as a memorial to Canada's birthday. I didn't have a paper route at the time, but a friend of mine was a paper carrier for the *Observer*, and asked me to give him a hand delivering this particular edition because of the bulkiness and weight the trees added. For my efforts, I was given three of the maple saplings to bring home. Dad and I planted them along the back fence of 884 Wellington St., and if you drive by that house today, you will see those same three trees have grown to over fifty feet in height. At the time of planting, there was no thought of me looking at those trees fifty years later. That act of burying the roots of those trees, we now know, has had a positive effect on the environment, and provides a tangible connection to my childhood growing up on Wellington St.

That summer was also the first time I got wind of a centuries-old issue: racism. To that point in my young life, it was never even a topic of discussion in our loving home and, having persons of colour as very good friends, was normal for us. The news told a different story, and it was scary. The city of Detroit, MI—only one hundred kilometres from Sarnia—was the scene of devastating racial riots all summer long. Out of control demonstrations, arson, looting, civil unrest, and even murder, were broadcast into our homes on a daily basis, to the point where it was sometimes incomprehensible to understand. In Canada, and especially in my little town of Sarnia, I felt safe. We still stayed out until the streetlights came on.

Probably the thing that stands out as so indisputably chaotic to me during my years at St. Margaret's School was the antics of my Grade 6 teacher who, for reasons, shall remain nameless. From the day I started the school year that September, until I was promoted to Grade 7 the next June, it was a tumultuous ten months. To this day I have often thought about why that man even entered the teaching profession. By today's measuring stick, he would be considered a tyrant, and an outright bully. Several times a day, he would walk up and down the rows between the desks with a wooden pointer in his hand. If someone was not paying attention, talking out loud, or just generally not doing what he wanted done, he would unexpectedly smack the pointer on the desk, and scare the shit out of all of us. Many times we were sent to the principal's office or made to stand outside the door as punishment for the littlest infractions.

Now, my good friend Rod, of broken leg fame, was not the most disciplined student in the classroom and could be somewhat of an instigator, to the teacher's chagrin. The day came when, during one of Rod's inattentive moments, Mr. G attempted to smack the wooden pointer hard across his desk, but Rod was fast. He grabbed the pointer away from the very startled teacher, and broke it in two over his knee. Needless to say, Rod was sent yet again to the principal's office, and Mr. G was beside himself for the rest of the day.

I'm pretty sure after the shenanigans of Grade 6, he did not return to teaching. It was probably the best for all involved. I can't help but wonder what circumstances in his life led to this kind of behaviour towards his students. The ten-year-old me didn't care for him at all, but now the retired me knows better and hopes he found some healing peace in his life.

All the while, I was hanging out with Paul every day, and my circle of friends was growing. I became very close to Roger Serratore, who lived one street over. We had some great times catching crawfish and tadpoles in the pond behind his house. He was from a big Italian family, and the food I ate while there was always so delicious. We lost touch for some years after grade school but have since become reacquainted and to this day keep in touch through social media.

Skip LeClair was another close friend. He lived a block away on Walnut St. That area was pretty rough and was known as the "low rentals" area of town. Actually, several of my friends lived over there and, looking back, I can say with confidence that it absolutely did have an influence on my life, in a positive manner. Even though we ourselves were poor, my parents taught us we were all equal, and just because they lived in subsidized housing, as most of that area was, it should not affect the way we treat others or want to be treated ourselves. I know Skip passed away around 2017. When I heard the news, I couldn't help but remember all the good times we had together.

Until this point in my life, I was happily hanging around my many male friends. Things would change soon enough—I was starting to notice girls too. Debbie Smith, Helen Jablecki, Patty O'Brien, and Lorraine Bronson were just a few of the girls we hung around with during those formative years. At the time they were buddies, but not for long.

The classic music we now know and love was being produced and released for the very first time during my school-age years. The Beatles released *Sgt. Pepper's Lonely Hearts Club Band* that summer—still a very relevant piece of music today.

Not that it was huge news in 1967, but the Toronto Maple Leafs won the Stanley Cup, beating Montréal for the title. The huge news today is that the Leafs still haven't won the cup again, as of this writing in 2023. Those die-hard Leafs fans are still waiting!

Just before Christmas of 1967, we received into our home another healthy baby girl. Veronica Noelle was born December 20th, and the doctors allowed Mom and Noelle to come home Christmas Eve. That was the best present anyone could ever ask for. Oh, how we loved the two little ones. Mom had given birth to ten children in fifteen years, from 1952 to 1967. That would prove to be enough.

8. The End of Innocence

From the joy of Christmas to the start of a new year, 1968 would prove to be a tough one for all of us, globally. I was by this time, starting to understand more of what made the world turn, and a couple of major events in the first six months really took away our innocence. Yes, the world was changing, and not for the better.

On April 4th, Dr. Martin Luther King Jr.—a well-known, and highly respected southern Baptist preacher, a leader of the civil rights movement—was assassinated on the balcony of the Lorraine Motel in Memphis, Tennessee. It was a catalyst for the continuing racial issues we experience today.

Unfortunately, the violence would not end there. Just two months later, in the late evening of June 5th, US Senator Robert Kennedy, brother of slain President JFK, was himself gunned down in Los Angeles after winning the California primary for the democratic nomination for president. The world mourned as my parents tried again to explain these horrible deeds to us. I was now old enough to understand the magnitude of such acts. In my heart I knew this unimaginable violence against the leaders of our free nations was bad for the world and could only breed more violence—pretty weighty thoughts for an eleven-year-old kid.

I was never so happy to be finishing a school year as that crazy one in Grade 6. I really had never experienced the tensions of hate and violence as much as I did in the first six months of 1968—school issues included. Thinking back on those times, it's ironic that the most violent year of my school career was also one of the most unsettling years the world had witnessed in decades. Food for thought.

To end that tumultuous school year on a high note, Dad borrowed his boss's car again—a Pontiac Parisienne station wagon, and the whole family travelled to Sudbury to visit relatives. That car was more comfortable than the previous one we had used for the long trip east, a few years earlier. The highlight of that family vacation was all of us standing in front of the Big Nickel. This famous attraction is a thirty-foot replica of a 1951 Canadian nickel and is the world's largest depiction of a coin anywhere. It was erected to commemorate the many nickel mines in the region—great memories.

I looked forward to my new beginnings, starting Grade 7 at St. Joseph's School on Stuart St. There was no such thing as busing for intercity kids, which meant I had to walk forty minutes each way to get to school, every day. To make it easier, I got a second-hand bike for the trek. Paul's house was on the way, so I would meet him each morning, and we would ride across town to attend classes at my old, but familiar school. The other thing that made it bearable was that all of us classmates were still together, even though it was a different classroom setting. It must have been an uneventful school year because I don't have a lot of recollection during that time.

Well, there was this one time. I was riding home from school when I overheard some of the kids talking about a secret stash of Freezies. Curiosity got the better of me when I followed a group of them to a building on Talfourd St. The door to the building was ajar. Looking back now, I can only describe it as some sort of warehouse. I could see boxes upon boxes of the sugary flavoured treats, stacked on pallets. The kids who had arrived before me were carrying away as many boxes as they could grab—all laughing as they ran down the street—and I followed suit. The advantage I had was that my bike was equipped with a wire carrier on the front, for the sole purpose of assisting me with the heavy newspapers I delivered every morning. At that moment, the carrier definitely got re-purposed. In went several boxes of the discovered stash and down the street I went also. Details are sketchy as to what happened to the loot I pilfered that day. I can tell you that at the time I did not equate my actions to theft, although that is exactly what it was. Fortunately for myself and my comrades, we never got nabbed for our crime of the century. I'm still on the lam!

Okay, there was one other time. Mom sent me to the grocery store to buy her cigarettes. Yes, at the time that was a legal thing to do. I approached the checkout counter with two people ahead of me. To my left, as is the case today, were racks of incidentals to incite last-minute purchases. Chocolate bars were ten cents apiece, and there were dozens of them on this rack. For reasons unknown—possibly feeling emboldened by my previous crime—I put a Coffee Crisp in my pocket. I paid for the cigarettes and left the store, only to be immediately approached by a store employee asking if I had paid for the item in my pocket. Busted! I was escorted to the manager's office and made to wait while she called home. Mom was informed of what I had done, and, after a brief verbal exchange, I was allowed to go home, minus the chocolate bar. I was never so scared to enter our house as I was that afternoon. She sat me down and instead of scolding me, explained how what I had done was wrong. She made me promise never to do it again—or she would tell Dad. That was it, my stealing days were over. I would no longer entertain future criminal intent. Nobody wants the wrath of their father coming down on them for doing that type of shit. I never stole again.

As mentioned, the bike did come in handy for my *London Free Press* paper route I had taken over from my brother. It was a morning delivery with about forty-five customers, so I would be at the corner service station to pick up my bundle by about 5:45 a.m. I delivered those newspapers through all kinds of weather, and in the end, I believe it made me a stronger individual. That was my introduction to the world of the workforce, commerce, overcoming diversity, and learning new disciplines. You have to know, getting out of bed at that age, and at that hour—every morning—was a chore.

It was around then I tried cigarettes for the first time—I never did say I was an angel! My mother and father smoked Black Cat #7's, so it wasn't long before I was taking a cigarette or two and sharing them with friends. We would sneak off to the Indian Road overpass, and in the relative safety beneath the road, alongside the tracks, we would smoke. Unfortunately, I would continue to smoke for another ten years before I quit for good. I consider myself one of the lucky ones to have realized the health implications at an early age. In an ironic twist, I quit smoking only a couple of months after my parents had finally given me permission to smoke in the house. Yes, that was a thing too.

9. A Budding Social Life

The summer between Grades 7 and 8—as Canadian rock star Brian Adams would eventually write about: "The Summer of '69"—saw significant changes in my maturity level. There was an area a couple of blocks over from our home on Wellington St. known as the tree streets, and as you may have guessed, each ribbon of blacktop was named after a different tree. I met several kids my age from those tree-lined streets, and spent almost every day that summer on Sycamore St. My first real girlfriend, Heather Basin, lived there. Even though I was dealing with the awkward feelings of young love at such a tender age—it was also a magical time. Heather, Martha, Carol, Cathy, Danny, Mikey, Dave, Owen, Tim, and Wayne were a part of the first group of friends I played Spin the Bottle with. It was also that magical moment in time for this young guy when, the stars aligned, the heavens opened, the earth shook, and I copped my first "feel." In an ironic twist, I became friends with her on Facebook a few years ago. Of course, she has no idea I remember this incident so vividly. Some things just stick in your mind—forever.

I was given much more freedom from home and took advantage of that fact—staying out late, experimenting with cigarettes, and learning the ways of the world in an accelerated way. It was also a time when long hair had become the norm for guys. Greg and I tried several times to get away with our hair being a little out of sorts, but it seemed just as we were thinking all was good, something would trigger Dad. He would lay down the law and make us get our haircut. It wasn't until I entered high school a year later that he finally relented. We had finally gained the freedom to grow our hair to any length we wanted.

Perpetual Motion

My first-ever rock concert that summer was an event that would influence my musical tastes going forward. It was at a very small club-style venue on Queen St. in Sarnia's South End. A very new and upcoming Detroit-area rock band by the name of The Bob Seger System was making the circuit and expanding their performance area. They went on to stardom—are now legendary in the industry—and I have seen that band, or a version of it, three times.

I met Claude Chaisson, a fantastic guitar player who owned an orange Gretsch, one of the sweetest-sounding guitars I've ever heard. He introduced me to a heavy metal band called Iron Butterfly. Their hit song in 1969 was "In-A-Gadda-Da-Vida" and was magical in its bass lines. Looking back on all of these snippets of such a monumental year, I am so happy I got to experience that history firsthand.

As my social life took hold, more girls came into the picture. Julie and Jill Dutrizac, Kathy Garvin, Debbie Smolders, and several of my friend's big sisters, were all getting attention. There was nobody finer in looks and personality than my friend's sister, Penny. She was a vision, and older than me—I was in love. Truth be told, she was the first female I saw who was less than fully dressed. Two for two!

Until this time in my life, I had not experienced any significant tragedy that affected me personally. Inevitably, it was going to happen at some point. The first noteworthy event of such magnitude took place that summer. My good buddy Dave and some friends made their way to Bright's Grove beach for a swim. They couldn't resist the temptation to do some diving off the metal seawalls that protruded out into the lake. What they didn't know was that a storm had come in the night before and deposited a mountain of sand just under the waterline next to the sea wall. Dave was the first to take the plunge. In a split second, his life changed forever. He broke his neck, and at that moment became a paraplegic for life. He was rushed to the nearby hospital for emergency care and after being stabilized, transported to a trauma centre in London. He eventually ended up at the London Rehabilitation Hospital for months recovering from his accident. Dave finally made it back home the following spring.

That accident affected me mentally, and I struggled to deal with it for some time. I continued to see him for a while after the accident and was happy to hear he had gotten his driver's license and a van to drive. This definitely gave him the much-needed mobility he was seeking. We eventually lost contact, as happens often with those we knew so long ago. I hope he is well.

Certainly one of the most historically significant moments ever, occurred in July of 1969. NASA's Apollo 11 and its crew, led by the ever-capable Neil Armstrong (of birthday fame) blasted off the launch pad at Cape Canaveral in Florida, and two days later, landed the Lunar Module *Eagle* at the Sea of Tranquility, on the moon. It was the fulfillment of a promise made by then-President John F. Kennedy in his address to Congress in May of 1961. He had committed to landing men on the moon by the end of the decade, and although many were skeptical of his comments, he achieved his goal. Unfortunately, he didn't live to see his dream come to fruition. As mentioned, JFK was assassinated on November 22nd, 1963 in Dallas, Texas while on the campaign trail for re-election to a second term as president.

I witnessed the moon landing that beautiful July day, at my Uncle Eugene's house down the street, watching history being made. This event was the catalyst to me taking a huge interest in all things space-related. I have followed NASA, and the changing tides of the space race, ever since.

The era of my coming of age was in full swing in the Sarnia/Point Edward area. The place to hang out was Rose Gardens, a wooden barn-like structure that housed a roller-skating rink on what is now the Sandy Lane Apartments at the end of Alfred St. It was cool to get a ride to the rink and spin around the floor to the tunes of the great bands of the day. "Green River" by Creedence Clearwater Revival was a popular song to test our skills, as was "Spirit in the Sky" by the one-hit wonder, Norman Greenbaum. Rose Gardens was open from 1951 to 1974 and provided many of us with the recreation we needed to expand our horizons. I remember it closing my senior year in high school—the end of an era, or so we thought at the time.

A short time later, Bob Barnes, our friend and neighbour, saw a need to bring the roller-skating scene back to the area after Rose Gardens closed. Being of the entrepreneurial spirit, he devised a plan to open a brand-new, state-of-the-art facility called Skate Country. This was located on a vacant tract of land on Upper Canada Dr. in Sarnia's South End. The biggest draw to this facility was its poured, orange-vinyl skating surface. Sarnia had not seen the likes of it before, as the former Rose Gardens barn was just cement. The new facility had a vast array of coloured lighting, a huge sound system, and a mirrored disco ball hanging from the ceiling in the centre of the rink. Brand-new skates were all the rage, and we got real good at all the flashy moves while getting much needed exercise.

As I had with Eric Flesher, someone you will meet soon enough, I worked for Bob on his construction site for a whole summer while Skate Country was being built, and subsequently was employed by him for a time at the rink. I was what was known as a cruiser, or one of the guys who attempted to keep everyone safe. While we were not skating, we worked the rental station, and at the end of the night, made sure the place was clean for opening the next day.

My eventual claim to fame at the rink was an incident on New Year's Eve, 1977. I was helping with cleanup in the kitchen when I inadvertently tripped the Halon fire-suppression system over the fryers. The mess that it made was crazy. White powder was everywhere—on every surface for yards around. Not only did it take us hours to clean it up, but the cost was enormous for restoration of the system—replacement of the oil in the fryers, and all food that was exposed—then thrown out. I did not win Employee of the Month, and most of us missed our planned festivities for ringing in the new year.

We continued to discover music in a very big way. The late '60s produced some of the greatest, most influential music ever recorded, and I was so fortunate to be in on the ground floor of this movement. To this day, I listen to classic rock—as the genre is now known. The likes of The Beatles, Santana, The Zombies, The Rolling Stones, Moody Blues, Pink Floyd, Crosby Stills & Nash, Neil Young, Deep Purple, Jimmy Hendrix, Bob Seger, CCR, Bob Dylan—just to name a few influencers, all of whom came out with hit after hit, and this was still on AM radio. I was too young to attend the fabled rock concert *Woodstock* in Bethel, New York in August of that year—now considered the greatest music festival of all time.

I was doing dishes one evening in late 1969 when I heard the song "Whole Lotta Love/Livin' Lovin' Maid" by a new band out of England.

They called themselves Led Zeppelin. The sound that night was coming from a tiny portable transistor radio on the counter, and it sounded great! I stopped my dish-drying activity and just listened—and listened—and listened some more. I was amazed at the length of the song. They had actually played two songs back-to-back for a total of about eight minutes of airtime, and it was magical—unprecedented until then. I'm not sure what genius producer or station manager decided on that arrangement but that is how it was played every time and is still known as a two-song track today. The FM airwaves were still underground and unknown to me for months yet, but I could feel things changing rapidly.

The tumultuous, and life changing '60s were finally coming to an end, and a new decade was upon us. What would the '70s bring? We were now grade-school seniors, and that meant some status back at St. Margaret's School. We were the prodigal kids returning from a year of exile, and there was so much to do to get ready for high school. Mr. Frezza was not only our Grade 8 teacher but the principal of the school, too. He was a wonderful, caring human, and I credit him for much of my early teenage development—and such a change from that grouchy old Mr. G!

10. High School Tales

It was time to start thinking like grownups. Picking our subjects and electives for our first year of high school meant deciding if we wanted to go the five-year Arts and Science way, or four-year General. It was, of course, pretty much decided for us by our parents—not only which subjects we were taking but what high school we were to attend also. Given the fact that we were Catholic, and there was only one Catholic high school in the city, the choice was obvious. St. Patrick's High School on Bright St. was it. What wasn't talked about much was that our crazy little group of grade school friends was about to be torn apart. There were four other high schools in Sarnia at the time, and the gang would soon be dispersed among them. I didn't have a clue what any of it meant to me then but could feel a dramatic shift was imminent.

Before any of that could happen, there was still a class trip to plan, another perk of being in Grade 8. Different options were presented. Of course, not like in later years where they'd go to Europe and such, but more reasonable options like skiing—or a daytrip to the newly opened Ontario Science Centre in Toronto. We chose the latter. Fundraising by selling chocolate bars and bake sales helped pay our way. It was a very good year. Friendships were solidified—the great unknown lay beyond, and I was ready—or so I thought.

The summer of 1970 had the significance of being my last vacation before entering high school. For the first time, I had the freedom to move about the city by any means possible and at that time, hitchhiking was the preferred method. The city was relatively safe and besides, all the kids were doing it! As a side note, and a subject discussed at great length further on, hitchhiking was to play a big part in my mobility around the city and beyond.

My hangout for the summer was Murphy Rd. Beach off Lakeshore Rd. on the shores of Lake Huron. It was at the far end of the city, which created an issue getting there at times when I didn't feel like thumbing a ride. My sister Lorraine was dating Art Brosha during this time. Originally from Nova Scotia, he was now working in Sudbury. On his week's break from work, he arrived in Sarnia driving a green 1968 Mustang Fastback—fully piped out, and fast as hell. I asked, and he obliged me with rides to the beach several times in that muscle car. My love for that genre of vehicle has stayed with me ever since. I am disappointed to say I've never yet owned a classic Mustang.

A notable encounter with Art happened fifty years later, in the fall of 2020. I found myself in Cheticamp, NS on Cape Breton Island, staying at the Laurie Motel. I ended up sitting next to Art and his wife for breakfast. We spoke for a few minutes and reminisced about that glorious green machine of his. It was nice to see him again.

I met many different people that summer who would become long-time friends but none more memorable than Jeff Zierler, a rich kid from Northern High—we hit it off right away. Jeff holds the dubious distinction of being the first person I knew who actually had illicit drugs on his person. He had three joints in the top left pocket of his jean jacket, which he showed me while we were at the beach. All I could hear was my mother saying, "Drugs are bad. Don't do drugs." At the time, and long before marijuana was legal, this was huge. No, I did not partake of his herb at the time. It also did not make him a bad boy. If anything, in my eyes, he was even cooler than he had seemed before!

Jeff would become a lifelong friend, and I was shaken to the core the day I found out he had not survived a bypass operation when he was forty-seven years old. I had breakfast with him the day before he was admitted to a London hospital. We planned to meet again in his recovery room after his surgery. That never happened. I was out on the lake when I got the call from his sweet girlfriend Judi, informing me that he had passed away on the operating table due to complications from his severe diabetes. A week later, my friends and I were attending his funeral. Yes, life can change in a second.

I also met Brad Goodchild, who was an incredible artist/animator, even back then. He would have his sketch pad with him most days, and we all enjoyed watching him draw his freehand characters. He would go on to work for many famous studios such as Disney and Dreamworks, and to this day, you can see his name among the credits for many projects. He was also engaged to my sister Valerie for a short while, but nothing became of it in the end.

The summer drifted by. The lazy days and nights hanging around the beach will forever evoke memories of laughter, sunshine, bonfires, and budding romance—not with anyone special yet, but the notion of "hey, I really like girls" was planted firmly in my mind.

One of the milestones to occur that summer was the addition of our first family car. Dad had never owned a personal vehicle. For all the years prior, he would have the use of the company truck to get us to where we needed to go, buy groceries—that sort of thing. So, when a shiny-new, baby-blue 1969 Ford Custom 500 arrived in the driveway, we suddenly became much more mobile. This car would play a significant role in my future high school shenanigans.

In September of 1970, I entered high school. What? Where had the time gone? It seemed the years were screaming by, and there was no way I could stop the rush to the future. For many years, the high school I was about to attend had a dress code policy. The students were required to wear the current ensemble of navy blue and white outfits. This policy had been contested by the students over the years, but it was always upheld by the school board. My first year at St. Pat's was the first year they finally eliminated the dress code—for the boys only. Even as I write this, I still can't believe such blatant discrimination was allowed. I have been told very recently that the dress code for the boys was again reinstated a few years back. I'm sure it will change again.

So there I was, walking to school in my new T-shirt, Levi's, jean jacket, snoot boots, and leather belt, all purchased in London the week before— for a whopping sum of sixty-five dollars. My paper route had been good to me financially, and I was thrilled I could buy my own clothes.

Classroom: 9F with Miss Lannon—at St. Patrick's High School—holy shit! I remember it like it was yesterday. New faces, new routine, new life.

Roll call, and seating assignments were dealt with, and most surprising was a cute little red-haired girl sitting right in front of me. Her name? Dana McEachan! I had never met another person with my name before—let alone a cute red-headed girl. We became instant friends. I saw her a lot over the years after high school, and if I ran into her today, I would recognize her with hugs and laughter all around. In a twist of irony to be played out much later, the red-haired trait would have a significant effect on my future love life.

I met Drew Parsons that day also. He was a quirky kid with a great smile, and an infectious laugh. We hit it off and became fast buds. I lost touch with Drew after high school but have heard recently he is alive and doing fine. With the advent of social media, it is sometimes easy to locate old school mates. I looked for Drew but to no avail.

School wasn't the only place where we were social. The previous summer at the beach produced many long-time friends. Monica Zub was one of those beautiful girls we loved to hang with. The upside to Monica's friendship was also getting to know her brother, Steve. Even though they both attended Northern High, Steve and I would become best friends. For many years, I frequented the Zub household where Momma Zub would treat us like family. She made the best cabbage rolls and perogies I had ever tasted. Steve, and Monica's dad, Dr. Zub, was the Public School Board psychiatrist. He kept to himself somewhat but was always pleasant to me. He had a very thick German accent and, at the time, not knowing about political correctness, we would often imitate him in the style of Colonel Klink from the hit '70s TV series *Hogan's Heroes*. Oh, the shit we got away with back then.

Grade 9 was definitely a time of discovery, especially when girls were involved. I met Linda, a pretty brunette who lived on Rutherglen Close, off Lakeshore Rd. I was smitten and started hanging around her often. The distance from my house to hers was about four miles, and—wanting to see her—I would hitchhike to the North End of the city after school most days. I would then have to do the same back home, late at night. I had my trusty jean jacket, and my thumb. All through that winter, I continued to wear that jacket. Sometimes a sweater underneath was required but very seldom. Ahhh, the things we did for love!

Perpetual Motion

Linda and family had a boarder staying at their place during that time. Sonny—I never did know his real name—drove a brand-new, orange-coloured 1971 model year Pinto with oversized tires on custom rims and a great 8-track stereo installed. One night in early spring, Linda and I went to the local carnival where Sarnia's Lambton Mall is now located. We asked Sonny to pick us up for the ride back to her place. He had a fantastic artist playing, Cat Stevens' now classic *Tea for the Tillerman* blasting through the speakers. I will never forget the feeling I had at that moment, listening to some great new music, sitting in the back seat of a brand-new car with my best girl—my first real love—free as a bird with seemingly no restrictions on my life—oh, the simpler times.

Later that fine summer, I etched a memory for the ages. Linda's mom owned a 1962 Chevrolet Impala, red in colour. I'm not sure why she didn't have it with her this particular weekend, but she was not home, and the car was—lucky for us. Linda's younger sister Sharon and her boyfriend Roman were hanging out at the house on this Sunday when Linda suggested we take the car for a ride. She needed something at the store. I was to drive. Of course, I had bragged about the fact that I had driven a car before and it was easy-peasy—so that is what we did. I was scared beyond belief, but my ego did not let me fail. The four of us made it to the corner store about a half-mile away, and very near our beach. When we pulled into the lot, several of our friends were hanging outside the variety store—there to witness me in the driver's seat of the car. My cool factor went up exponentially. I often wonder how Linda's mom would have reacted to our little road trip. I'm sure she never found out, but can imagine the outcome would not have been a pleasant one if she did.

Just for clarification, I had only driven two cars prior to that. The first time was way back in 1966 when I was about ten years old. One of my parents' friends, Eric Flesher, and his wife, Shirley, were just starting to build a modular home out on Egremont Side Rd. northeast of the city—about a half-hour drive from our current home on Wellington St. It was summertime, and I was going out to the job site most days with Eric so I could help him with the build. In all actuality, I was picking up scrap lumber as it was cut and putting it in a pile to be burned on the weekends. I really did think I had an important job. On this particular day—heading to the construction site, Eric stopped the car just as we made the turn onto Egremont. He asked me if I wanted to drive the car the rest of the way to the house. To me, that distance might as well have been a hundred miles, but it was about a half-mile at best—on a very straight dirt road with nothing to hit or crash into. The car was a 1957 Plymouth Fury with push button gear shift controls on the dash. I drove that car—very slowly I might add—to the driveway, turned in and pressed the "P" button for Park. I was never more proud of myself in that moment. That memory has stuck with me, and I had remained friends with Eric for years until his recent passing.

The second time was with Linda's stepfather, Bill, a few weeks earlier. He owned a 1969 Volkswagen Karmann-Ghia convertible—complete with manual transmission. He took Linda and me out for a ride in the country, and allowed me to drive the backroads. It was the first time I drove a standard model car, and it was sporty to boot—again, a very memorable experience.

Linda, and I would continue to date for about a year or so with an intensity I hadn't experienced before. She taught me many life lessons about intimacy and relationships that I would take into adulthood—yes, she was truly memorable.

I was crushed when we broke up. I had now experienced my first love, and my first heartbreak. Unfortunately, it would not be the last. I remember thinking that my world would never be the same—and looking back, it wasn't. My father walked into my room soon after, saw me crying, and asked why. He tried to console me and through my sobbing breath I blurted out, "But I loved her!" And at the time, I truly believed I did. I only saw Linda a couple of times after that, with one memorable tale told further into my story.

Those times would set the pattern for my life of dating. In retrospect, I seemed to date long and hard. I would meet someone, fall head over heels for them, put them on a pedestal—and make them the central part of my life. When things did fall apart or come to an end, I fell hard down that rabbit hole. Hints of a depressive nature started to emerge. It would take me another forty-five years to finally figure that shit out.

I was introduced to the recreational use of cannabis in Grade 9. Nothing that is now illegal but decades ago—certainly taboo. I had resisted the temptations for months, ever since Jeff showed me his stash. Marijuana and hashish were readily available now that I was in high school. I experimented sparingly but never got into the drug scene heavily. I did however witness some things that probably steered me clear of anything that would have been detrimental to my health. Acid, cocaine, magic mushrooms, and at the time, probably some heroin—although I didn't know it, were always available on the street. After all, this was the early '70s, the start of a new decade, and if you take the time to read some history involving the drug trade of that era, it is not hard to fathom the types of things that could have influenced me. Again, my mother's mantra from several years earlier, "Drugs are bad, don't do drugs," was always, and ever present in my mind. She was a smart lady. Thanks, Mom.

The first time I bought hashish was late December. My buddy, Mark and I were to babysit a friend's son on Brock St., an older part of the city. Some of the weathered homes in that area had seen better days—this one was not in the best of condition, for sure. We thought it would be wise to have a little something to pass the night away after "little Johnny" was in bed. I'm not proud of these moments but yes, we smoked the hash and had a great laugh for several hours. The funniest thing about the evening was the decrepitly slanted floor in the living room of the old house. Walking around added to the hilarity of the situation, and I guess that is why it is such a memorable occasion—ok, ok, you had to be there.

The beginning of the new decade brought many more firsts to my upbringing. I tasted alcohol. A beer or two had been consumed here or there but not much, and then I tasted Golden Wedding, a Canadian rye whisky I got from my brother Greg. It was a mickey, or a fifth, or a pint, whatever you want to call it—but it was raw, and it was real, and it burned all the way down my throat. That first whisky buzz was truly a delightful experience—for a few hours. By the time the pint was gone—so was I. I giggled, laughed out loud, slurred my words, stumbled around the neighbour's apartment for a while, and in the end—got violently sick. At least that is what I believe happened. I wouldn't know because for the first time, I was drunk. The next day wasn't pretty. Somehow though, I avoided the all-knowing inquisitive stares of my parents on that momentous occasion. I had seen many times how they taunted my older siblings when it was their rite of passage to feel the wrath of the dreaded hangover. Usually, a warm beer on a tray presented to the aggrieved child—while they were still in bed, saddled with a migraine-type jackhammer headache—was the norm. Dad, I believe, relished in this ritual, knowing that it was harmless to us in the long run.

Alcohol became a part of my fabric as it did for my friends, siblings, my parents before me, and their parents too. My friends, and my social circle were my biggest influencers, and so, I classified myself as a social drinker. I don't believe I ever truly abused it. That's not to say I didn't consume too much on occasion, or use it as a crutch during some desperate times in my life, but I can say I never ever felt I had a problem, and that I could stop drinking altogether if I wanted to—I just didn't want to.

Around Christmas, I was hanging with some friends at a house party in the tree streets. It was the festive season, so we as a group were trying mixed cocktails—a very new experience for me. Someone poured me a Black Russian, and then probably a few more. I woke up early the next morning in a bathtub—empty, thankfully—and had no idea where I was. It was the first time I had blacked out from drinking. I was hung "to the nines" as the saying goes, and as we all do on such occasion, swore I would never drink again—if only I could feel somewhat normal. I believe it took about twenty-four hours for me to function. There was a definite lesson to be learned in that episode, and I believe I understood what it was. It just took me a few more years to put that lesson into action. After all, it was the '70s.

Besides my London Free Press paper route I'd had a few years back, I was also now a seasoned worker. I spent more than a year working for the St. Vincent de Paul Society on Front St. My job was to sort used clothing into different categories, the absorbent material separated—to be cut up, and used for rags. I would then bundle them and prepare them for shipment to industry. My wage was fifty cents per hour. This was my spending money, and in high school we all needed spending money to be cool.

The kind ladies who worked the store would make sure I had a portable radio with me so I would not get too lonely. This fact is entirely significant because I heard Don McClean's now iconic "American Pie" for the first time while sorting those rags. The influence of music was powerful then and continued to be a huge part of my life.

Perpetual Motion

I was in my first traffic accident while working for St. Vincent de Paul, and not once but twice with my co-worker, Jeff. He was the pickup driver for used furniture and other donations. We would go out on Saturday mornings with a list of addresses to pick up the donations—Jeff always drove very aggressively. Both accidents were probably his fault. Fortunately, we were not hurt, but after the second mishap, I refused to venture out with him again. It wasn't long before he moved on.

The first FM rock station to air locally was WRIF out of Detroit, and to this day it is a powerhouse station for rock and roll. What are all now considered classic rock songs were played on that new radio format for the first time. This new genre of music started to influence me greatly. The "in" thing to do in my crowd was to attend live concerts to see these influential bands, and I enjoyed that activity much more than most. This pastime became a regular occurrence during my high school days, with a concert being attended, usually in the Detroit area, about every second week. A special treat would be to travel to Hamilton or Toronto to see a favourite band—not only because of the music, but for the whole friendship bonding experience. I lost count after about four hundred concerts and still enjoy attending live events today.

Grade 9 came and went. I had long hair. I excelled at forming new lifelong friendships, learning how to become a social being, and understanding the ways of this new world I had entered, temptations and all. I had enjoyed the hell out of my first year of high school—but I failed miserably at being a high school student, getting very poor marks in most subjects. I still have the report cards to prove it.

The only subject I excelled at was typing. Think about that for a second in the context of today's society and remember: We had no internet, no home computers, and no cell phones. They were yet to be thought of, let alone mass-produced. To be honest, we were lucky if we got to use one of the few electric typewriters in the classroom. I took the course because I thought it would be an easy filler for my electives, and besides, Mr. Sakerak taught the class, and he was cool. It turned out to be the one skill I still get practical use of daily, and I have been out of school for fifty years.

The summer of 1971, between Grade 9 and 10, was a blast despite the loss of my first love. My friends and I continued to hang out at Murphy

Rd. Beach and, sometimes stayed out all night. We would have our bonfire by the shore and then sleep in the sand until either daybreak or the police came to tell us to make our way home. I was starting to notice, and really appreciate my newfound freedom.

Our core group of friends grew also. Joan was about to enter St. Pat's, which meant the crowd hanging around our house would get bigger with the addition of her pals too. As much as I knew several of Greg's friends, I was still a little too young to be seen with them. That would change in a year or two when our circles would merge to the point of us hanging out together—now that was progress!

It seems I was repeating a pattern, also. Greg was the original owner of that previously mentioned *London Free Press* paper route, and when he did not feel like doing it anymore, I had taken over. The same can be said for his job at Sanitary Maintenance. I took over that one too. It consisted of evening work cleaning and waxing floors in doctor's offices, professional buildings, and any other building where I was needed. I hated it, but it was better than getting up at five o'clock in the morning. Although it was minimum wage, it put money in my pocket to be able to do the things teenage boys at the time did. I think the wage for that job was two dollars an hour.

As I got older, the privilege of freedom to be me—to explore the world around me with no boundaries—was very liberating. My parents had trust in each of us, and until we abused that trust, it would remain—faithfully. I can honestly say that even though I may have done some things they may not have approved of, I never gave them reason to not trust me.

Ok, there was this bar on London Line—locally known as Sarnia's Golden Mile, called Huey's Junkyard. It was located in the former ballroom of the Holliday Hotel (no affiliation to the Holiday Inn chain). This venue was the most popular nightclub in the area at the time. Local bands—and there were many great ones—would play on weekends to a packed house. Door bouncers and age-of-majority cards were virtually non-existent, so we would devise ways to enter the club even though we were minors. (I turned 15 that summer) We succeeded on several occasions, even if at times that meant climbing through the bathroom window someone would inevitably leave unlocked. We may have been influenced to try this method of entry by the current Beatles hit on the airwaves at the time. The mega-hit, "She Came in Through the Bathroom Window" was recorded and released by the supergroup in July of '69.

Probably the most memorable of those illegal visits was on a Saturday afternoon matinee in the late summer of '71. Several of us managed to enter the lounge at about noon and began to enjoy the local musical talents of the Stutt Brothers, a band known for some hard-driving rock and roll. Two songs stuck out that day, "Long Train Runnin'" by the Doobie Brothers and "Whipping Post" by The Allman Brothers. To this day, when I hear those tunes, I am floated back to that Saturday at the Junkyard.

The bar was about half full, maybe a hundred people. The band was loud, and on point. The weather that day was perfect. The next event will always be a crazy memory because it just doesn't happen today. One of the bad boys from the rough side of town decided to ride his Harley through the big double doors, into the bar, and when he and his machine reached the dance floor, everyone scattered. Jake then proceeded to do donuts round and round in a wide circle, all the while squealing his tires on the parquet tiles. The smoke from the burning rubber filled the area. After about a minute of his shenanigans, he existed through the big doors at the end of the bar. Everyone knew who it was, and to my knowledge, nothing was ever done about it. The smoke cleared, and we went back to our beer and music—like nothing had happened.

That same day, there happened to be a young musician sitting at the table beside us enjoying the offerings of his friends on stage. He seemed to have a grasp of the music and would sing along to each of the songs as if he were on stage himself. A couple of hours went by, and we had now struck up a friendship with this skinny rocker. The matinee was over but none of us wanted to end the day, so he invited us back to his parents' place in the North End to spin some vinyl. He had introduced himself as Kim, and I remember thinking it was such an unusual name for a guy. When I introduced myself, he commented on the irony of our names being girls' names also. We went to the lower level of his parent's house, where the whole rec room was covered in freight elevator padding. This apparently was so he could practice his music without disturbing the neighbours.

Kim Mitchell went on to form the band Max Webster in 1973, and after a very successful nine year run with that band, enjoyed a fine solo career. His only #1 hit, "Go for a Soda" is as popular today as it was back then. I cherish the memories of hanging out with this guy before he was famous, even if it was only for a day.

On yet another afternoon, after the fun and the music at Huey's—while hanging out at a buddy's house—he thought he'd put on a new record and asked us if we had ever heard of a band called Little Feat. We hadn't, so he played his copy of *Feats Don't Fail Me Now* in its entirety, very loud, and very aggressive. The mood was festive, fuelled by the beer and pot. I'm sure this had much to do with the enjoyment of the tunes. That vinyl instantly became one of my all-time favourite albums—ever. Since that memorable day, I've owned two vinyl copies, one cassette, and two CDs. Yes, I have played this set of songs so much I have worn through each unit.

Oftentimes, I look back at the things I did as a teen and just shake my head. Even though I had survived some stupid antics, it still didn't make them smart. One such ridiculously wrong habit I was privy to was when my very good friend, Paul would steal his mother's car while she was at work. She worked about two blocks from home so would walk for the fresh air and exercise many of those days. She owned a tan-brown 1970 Ford Fairlane 500. It was sleek, and it was fast. The lure of cruising around town, tunes cranked, windows down, proved too much for Paul. He would "borrow" the car, pick me up, and we would drive around as if we owned the city. No, Paul didn't have his driver's license, and neither did I. We were only fifteen. This went on for most of the spring and summer of 1971, and we never got caught. I still don't know how that happened. Mrs. Butler must have realized there wasn't as much gas in the car as when she had left it last. I certainly don't remember ever stopping to fill the tank, and that car was a gas guzzler.

We had quite the party on the beach all of that Labour Day weekend in the waning days of our fabulous summer of '71. It seemed to me, most of the high school kids in the city had discovered our treasured secret we had kept for the last couple of years. The influx of new bodies of course, meant that I was meeting other kids from the five different schools. The classifications for each of the schools was known city wide. The Northern kids were the rich bitches. The St. Clair kids were the farmers. The SCITS kids were the greasers. The Central kids were the hippies/jocks, and we at St. Pat's were the stoners. The beach was packed with us regulars, and many newcomers. Some of the time, it got out of hand with the drinking and the pot smoking. The police were called and visited us several times during the weekend, but all went relatively smoothly. No harm, no foul. Sadly, it was time to get back to school, and Grade 10 was going to be harder than Grade 9. I needed to buckle down and improve my grades—the challenge was on.

Grade 10 started with a great surprise. The first day of class saw us heading to our new homerooms to get settled in. Imagine my surprise when my friend, Monica's brother—my Northern buddy, Steve Zub—came bouncing into the classroom. He had transferred to St. Pat's because he thought he'd like it better. I guess that was a legitimate reason back then.

Steve was so charismatic. He always wore a jean jacket he had painted and bejewelled, and his hair was long. He was a big boy at about six-foot-one. His signature look though, was very tall, high-heeled leather boots that he had custom painted in bright colours. Influenced by the Detroit rock band Kiss, he had several pairs of these flashy boots, and when worn, they made him at least three or four inches taller. The girls loved him! I knew immediately this was going to be a stellar year. My first thought was that, again, I may not fare well in the academic arena, but at that time I didn't care. My buddy was here, and look out! We would go on to enjoy the rest of high school and beyond together and create some of the best memories ever.

As tight-knit a group as there ever was, alongside Steve and me, the ever ready-to-party duo of Mike McCaffery and Larry Chynces added to the wonders of friendship. We would go on to be inseparable for most of the next several years.

One of many such memorable occasions, involving mostly illegal shenanigans, happened in the spring of 1972. The new 400 Series Highway 402 would eventually make travel much easier and faster from Sarnia to London, but in the spring of that year, it was just a mud-track of construction—half-built overpasses, and no access except for heavy equipment. The main section from Modeland Rd. in Sarnia to Highway

81 at Strathroy had progressed farther than the two connecting sections to the west and east but was still not fit for vehicles of the streetworthy kind. That, of course, did not stop Steve, myself, and the others from attempting the near impossible. Coming home from an evening in London was about to get crazy. I'm not sure how we managed to get into the construction zone or where we accessed it along the way, but we managed to somehow find ourselves travelling west towards Sarnia, through and around barriers at quite an elevated speed. We were in Steve's Montego station wagon, one of the many vehicles he owned during those memorable high school years. I wish I could tell you we made it all the way home without incident, but that would be a lie. We almost made it home. Just as we were attempting to exit the mud encrusted highway overpass at Modeland Rd., our last hurdle to freedom, Steve lost control of the car, slid sideways, and ended up buried up to the rear axle part-way down the steep embankment of the unfinished abutment. Lucky for us, no one was hurt. We laughed at our predicament and next tried to figure out how to get out of there. If that act had been tried today, we would all have been arrested for sure. But as it was late in the evening, and under the cover of darkness, we had time to get the car removed by the many friends we solicited for the extraction—finally getting the vehicle to a car wash to remove any evidence of our foolish act. There is a snapshot of the car resting askew in the mud somewhere.

Steve, Mike, Larry, and I were pretty well inseparable for most of high school. We hung together every chance we had, and although not always in the safest of manner, we had each other's back. Most episodes or exploits involved alcohol, some pot thrown in for a laugh, and some of the greatest emerging rock and roll to ever grace a radio station or record player—all the makings of the best times during my formative teenage years.

We did, of course, eventually go our separate ways a few years after high school, but the things we did, the memories made, are a lasting treasure. I will continue to laugh when I think of our antics, and the fact that each of us is still alive!

I truly don't think anyone, especially our teachers, would have predicted the outcome of our lives. They saw us as a rag-tag group of misfits who were not going to amount to much. How wrong they were.

For the record: Steve started working for CN Railway while still in high school. The last time we spoke, he had moved up the corporate ladder in Montréal and was about to retire from the same CN after over forty years of service. I'm sure he's enjoying his retirement now.

Mike entered the military right out of high school and spent twenty years serving his country in many war-ravaged areas of the world as a peacekeeper with the Canadian Forces. He is now retired, and I believe, living in Sarnia.

Larry eventually moved to Miami, FL and opened his own construction company, and the last report on him was very positive. He has run his successful business for over thirty-five years.

As will be recounted in much more detail in later chapters, I did my thirty-five years in service to the City of Sarnia as a firefighter, retiring as Deputy Chief. Not bad for a bunch of misfits. I miss those guys.

Another notable character in my Grade 10 class was a skinny, long-haired kid named Mike Bradley. He was quiet, unassuming and kept to himself. Mike would go on to sell real estate for a short period after high school, and as fate would have it, he knew a gentleman by the name of Bud Cullen who was running for the Ontario legislature. Mike was asked to be his campaign manager, and they went on to victory. Now having a taste for politics, Mike ran for a seat on Sarnia city council, and won. The one-term counsellor then set his political sights even higher when, in 1988, he assumed the title of "Your Worship" as mayor of Sarnia. This holds significant meaning for me, considering the Corporation of the City of Sarnia became my career employer—with Mike at the helm for most of it.

As I write today, Mayor Bradley has been elected to an unprecedented eleventh term as mayor of Sarnia. He is now the longest-serving mayor in Sarnia's history and second-longest-serving mayor in the Province of Ontario. Kudos to you, old friend.

Music continued to dominate my life in Grade 10. I was going to concerts in Detroit and the surrounding area often. The likes of Deep Purple, Jethro Tull, The Rolling Stones, Yes, Mott the Hoople, ZZ Top, Alice

Cooper, Black Sabbath, The Allman Brothers Band, and so many more all came out with incredible rock and roll. I would buy the latest vinyl for about five to seven dollars each, which added to my growing collection of records.

There was a different genre of music getting lots of local attention also. The St. Pat's theatre troupe did three very memorable operatic plays around this time. The first was *Pirates of Penzance,* followed by *H.M.S Pinafore,* and lastly, *The Mikado.* An extremely talented group of students performed these plays flawlessly and received much recognition for their efforts. I believe Cecilia Mallon played the lead heroine in all three musicals, and she could sing beautifully. I would love to tell you that I co-starred in these plays but alas, I would be lying—I worked on props, and backstage.

One of the best moments of the year, musically, took place during the Lambton County Live Theatre Review at the SCITS auditorium. Each year, besides St. Pat's, area high schools would practice and perform chosen plays in their own interpretation. St. Clair High School submitted their version of the album by the band The Moody Blues, *A Question of Balance*, produced by Frank Casey, a good friend of the family. They won first-place hands-down in that competition, and deservedly so. It was as well done as any professional theatre I have seen since. Many years later, in 2018, I finally saw The Moody Blues in concert, in South Florida. All the original band members were on stage that evening and sounded amazing.

Image was becoming a thing for me, that school year. Girls were hanging around more, and I liked it. Even though I had dated Linda for the first part of high school, this was different. Paddy Cunningham, Judy Kanyuk, Mary T Marcy, Cecilia Mallon, Wendy Teskey, Janice Baird, and so many others all played a big part in those formative years. I was hanging with some jocks—one of them had a full home gym in his garage—so I started thinking about working out. In the beginning, I was not even sure what that entailed, or if I ever got good at it, but things happen for a reason. John, Jamie, and Paul were but a few who would meet two or three times a week to get sore. Eventually, my participation in all that physical activity would help me greatly with the rigours of my chosen career. It has done me a world of good. I have participated in some form of physical exercise ever since—having had several gym memberships—loved weight training, running, and now, long walks.

I had also taken a liking to a feisty young lady that spring of '72, and we were hanging out regularly. Caryl was my doctor's daughter and, coming from the north end of town, would be considered a rich kid. Actually, in our world, anyone who lived north of the highway dividing the city was a rich kid. Daddy had money, so Caryl had the use of one of the family cars. It was a '71 Plymouth Scamp, and the perfect cruising car. We drove that car into the summer with our sights set on great times, and great weather.

The Grade 10 school year had ended with about the same scholastic results as previous years, a passing grade—but barely. I had been promised by my Grade 10 French teacher, Mr Kerr, that he would pass me in that subject if I never took French again. Yes, it was that bad. The social aspect of school, to me, seemed much more important. Lifelong friendships were solidified. I was halfway through my high school career, and looking forward to the great beyond.

It was time to celebrate my milestone sixteenth birthday. I came home that afternoon to find a note inside my birthday card informing me I was to participate in a scavenger hunt for twenty-four bottles of Molson Canadian beer. The surprising thing being—the card was from Mom and Dad. They had hidden the bottles throughout the house, and I couldn't drink my first until I found all of them. They even had the smarts to hide a couple of cold ones in the fridge for when I completed the hunt. Keep in mind the drinking age was eighteen—for me, two years away. My parents were just cool that way. Besides, they had a very good reason for doing this. In their minds, it was safer to buy me a treat, and allow me to drink a few at home, than to know I would go out and drink beer anyways—possibly getting in trouble or hurt. I guess I can't fault their logic. If you were to now ask my adult children, Stephanie and Shaun, they would tell you this was the way I treated them also.

By now, my hair was long and fell over my shoulders in a mass of curls. It was a sign of the times—without a care in the world. After all, I was sixteen, old enough to drive—surrounded by great friends, and damn it, my hair was cool. What more could a guy ask for.

Turning sixteen also meant I could actually get my driver's license for real, and use the family car—or so I hoped. The following day, I went to the license bureau on East St., and wrote the test for my beginner's permit. It was such a thrill to walk out of the building with that document in hand. My world was rapidly expanding. Not only would I be the first kid in the family to learn how to drive, but the first to get my full license and, possibly borrow Dad's wheels on occasion. My older siblings either didn't have the drive, no pun intended, or they were off doing their own thing—not showing any interest in increasing their mobility.

Dad was a great driving instructor. Many lessons and skills were taught during that late summer, with one lesson in particular standing out above all. We were driving east on London Rd. in Sarnia in what is now known as fast food alley between Murphy Rd. and the Lambton Mall. At the time, the road was only two lanes wide.

The lesson was conveyed this way: "When you are driving a vehicle, you have to drive the car in front of you, on both sides of you, and even behind you." His reasoning was clear. The other drivers may or may not be paying attention, so you have to do it for them. "Always be aware of your surroundings, and check your rear-view mirror—often."

Wise advice from a wise man. I think of those words often when in traffic. This advice probably saved a scratch or two on the many vehicles I have owned over the years. I continued to practice.

In late August, Caryl, Steve, and I took the train to Toronto. This would be another first. I had never ventured that far from town on my own before and, other than the train ride from Nova Scotia to Sarnia when I was three, this would be my first one since. We were going to do some shopping, and on a personal note, I was going to get my first professional haircut at one of the new-style salons that were popping up in Toronto and other metropolitan centres. This salon—unlike a barbershop, was unisex, and all the rage. Head Hunters was billed as the "in" place to get your hair styled. That fact should have been my first clue. I can now only describe my haircut at that time as the coolest on the planet, and in hindsight, the ugliest, most ridiculous looking haircut I have ever had. It was immediately labeled the poodle cut. You might know it today as a mullet. It was cut quite short on top and left long in the back but with a tapered look—oh, the embarrassment of it all. Just look at my Grade 11 class picture.

Shortly after our return, and as fall approached with another school year on the horizon, it was quickly noted that Caryl and I were more friends than an actual couple, so we chose to go that route. Although I don't see her often these days, I still consider her a friend.

Meanwhile, I was getting antsy. I had no intention of waiting much longer to take my actual driver's test. I probably hounded my father much more than I remember, but he didn't seem to mind taking me out for some roadworthy practice. The only other person to trust me with his car was Kevin Hoffman, a friend from school. He had a little Datsun 210, and was more than happy to help me practice, even after I scraped his door trying to parallel park. This was the vehicle I finally did use to pass my road test.

Shortly after getting my license came the first challenge. Greg had asked me if I would drive him and several friends to Pinery Provincial Park on the shores of Lake Huron so they could do some camping. If I agreed, he was to ask Dad for permission, and see where that went. I assumed the answer would be no, but I was wrong. With a pep-talk, and some mapped-out directions, we set out for the forty-five-minute drive to the park. I was thrilled but scared at the same time— having never driven beyond the city limits. After successfully dropping them off, I managed to navigate my way home without issue. This was huge. Again, my world grew exponentially.

It wasn't often, but on occasion I was allowed to come home after school and get the car to run errands. My first errand most of the time was to head directly back to the school to pick up my friends so we could go cruising. Cramming seven or eight of us into that big blue Custom 500 became a treasured ritual when Dad felt generous.

My parents started travelling more now that they had a reliable vehicle and we were getting older. Each summer they would head east for two weeks. In those early times, Lorraine, being the oldest, was put in charge of making sure we didn't destroy the house. She was given quite a lot of responsibility. Most every time, we would have ten to fifteen friends hanging out in the park behind the house the afternoon Mom and Dad left. Of course, each of those hooligans had a case of beer with them—what was affectionately known as a two-four. The moment they left, the gang would hop the fence, and the two-week party would begin. Mom's friends would unexpectedly stop by the house on any given day. I know for a fact this was by design, and not by chance. They were checking up on us—sometimes even staying for a beer. This whole routine went on year after year, and several more after I eventually left the house. Martin and Noelle continued the tradition—sure made me proud.

Around this time, I got my first car—given to me. My father's brother, Uncle Tony, owed him some money, two hundred dollars to be exact. In exchange for that debt, Dad received Tony's old car which had been a hand-me-down from his boss some years before. It was a very rare, 1961 Chevrolet Nomad station wagon. It came equipped with power steering, power brakes, power windows, and automatic transmission. The best part—it was all mine. The freedom that car afforded me was endless and made it far easier to actually go on a date. Unfortunately, it was also subject to mechanical issues, so it was not very reliable. I drove it off and on for about a year. Knowing what I know today, having that car restored would have made it worth many thousands of dollars in the present classic car market—yes, another missed opportunity.

11. Time To Get Serious

Grade 11—Mr. Oakes' class. I knew I was running out of time and just had to buckle down to get some decent marks—average or above. I still had no idea what I was going to do after school, but the pressure was on to start figuring that out. The problem facing me was a very full social calendar—again. I had many good friends, and many more acquaintances, and felt the need to hang out with the crowd more than I felt the need for an education. Don't get me wrong, I was very aware that my education should have been a priority, but outside influences were the current bane of my existence. A pretty girl's smile, an invitation to a house party or just about any other excuse would do it. At this point, music continued to be monumental, and another wild distraction. I had been to over one hundred concerts by this time and saw no relief in sight for such activity.

And then it happened, one of the most significant moments from my high school days. It was shortly after the first term started that September. A new group of students were starting Grade 9. One such young lady's name was Kathy. The day she walked into St. Pat's was the day she became the most beautiful girl in the school—not only gorgeous, but intelligent, outgoing, and carefree.

A tradition in high school, continued from the "bobby socks" era, was to have dances every Friday night. Each school in the district would take turns hosting a dance. Usually, as was custom, the first dance of the year was called the Sadie Hawkins dance. The one rule applied was that the girls got to ask the boys to the dance—just this once.

I was home one evening watching Elvis Presley's *Aloha From Hawaii* on TV—along with a billion other people in the world. The phone rang, and to my wide-eyed, gaping-mouth surprise, I heard Kathy's voice on the line. The conversation was short, sweet, and in the end, I had been asked to escort her to the Sadie Hawkins dance. This was huge. Out of all the eligible guys in high school, this beautiful young lady asked me to go to that dance. That was to be the start of a year-long love affair, and we found ourselves spending most of our time together. I am quite sure her folks didn't approve of this long-haired hippie hanging around their beautiful young daughter—picking her up for school, dropping her off at the end of the day, sometimes late into the evening. Although at times cordial enough, I never felt quite at home in their presence.

Life went on in sort of a trance. I was smitten by my queen, and most nothing else mattered. In years to come, this would be finally recognized as a destructive pattern in my life. As recalled earlier, whenever I would get involved in a relationship, it seems I intended to block everything else out, and only pay attention to my significant other. Many years later, I would be called out on this fact, and I now believe that that is what eventually broke the cycle.

Kathy was a good influence on me in my senior years at school. Her intelligence was rubbing off. I became more interested in some of my school subjects—mainly English and History. Maybe it was my teachers, Mrs. Stellmaker and Brother Peter, who made those classes interesting—maybe a combination of both, but whatever was happening to me was good. My homeroom teacher, Joe Oakes, who also taught me math, saw my renewed potential, and I started to improve in that subject also.

Kathy and I continued to date through Grade 11. A couple of influential songs that bring back memories of those times with Kathy are "My Sweet Lord" by George Harrison and "Diamond Girl" by Seals and Croft. We would drive around in my Nomad for hours on end singing those songs—feeling like we were invincible. On one occasion, she and her girlfriends rented a cottage up the lake at Kettle Point and needed a ride there. My trusty station wagon came in handy, and I ended up staying with them for two days. We swam, ate, drank, and barbecued all weekend. Those were fine times. That early fall, as the weather turned colder, she would bundle up—calling the changing season "turtleneck and jacket weather," in reference to the style of the day.

Perpetual Motion

The one constant in this world is change, and there would continue to be much of that in my life. I don't recall the hard reasons for Kathy's and my demise, but surely it must have had something to do with us continuing to grow up and wanting to explore new horizons. I know we weren't dating when I entered Grade 12, but I can truthfully say that being with Kathy for that period was a time of real personal growth. We remained friends for several years after high school, and ironically, she eventually married the guy she started dating after we broke up.

Part of the curriculum in high school was speech writing. I had previous experience with this genre as far back as grade school, so didn't shy away from public speaking. I also loved pushing the boundaries with my subject matter. I knew I was going to push the envelope with this one too. My Grade 11 speech was titled "The Art of Smoking." On the day my name was called, I stood, walked to the front of the room, and addressed the teacher and my classmates—some of them had smug looks of anticipation, having had a sneak preview of what was about to transpire. I began by giving them a brief history of cigarettes. The difference between my speech and others was, unbeknownst to but a select few in the classroom, I was going to do an actual demonstration on how to light and smoke a cigarette. A well-known fact was that our English teacher, Mrs. Stellmaker, was a very heavy smoker, so I presumed she would understand. I continued, explaining how a cigarette was constructed, what caused the thermal reaction as the flame touched the end of the rolled tobacco, how to draw your breath when you ingested the tar and nicotine deep into your lungs, and the intervals between each inhale of toxic smoke. Not only did I explain this verbally, but I actually performed each maneuver as a visual demonstration. The audible gasps coming from the assembled students was the reaction I had anticipated. Nobody in the history of the school had ever had the balls to actually light a cigarette in any classroom, let alone Stella's! I was keenly aware of her intense observation from the back of the class. Once I had demonstrated the art of lighting the cigarette, I held it in my left hand, and at approximately fifteen second intervals, inhaled again deeply on the cigarette. After the third such action, the teacher's smoke-stained, gravelly voice came from the back of the room: "That is enough of the demonstration, Mr. Pitts. You may put the cigarette out and continue your speech."

I was euphoric. I had actually pulled it off in front of, most likely, the strictest teacher in the city. Two good things happened because of that speech. I got an A+ for my effort, including very positive comments on my overall presentation. I also became the talk of the school after word rapidly spread of my bold decisions and choices made, in front of "Stella." Being defiant had its perks!

Pink Floyd's album *Dark Side of the Moon* was released in the spring of '73. Now considered arguably the greatest album ever recorded, at that time it was just another spectacular piece of music. Saturday mornings, and headphones were made for that piece of vinyl, and I took advantage of it many days over. One of the greatest concerts I have ever attended—even to this day—was Pink Floyd performing live at Ivor Wynne Stadium in Hamilton, Ontario in late June of '75. After several opening numbers, the band started into their newest studio recording. From the melodic opening notes of "Breathe" to the haunting crescendo of "On the Run," they played it in its entirety. The theatrics on stage that afternoon were only eclipsed by the giant airplane prop that crashed into the stage at the end of the song "Money." I still rate that concert in my top five.

The other significant piece of music that made it big in 1973 was Andrew Lloyd Webber's adaptation of the life and times of Christ. *Jesus Christ Superstar* was a two-disc vinyl set composed as a rock opera and released in 1971. The original Broadway musical brought this piece of music to the forefront, and it became very trendy. Since then, it has become infinitely famous and been redone many times over. I have seen at least ten live renditions of this play since its inception—most recently in Wolfeville, NS with a stellar performance by my nephew, Bradley Cameron, playing the part of Peter. It has also become the soundtrack I listen to most often when needing some spirituality in my life.

Although I had written book reports in both Grade 9 and Grade 10, I had not read any actual books since my junior years at St. Margaret's School. Book reports were easy. I got creative, used Cole's Notes, and basically made up stories. I recall getting decent marks too. My dislike or disinterest in reading changed in 1974 when a young American author,

Stephen King, published his first book, *Carrie*. The horror genre was unfamiliar to me, so after several friends had recommended the read, I knew I would delve into it. Of course, that was the beginning of a lifelong love affair with his style of writing—and books in general. I now have read everything of his I have been able to get my hands on—and there are only a handful of authors I can say that about. Along with *Carrie*, the likes of *Salem's Lot*, *It*, *The Shining*, *The Green Mile*, *12/22/63* and so many others are just classic King.

Events of the day that were talked about in and around school and have since become historically significant, included the likes of the Vietnam War and the Watergate scandal in US politics. We were well aware there were protests at the college and university level to end the war in Southeast Asia. That conflict was the first to be nationally televised into our homes each evening. It brought the horrors of war to life. Fortunately, after approximately twelve years, fighting ceased, and the war ended in August of '73. The protests turned to jubilant celebrations, which were also televised nationally. Kids my age had been dying in the jungles of the far-east for all those years—and to what end?

Edwin Starr, an American Motown artist, wrote an anti-war song in 1970, aptly titled "War." It had very poignant lyrics that spoke to the notion that life was precious and much too short for nations to be fighting wars every day. He melodically explained how the brutal act of war was responsible for taking away so many of our youth when it was just not necessary. The message in his song has aged well. Looking back on this period of unrest—and even with the current conflicts of today—history has proven him right.

We were not immune to the fact that war did not accomplish anything except death and destruction. The constant bombardment of this type of news had a profound and detrimental effect on many young minds—including mine.

As it is today, with twenty-four-hour cable news, internet saturation, and social media of all kinds reflecting the so-called importance of every significant event happening around the world, all piped into our ears and minds through the ever-present earbuds—we have become almost immune to what is actually significant. What is the truth anymore? I really wonder if *fake news* will ever not be an issue again. I can honestly say I was acutely aware of what was happening in the world at that time but, being physically removed from it, I don't recall my lifestyle being adversely affected. I am very thankful for that.

Since Richard Nixon had become the US president in 1969, the war machine seemed to have escalated, and politics was getting out of hand. The Watergate Affair in 1972 was the result of this delusion of power by one man to do what he pleased and be damned to the rest of the country. This too was fodder for the nightly talking heads. As the details of the break-in to the Watergate Convention Center became public, concern grew that the President of the United States—the most powerful man in the free world—was involved in a political cover-up. As we now know, this was but a brief glimpse into the insanity that would mire a future leader of the free world some forty-five years later.

I don't totally recall the whole Watergate Affair involving Nixon during his second term of office. I took it in like most others but always had the ability to fringe it. It was most often the lead story on the evening news for two long years, and in the end, way up in Kitimat, BC, alongside Jim Butler, Al and Frank Sowinski, I sat and watched the televised speech that hot August night in 1974 when Richard Nixon resigned his presidency—a historical first.

Maybe it is a coincidence that I became interested in all sources of history at a time when history was being made right on my doorstep. However that may be, those early influences of watching the evening news have remained with me to this day. The likes of Walter Cronkite, David Brinkley, Sam Donaldson, Barbara Walters, and many other trustworthy newscasters were where we got our credible sources of the day's events. Of course, the evening news has been redefined many times over. My favourite news cast is now a short, half-hour broadcast entitled *ABC World News Tonight* with David Muir. This is all I need most of the time. He is a professional and does not sugar coat the events of the day. He tells it like it is, and after that brief half hour, I feel like I have all the information I need to be informed. As will be stated in later chapters, I sometimes still tend to fall off the rails somewhat when I get fully immersed in spectacular events of a given day or time period.

Meanwhile, the old '61 Chevy I was so proud of finally broke down for good. Having no money or the knowledge of how to fix it, my car would occupy half the driveway for the next two years. We did use it for the occasional toke when the folks were home. Fortunately, Steve still had a car, and that would continue to be our mode of transportation into the future.

Grades 11 and 12 were considered senior years at St. Pat's. An addition to the school had been built as a stand-alone structure, which included several new classrooms and a lounge area for the senior students to gather when not required to attend class. This lounge would become a significant part of my scholastic life. We used it in fair and foul weather to smoke cigarettes, hang with our friends, play euchre, or listen to the many talented students playing their chosen instruments. It added an element to our social lives that I don't think the other high schools had.

The summer of 1973 finally dawned. It had been a long school year, but with the success of my marks, I was ready to let loose. By this time, Steve, Larry, Mike, and I were truly inseparable. Trish Woodcock, Monica Pearl, Caryl Clift, Wendy Teskey, and a large group of others had now bonded and were fast becoming lifelong friends. Al Sowinski, Jim Butler, Jeff Zierler, and John Rawlings, with his AMC Gremlin, all continued to have a major influence on my teen years.

That summer consisted of lots of social activity, including several more concerts, house parties, trips to the beach, and opportunities to live life to the fullest. We were healthy and carefree. I don't recall any one of us outwardly discussing anxiety or depression. We had never heard of being gluten-free, having peanut allergies, being vegan or vegetarian, or any other of the significant issues facing teens today. I'm not sure I even knew the meaning of the word "suicide." I can state for certain that I knew of no one who took their own life. That would not become a reality to me until several years into my eventual career. I'm not sure if it's the hormones in the food we eat today or just what it is, but times seemed to have been much simpler back then—and much harder on the kids now.

One of the advantages of living in simpler times, and quirks, if you will, of coming from a large family, was that there was always a houseful of people. My siblings and I, along with my parents, often contributed to this seemingly overcrowded space. The house we grew up in was a side-by-side duplex that I believe was less than a thousand square feet. We somehow made it work. Over the course of the four years I spent at St. Pat's, our little abode on Wellington St. had become the high school hangout—and my parents were cool with that. Most of our friends would call them Mom and Dad, and several were comfortable enough to just walk into the house, open the fridge, and indulge at will. One such friend, Jim Butler, recounts this fact often—even to this day.

For many years—and long before high school—our family had one of the greatest traditions I have ever taken part in. Every Christmas Eve, there was an open invitation to a festive gathering at the Pitts' residence, and it seems everyone showed up. Many of my parent's friends were there in the beginning, but as we siblings got older, they became the minority. One of the attractions to such a large crowd was Mom's famous rabbit pie. She would spend all day Christmas Eve at the stove, preparing the wild game in a large stock pot with big chunks of salted pork fat. The smells of that day were so intoxicating to us as we counted down the hours to the feast. But there were rules. The stipulation was that the rabbit pie would be served after coming back from midnight mass. Our diehard friends, most of whom probably didn't go to church on a regular basis, would attend the mass at St. Benedict's church in anticipation of a sliver of pie upon return. It must have been worth it, because there was always a crowd after mass. All I can think of is the Biblical story of the loaves and fishes. I don't know how she did it, but Mom always seemed to have enough—not only during this very special occasion, but at any time a meal was served. There were always extra bodies around the dinner table, and no one was ever refused a seat.

And then I was in Grade 12 —my senior year. I still had no idea what I was going to do after graduation, or if I would graduate at all, for that matter. Was I going to pursue a post-secondary education, such as college or university, or was I going to enter the workforce? I thought about this but again didn't put the greatest effort into resolving the issue. In the end, it came down to just not liking school, or at least the curriculum-based part of it. I applied myself in Grade 12 and came away with decent marks. This was most likely due to my maturity level, and the fact that I did not have any girlfriend-related distractions. Mary T. Marcy and I went to a concert one time in Detroit and had a great time, but as had happened with Caryl and me, we just became very good friends, and so I left it at that. I hung out with my friends, continued to do well in school, and tried to mentally prepare for the future.

That all changed when I finally took notice of a little blonde girl walking the halls. Her name: Nancy Kanyuk.

Nancy was a year my junior and in Grade 11. Her sister, Judy, had been in many of my classes over the years. This strikingly beautiful lady was petite, cute as a button, and very flirtatious. It all started innocently enough, but I found myself going out of my way to cross paths with her in the hallways—just to be near her. I went as far as to study her class schedule so I knew just when she would appear, and from which classroom door. We started to hang out after school and on weekends and eventually we acknowledged we were a couple. It felt good to be back in a relationship. This was my comfort zone. I was in love.

Nancy and I dated for many months, and again, I was smitten. Her family was wonderful to me—making me feel very much a part of her life. My upbringing taught me to treat women with respect, and if ever I did do that, it was with Nancy. We enjoyed many flirtatious activities, some quite emotionally and sexually charged for two teens in love, but in the end, we remained strictly platonic. I truly could have married that girl. She now lives in the United States with her awesome husband Kirk and family, and we still converse several times a year through social media.

Along with all the usual suspects, Jim Butler and I were starting to chum around quite a bit more. Jim was tall, athletic, and with long red hair, was dating the most beautiful girl in Grade 12. Jim and Paddy were the Barbie and Ken couple that seemed to have it all. I always thought they would end up married, but it was not to be.

He and I were sitting around one night having a couple of beers when we got into a conversation with my brother, Greg about his previous experience hitchhiking to the West Coast. Greg and his buddy Kelly had thumbed their way out west the year before—a fact that peaked Jim's and my interest. I absolutely looked up to my big brother. He was a track star, a basketball star, a chick magnet, a free spirit, and my buddy. Needless to say, he had quite the influence over me. And so, with that, the stage was set. Jim and I began planning to do the same.

This new obsession occupied much of my free time. For the next several months, it seemed everyone my age was making plans to do something. Most were plotting their move to higher education, while some of us—the more adventurous ones—were scheming to get out of Dodge. Is it any wonder my memories are sketchy during this period? It seems I had one goal in mind: I was going to make my way to Vancouver Island.

My parents were less than impressed, as was dear Nancy. Not only was I not considering post-secondary education, but I also didn't have a job, so how was I going to pay for this adventurous trip to the west? They had a point. I was told in no uncertain terms that I was paying my own way, and that I needed a substantial amount of money in my pocket before they would let me embark on this journey. Challenge accepted.

I continued to do well scholastically, and in June of 1974, I passed my required courses, receiving enough credits to earn my secondary school diploma. For the first time in my four years of high school, I didn't have to write any exams to make the grade. I had already made the decision to take at least a year off school before determining my future. Now all I needed was a job so I could earn enough money to implement our travel plans.

PART 2

12. Freedom On the Open Road

Jim and I applied for and were hired locally with an industrial company based out of Toronto. We were contracted to do some maintenance work on several large oil tanks at one of the facilities on the outskirts of Sarnia. Heath Co. paid us $4.25 an hour to spend all day in a full-body canvas jumpsuit in the late June heat, sandblasting the paint on the outsides of those very large oil-laden vessels. It was brutally hot work. It didn't take us long to realize we needed to make our money and leave, and in short order, we did.

Our departure date was July 9th. I showed my mother I had earned the needed cash to sustain me for the foreseeable future. I bought a hiker's backpack and a lightweight sleeping bag, then packed the few essentials I anticipated I would need. I said my tearful goodbyes to Nancy with a promise to write often. On the morning of July 9th, 1974, with $220 in my pocket, Jim and I hit the road.

Steve Zub had been working part-time for CN Rail for several years and was now going to start full-time after graduation. He was on a training course in Toronto, staying at a downtown hotel. That was our first stop. We stuck out our thumbs at the entrance to my future and waited for our first ride. We made it to Toronto in good time—finding Steve's hotel easily. A little celebration ensued now that we were officially on the road.

One of the things I vowed to do, and was very successful at, was keeping a short diary of our daily adventures to the west and back. It was to be a keepsake for me but also a record of the things we experienced so I wouldn't forget. Upon our return, I had that diary put away somewhere, and it was subsequently lost for many years. I know I teased my children about it. They wanted to read all about my adventures, but I kept telling them they had to be at least twenty-one, in adulthood—only because some of the content may have been a little R-rated for their young minds. As I write this, my kids are in their mid to late thirties, and have yet to read the diary. I did find it in 2020 and had fun re-reading the scribblings of my youth. Surprisingly, I had near total recall of the goings on, the craziness that ensued, but ironically, there was nothing risqué. I have used those writings as a reminder of events and have thus expanded on them here. My memories of that crazy summer of travel are now preserved next, for all to read.

Our first night in Toronto was typical. We had finished high school, were free to do anything we pleased—on our own in a great big world—and we were spending the night in one of the biggest cities in the world, with great friends. What more could you ask for? What could go wrong? For most of the night, nothing, and then after having consumed many stubby brown bottles of barley, an altercation took place not far from the hotel. Someone, a single male, tried to hit on Jim and me, and, after failing to lure us into no good, became rather agitated. It seemed he didn't like being rejected and started to get aggressive. Being young and somewhat naive to the ways of the big city, I was definitely not comfortable with his menacing posture. Things quickly escalated. Jim and I found ourselves in a position of having to defend ourselves physically. I have never been one for violence or aggression of any sort, but this called for action. It didn't take much between the two of us to put an end to his antics. We left him a little worse for wear and made it back to Steve's hotel. After recalling our encounter, a few laughs, and a couple more beers, it was lights out on the beginnings of what was to be an amazing summer.

The next day, a little hungover, with the rest of our lives in front of us, we left Steve, stuck out our thumbs, and headed for North Bay. At the time—because our singular mode of transportation was hitchhiking, we had no timetable, and no agenda. We just knew we had about two months to do all the things we had talked about. One of these things was staying in organized hostels all over the country. Hitchhiking was huge in the early '70s and was accepted by everyone. The general public was not afraid to pick up scraggly-haired strangers on the side of the road back then, and so it was that many governments and private organizations alike had created this vast network of very cheap accommodations for the youth of the day—to have a safe place to stay while on the road. Mainly, these hostels consisted of army-style tents set up in some available spaces around town, such as vacant schoolyards or green spaces. They would be equipped with cots and sparse amenities for the comfort of all. It was so well-organized, with brochures printed up listing every facility in towns across the nation. The cost per night: maximum fifty cents. This included a hot meal most of the time. If it wasn't hot, the sandwiches and cold snacks were readily available. There were no rules as to who could stay or not. They accepted everyone—all humans, and their pets too, and because they were designed for the hitchhiking traveller, the hostel became a place to meet other transients experiencing the same lifestyle we were.

Looking back now, I never felt threatened, violated, or intimidated by anyone while staying at any of these facilities. The incident in Toronto was in no way a reflection of events to follow.

We arrived at the hostel in North Bay, and because it was our first, didn't really know what to expect. But pretty much as anticipated, through many conversations with other travellers on the road, the hostel was great—located in a school. We were fed, watered, and bedded in a great location with several dozen others doing the same thing. Jim and I were excited to meet so many people with the same agenda and from so many different countries.

The next day, it was on to Sudbury. This one was made up of several large green army tents decked out with surplus armed forces cots. The whole site was set up on the shores of a lake just outside of town. It was beautiful. So nice in fact that we decided to stay for two days. This may have had something to do with the fabulous weather, the floating lawn chairs provided, the readily available alcohol and pot, or just the fact we were in no hurry to get anywhere fast. It was like camping, and we were ok with that. We even ran into a guy from Sarnia, some shady character named Pat that Greg and I knew.

The anticipated good times would soon come to an end. We went from euphoria in Sudbury to the worst day on the road in the two months we were gone. Again, with no destination in mind, the next morning, we were dropped off in small groups by the organizers, and at different intervals along the highway, so as not to be crowded together. I suppose this helped the travelling public to choose who they wanted to offer a ride to. We were in for a couple of long days. Each group managed rides at a regular clip, and we were on our way westbound shortly after securing a ride with a guy doing some sales calls. He wasn't going far but got us safely to the little town of Spanish, on the north shore of Georgian Bay. We had travelled about one 150 miles and were ok with that. Considering we had been removed from the pack of travellers, who were now, nowhere in sight, it would be easier to get rides.

And then we waited. And waited some more. It was hot, very buggy, and desolate. We waited, all told, just under twelve hours, seeing maybe a dozen cars in that time. It was getting real late, dark as night can be, in the middle of nowhere, and now trying to figure out where to lay our sleeping bags. Fear of bears, wolves, and every other wild predator lurking in the trees became all too real. This was the stranded scenario we didn't even think of—damn.

Miracles do happen, or at least we took it as that. Headlights appeared in the distance, rising over a crest in the road, illuminating our weary bodies. We frantically waved our arms to get the drivers attention. She stopped. I will never forget the vehicle, a very large, mint-green 1974 Chrysler New Yorker—the most beautiful car I had ever seen. Our chariot awaited. As it turned out, this lady was the proprietor of the next hostel down the road at Algoma Mills. She was coming in to check on things that evening, and just knew we needed a place to stay. After a shower, and safely tucked into a nice cot, it wasn't long before both Jim and I were in slumberland.

Sunday dawned onto a beautiful morning, and at about ten o'clock, we were again standing on the side of the road with our thumbs out—wondering just what the day would bring. From Algoma Mills, our route across the north of Lake Superior would prove to be another challenge. We knew we were traversing some very uninhabited lands, so we prayed for a safe ride to the other side of the lake at least.

A blue sedan pulled over, and we jumped into the back seat. A very nice middle-aged couple began the conversation by asking Jim about his guitar, and musical influences. The driver was a rock and roll disc-jockey for a local radio station in Sault Ste. Marie. They were returning from Sunday service and about to cook a large breakfast—would we care to join them? Well, of course we would. Arriving at a well-appointed suburban home in a fairly new subdivision, we were invited in as their guests. In 1974, this was a normal thing to do. Although there was crime and other nefarious things happening all the time, it was also a time of trust and freedom. Nowadays, this behaviour is unheard of, which unfortunately is a sad commentary on the way the world has evolved over the last fifty years.

"Mom" went into the kitchen to start breakfast. Jim and I followed "Dad" into the den where a truly awe-inspiring surprise awaited us—a collection of pristinely preserved vinyl records stretched from wall to wall and from floor to ceiling. There were close to five thousand albums, from every imaginable artist you could think of. Off to the side was a stereo setup I had never witnessed before. We were in heaven. We were given permission to play whatever we wanted for as long as we felt comfortable doing so. Wow again. The breakfast was superb, and the music was beyond our dreams. Two teenage boys who couldn't afford to buy records on a regular basis had been given access to a library of music—every one a classic now, but then, mostly new bands of the early '70s. This was the first time I heard the band Audience, and it was placed on regular rotation at Jim's house after we got home. We hung out until early afternoon, thanked our hosts for the incredible morning, and parted ways—with full bellies and memories to last a lifetime.

Finally getting picked up on the outskirts of town, our driver informed us he was going about three hundred miles. Happy to hear that, Jim and I settled in for the long ride. Little did we know, given our lack of geographic knowledge of the immediate area, we would be re-located to the middle of nowhere—again. We stocked up on water and snacks in Wawa, our last town for the foreseeable future, and then we were deposited outside of White River as late afternoon approached. The sun was beating down on us, so we made sure we had some treed shelter beside the road for protection. It would be several hours before we got our next ride, and what a memorable ride it was!

Dusk was starting to settle over the north country, and we didn't want to be anywhere near our current location when that happened. We prayed our luck would change, and finally, about seven o'clock that evening, an old pick-up truck pulled over. At first glance, we could see two men in the cab of the truck—a single cab to be exact, with no apparent room for two more passengers. We wondered aloud what they had pulled over for. Rather boisterously, the man on the right stuck his head out the window and asked us where we were headed—and did we need a ride? Well, yes, we needed a ride, but how was this going to help? After some friendly banter, we were told these two guys had been at a house party in Cole Harbour, NS two nights earlier, and, on a whim, decided to drive to Calgary to attend the famous Stampede, something they had never done before and always looked forward to seeing one day. They offered us the flatbed of the truck to ride in. This adventure had just gotten a lot more crazy. We accepted the offer, suggesting that we would at least go as far as we were safely comfortable with. We also knew it was going to be a chilly ride around the lake, even in July, as it routinely got down to single digits late at night. To make matters even more interesting, the early model GMC had wooden floorboards for the bed liner, complete with two gaping holes showing the passing highway beneath us. We bundled into our sleeping bags, and headed on down the road. All the while, the sound of good old Celtic music came from a very primitive 8-track stereo mounted on the floor of the truck. The one luxury item this old farm vehicle had was a slider-style window between them and us. I can't imagine it having been standard or even an option for this model of vehicle given its age, but somehow they had found one to install. Every once in a while, a part-bottle of rum or whisky would find its way through the window for us to swig from. I think it was the only thing that kept us warm that night. There certainly wasn't much sleep, not because we weren't able to, but because the truck burned more oil than gas, and every hour or so, we would have to stop to top the engine oil to full again. Sometimes we did both at once.

We must have slept somewhat in fits and starts, because I remember waking up to a flaming sunrise over the back tailgate of the truck. We had established earlier in the evening that if the old truck—and subsequently, the two intoxicated inhabitants of the cab—made it to Winnipeg, we would be forever grateful, and as luck had it, we arrived safely to the outskirts of the city somewhere around 9 a.m. It had been a very long, cold night, but knowing what lay in store for us that day, it was totally worth enduring the relative hardships of a very memorable night under the stars in northern Ontario.

Jim's sister and brother-in-law lived in Winnipeg and had made sure we would have a warm shower available, lots of good food, a clean bed to sleep in, and some fun activities planned if we wanted to stop for a few days. My Aunt Pat and Uncle Bruce were also stationed at the Canadian Forces base in Winnipeg at the time, so we were going to spend some time with them too. After the trip from hell we'd just had, this was going to be heaven. I really needed to get cleaned up. The hygiene factor was starting to wear thin. I hadn't realized it, but my feet were in pretty bad shape. Athlete's foot had taken hold, and it was going to take some soothing talc and maybe a bit of medication to find some relief. I was in luck. Jim's brother-in-law was also a doctor, so relief was quick.

That first night was spent at a CFL Blue Bombers game. I had never before attended a professional sports event, so I really enjoyed the show.

Actually, Jim's brother-in-law was a Doctor of Anatomy at the University of Manitoba. That in and of itself was really cool, but what made it even better was that he actually taught medical students to be doctors. More specifically, he taught his students the techniques of surgery by using cadavers, bodies that were donated upon death and used in the Gross Labs (as they are called) for dissection, and learning. I found it fascinating, and we talked about it for hours. The evening of our second day, after some more discussion about his line of work, he offered to take Jim and me to his anatomy lab to view his place of work up close. I was beyond excited to be able to see this for myself. I was seventeen and very impressionable—so I hardly slept a wink that night.

The morning dawned, and after another long shower to freshen up for the day, we toured the Winnipeg Zoo, spent some time touring the university campus, and did a bit of sightseeing. Later that evening, we arrived at the medical centre where the good doctor worked. Upon entering the building, I felt a sense of awe. I just knew this evening was going to be memorable. Being the summer, there were few students around, so we had free rein of the campus. After a tour of the facilities, we stopped outside the doors to the Gross Labs. Giving assurances once again that we were both totally ok with what we were about to see, we entered the sterile environment.

If my memory serves me correctly, it was pretty chilly in this room—the temperature was kept low to preserve the subjects lying on the tables around the room. There before us lay several cadavers, albeit tucked away in their body bags. After some explanation as to what actually occurs in such a room, we were asked if we wanted to see one. Hell ya!

What happened in the next fifteen minutes literally blew my mind. Once we got comfortable with our immediate environment, we were given a demonstration of surgical scalpel techniques on an actual cadaver. The next question was unexpected. Did we want to give it a try? Under direction, of course. We sure did!

I won't go into detail as to what I actually did with that scalpel, but suffice to say, it was a transformative experience in every sense of the word. The physical actions performed by me that evening have left an indelible impression on my memory. It was that intense. Thinking back, I still can't believe I had the opportunity to do such things. How else was a seventeen-year-old kid—thumbing his way across the country—ever going to have a profound experience such as it was, if not for the circumstances of that moment coming together to create the opportunity of a lifetime. It opened my eyes to a whole new world—and in some strange way, I believe it had a major effect on subsequent decisions made in pursuit of a career path. Wow, even writing that story brings it all back to life again as vividly as if it had just happened.

Mom's sister Pat and her husband Bruce had lived in Winnipeg for several years. Both of them were career Armed Forces personnel and had moved around the world at different stages of their careers. I have many good memories of the Alexander family visiting us in Sarnia. Way back then, my cousins Debbie, Kevin, Trent, and Brent, along with their mom and dad, would arrive with the force of nature, immediately mixing with our large crew to fill our small semi-detached home to the rafters with love and laughter. Our families got on great in those early days.

The next twenty-four hours were quite relaxing, and we enjoyed the hospitality shown by my extended family. Aunt Pat, a little quieter than I remembered, stayed somewhat in the background but cooked up some delicious meals for us, which we greatly appreciated. A highlight of our stay was when Uncle Bruce took Jim and me to the base mess hall for a few rounds of beer—somewhat illegal at the time, considering I was still underage.

It was time to carry on. I couldn't think of anything I could do to rival what had transpired in the last few days, but here we were, heading down the road to new adventures. We were dropped close to the on-ramp to the Trans-Canada Highway once again, and off we went to see the rest of the country. Over the next couple of days, thanks to some generous travellers, we managed to keep moving at a decent pace. We had stayed in another hostel that Friday night, with the usual shenanigans going on. Some wine flowed, some bud smoked—all the while, Jim played his guitar. He was such an entertainer, even at the tender age of eighteen. Most of the stops during our cross-country excursion developed into a jam session of a rag-tag bunch of travelling hippies enjoying the skills, talents, and vocals of the many overnight visitors.

On past Regina. The plan was to get across the prairies to our next destination, Banff, Alberta. We made our way further west, accepting several different rides en route to the mountains. All were pleasant and much appreciated—nothing to write home about. Well, except for one ride.

We were west of Moose Jaw when we got picked up by a scruffy fella, somewhere north of thirty, driving a red 1973 Toyota Celica GT. I know this for two reasons. I was really into cars at the time and could name the make, model, and year of just about any car on the road—and this car was a real hot commodity, being one of the more stylish but affordable sports cars available at that time. Jim and I were impressed. Considering each of the vehicles we had the pleasure of riding in that summer, this was a winner for sure.

Our driver, for the next couple of hours, was rather quiet. He seemed a bit nervous, perspiration staining the back of his collar. He checked his rear-view mirror excessively—something I had come to notice since I was a newly licensed driver and had had that skill drilled into my head. After some time, we got to talking, and he finally started to open up a bit. The next thing I knew, he was brandishing a handgun—waving it around nervously. From my vantage point to his right, it looked bad. I saw this nightmare unfold before Jim had a chance to see what was happening from the cramped confines behind me. Whether to just scare us or what—I

Perpetual Motion

don't recall, but "this is not going to end well" was my immediate thought. He began to ramble—giving us sketchy details of his recent escape from the notorious, Kingston Penitentiary, and how he was now considered a fugitive, on the run from the law.

Damn—this really wasn't going to end well. I remembered from the news that the maximum-security prison in Kingston, Ont. was one of the federal facilities where they housed the bad guys. If this guy escaped from there, then he might be the baddest of the bad. Obviously it ended well because I have penned this story, but at the time, I may have been somewhat scared shitless. He talked about his life on the lam over the last several days—and assured us that no, he wasn't going to hurt us. He did make us promise not to report him to the authorities when he dropped us off. I can tell you wholeheartedly, Jim and I readily agreed to abide by that pact. We were finally let off on the outskirts of Calgary—lying to Mr. Fugitive by telling him we were staying with friends in the city. Too scared to mention the episode to anyone, Jim and I kept it a secret between us for quite some time.

We found out later that his tall tale was just that—all bullshit. In actuality, there were very few escapes from this prison, it being a well-guarded facility, surrounded on two sides by Lake Ontario. But of course, at the time, I was young, innocent, and not very worldly. It was definitely my scariest event of the summer—and that damn gun was real! I can't help but still think about him most likely laughing his ass off after we got out of the car.

Kingston Pen was eventually closed for good in September of 2013, as it was in such a decrepit state. I did, however, get to tour the prison in 2016, and yes, it was every bit as horrid as the stories made it out to be.

This being our first time to the west, both Jim and I had only seen pictures of the spectacular views that were the Rocky Mountains. Those photos would not do it justice. Minutes outside the city limits of Calgary, we started to make out the foothills of this vast network of shale and limestone monoliths immersing us in another world. I had never dreamed there was a more beautiful place on earth.

Our next scheduled stop was Banff. We had heard good reports about this small mountain town, so we were really excited to finally arrive. What blew me away then—and still does today, causing me to repeatedly say, "WOW"—is just how beautiful the whole area really is. By the time we arrived at our hostel, we were mesmerized by our surroundings. Mount Rundle, the infamous mountain on the outskirts of the city, rose above us in all its majesty. We just knew this was going to be a great stop on our grand adventure. For the next week we planned to entertain ourselves by doing as much as possible during our brief stay. Our first stop after getting settled was beers at the King Edward Hotel, a local landmark that had been serving six-ounce glasses of draft beer for ten cents each for many years. Ten beers for a buck, how could we go wrong! We were pleasantly surprised at the price because our local establishment back home—the Balmoral in Point Edward, had just raised their prices for the same beverage to fifteen cents. It was a great introduction to the mountainous leg of the journey.

The next morning, as the sun rose above the mountains, we started making plans to find Nancy's sisters, Judy and Debbie, along with our friend, Mary T. They had made the move west earlier and were working summer jobs in the area. We were also going to take a walk through the town corridor to do a little shopping. Jim and I were walking along the sidewalk, passing the shops, when I noticed some camera bling in the window. I stopped to look at it; I was interested in photography even back then. What transpired next was straight out of the twilight zone. Jim hadn't seen me stop. As I stood eyeballing my possible purchase, I heard him calling my name. He was doing so while staring across the street—not at me, a few feet away. I followed his gaze to the far sidewalk, and there I was, same build, same hair, same clothes. I was truly seeing my reflection. I reacted by calling his name. When he turned and saw me, yes, the real me, standing behind him, he was quite bewildered. Without hesitation, and both thinking exactly the same thought, we bolted across the road to catch up with my twin. Taking that split second to make sure no traffic was coming in either direction, we had briefly taken our eyes off the stranger. When we made it to the other curb, he had vanished. We both thought he must have gone into one of the shops, so like two frantic fathers looking for a lost child, we entered each of the stores in the vicinity, trying to locate him. After several minutes of this, we finally admitted defeat, stopping on a nearby bench to recoup. The whole episode was too surreal. If I hadn't seen it for myself, I would have thought Jim was a little crazy at that moment, but if he was crazy, then I was also. We definitely agreed on what we had seen and were disappointed not to be able to find the other me. We hung out along Main St. for a couple of hours hoping to see what we so surely saw earlier in the day. It was not meant to be.

What that experience did was prove to me the existence of a twin—a doppelgänger—for each of us. I saw mine and only wish to this day I had had a chance to introduce myself to him. Who knows, our stories may have been similar too.

We finally located the girls and spent a couple of nights hanging out with them before it was time to head on down the road. For our final day in Banff, we hiked part way up Mount Rundle for some exercise and a view of the surrounding area. We then made our way out to the hot springs for a soak in what could only be described as nature's hot tub. Having spent a couple of days with Nancy's sisters only increased the fact that I missed her so much. It was a great few days in a place I swore I'd return to someday. It would take another forty-four years to fulfill that promise.

We left town on a clear morning with plenty of sunshine and a spring in our step. It had been a leisure-filled week in Alberta and things were only going to get better. Our next destination for an extended stay was on Vancouver Island. Jim's sister, Janice lived in the little town of Cumberland—outside of Courtenay, on the fabled island. She had a log cabin on Maple Lake, and the plan was to stay for a week.

What happened next was completely unplanned. We became three. Not too far west of Banff is a small town named Golden. I will always remember the name of the town because that is where we got our dog, Carly. She was a mixed-breed puppy, half St. Bernard, half German Shepard, and yes, she was pure gold. Jim and I had joked about this possibility the night before after seeing a pinned adoption notice on the message board at the hostel, but did not intend for it to happen. She was so damn cute though, and played to our vulnerabilities with her puppy dog eyes. Without too much fuss she became ours, and off we headed further west, now affixed to this journey of three.

Over the mountains we went, making our way to the Pacific Ocean. The initial concerns of us not getting rides because of the dog proved false. She didn't slow us down in the least. We made it to Vancouver, and after getting our tickets for the late ferry ride to Nanaimo, had a much-needed siesta in Stanley Park. The city of Vancouver holds few memories—we really didn't hang around long enough for me to form an opinion, good or bad. However, it must have made an indelible impression on Jim, because years later, he moved to that city and has remained there to this day.

The ferry ride to Nanaimo was enjoyable. Crossing a body of water such as the Strait of Georgia by boat was something I hadn't experienced before—anywhere. I remember it fondly. We were minor celebrities, our puppy being the star—she drew all the attention wherever we sat. Of course, I am remembering this part of the summer from several decades in the future. I'm sure some of the rougher parts of having an eight-week-old puppy have slipped my mind. Well enough, not every detail is recorded here anyways.

Time spent at Janice's place in Cumberland could have been scripted for a movie. After all, it was summertime on Vancouver Island—in a small village—in a rustic log cabin on a beautiful lake, with a cute puppy in tow, and family. I was seventeen, not a care in the world, my whole life ahead of me, and no clue what I was going to do with those facts. We had a great week. We played with Carly, attempted to train her, and got quite used to having her around. We canoed Maple Lake, the sun glistening off the rocky bottom sixty feet down; the water was that clear. I didn't know it then, but spending time in the great outdoors would become a way of life. My adventurous spirit was just ramping up.

We had been on the road just shy of a month. It seemed longer—I was missing my girl back home. Remember, we didn't have cell phones, social media of any kind, or any other way to communicate—except for landline telephones, and letter writing. With those two methods, I kept in touch with Nancy as best I could.

The actual planned part of our trip now over, we turned our thoughts and ideas to what lay ahead. What came next was a pretty bold adventure on its own. Our friends Al and Franco Sowinski had relocated to Kitimat, BC earlier in the summer. They had landed jobs at the Alcoa plant working with raw aluminum. Alcoa paid a handsome wage for attracting out-of-town workers due to the remoteness of the town. Jim and I discussed hitchhiking north. The highway would take us through the heart of British

Columbia—forest laden and desolate at the best of times. The pros outweighed the cons, and with that, we headed off the big island at the end of July.

The guys were over-the-moon excited that we were hiking the Caribou Highway, about fifteen hundred kilometres straight north, just to visit them. They were ready. The scenery was spectacular the whole way. The rides came at decent intervals; we never had to wait too long in one spot. The first night on the road, we pitched our tents in the middle of a fenced-in ball diamond in Hope. This was our best bet for any semblance of protection against roaming wildlife. It obviously worked. We didn't get eaten by any bears or wolves.

From Hope, we headed north to Quesnel, camped on the banks of the Fraser River, then to Prince George, sleeping in our tents for the couple of days it took to get there. We headed due west again on the Yellowhead Highway to Terrace and then finally to Kitimat. What an adventure that was, hitchhiking through some of the most rugged terrain Canada has to offer.

Jim and I were walking into town just after being dropped off. We were looking for a pay phone to call the boys to come and get us. Franco's car was called the *Danger Mobile*, a 1965 Meteor Montcalm that had definitely seen better days. Its dark blue paint was faded and rusting, the chrome pitted and dented. The most distinguishing mark on the car was a vinyl "DANGER" sticker on the cowling above the missing front grill. Franco had managed to get one from somebody at Ontario Hydro, and it defined this car perfectly. The next scene was something out of a Cheech and Chong skit. There, rolling onto us was a sight we welcomed with open arms. The battered Meteor was pulling to the curb—its two characters, contained within, hooping and hollering like madmen. Al had an ice cream cone in his hand, and when he saw us, he hurled it at the front windshield of the car, its contents coating the interior glass with its sweet stickiness. The car stopped—barely, and they were out, tackling us to the ground in joy. What a welcome! A scene staged like that today would draw law enforcement in minutes. Back then, it was just a bunch of long-haired hippies having a good time, and a good time was about to commence—and continue for days.

Over the next week, we partied our asses off. Lots of beer, some hard liquor, and many joints were passed around. The Sowinski boys still got up in the mornings, and went to work—leaving Jim and me lots of time to explore, play with the dog, and prepare for that evening's festivities. Those were Utopian days.

The noteworthy story to tell from this part of the journey is the date, August 5th, 1974—my eighteenth birthday. I was finally legal to drink—in Ontario. The problem was, I was in British Columbia where the legal age was nineteen. I'm sure you know the outcome to this dilemma—that being—there was no dilemma. ID and Age of Majority cards were not a factor in 1974, especially in a frontier-town like Kitimat. When the boys got home from work, we went out to the only pub in town and celebrated until closing time. I made short order of destroying my liver that night and could think of no better crew to help me ring in my coming of age.

For days, we hung out—ate, drank to our hearts' content, and did very little of anything else. It was starting to get stale. We did take a drive across the border to touch our toes on Alaskan soil, just to say we were in that far northern state during our hitchhiking adventures to the west. We also toured the Alcoa plant to see what the boys did for all that hard-earned cash.

After doing a little survey of our own dwindling finances, Jim and I decided it might be time to make our way across the country again—back to Ontario, and the potential of jobs awaiting us after Labour Day. We discussed this issue with the brothers, and Franco decided he wanted to head back to Ontario also. If this were true, it meant we had a ride all the way home, something we definitely had not anticipated. Another day or two went by, and it had been decided that yes, the three of us, with the dog, were heading out the last week of August. Al had decided to stay for a few months to make some extra money. He had a genuine reason for wanting to do so. He had his sights set on a 1971 MGB convertible, and with that extra influx of cash, his dream would be realized. With that, he took over Franco's job at the mill.

The night before we were to leave, we went out for one last celebration. I could tell Al was not at all comfortable about staying the extra months by himself; several comments spoken during the evening indicated he might change his mind. It was not to be. The morning of our departure, it became obvious he would not be a willing participant in the impending trek across the north part of the continent—down the Yellowhead Trail to the east, and on to familiar parts known to all of us.

The ride home was another adventure for the ages. The car itself protested, groaned, and quit on occasion, gave up several tires, drank more oil than gas, and generally moved along at its own pace. It worked when it wanted to and rested when it needed to. We swore it had a mind of its own. I was sure it was possessed of human emotions and exercised them on a regular basis. Jim and I saw the irony in these setbacks—recanting similar tales of our adventurous ride through the night, in northern Ontario a few weeks earlier. Of the several times we were pulled over by law enforcement, the Danger Mobile only failed to restart once. After establishing a rapport with the officer involved, he was kind enough to give us a boost—sending us merrily on our way.

I don't recall any discussion on whether we were driving straight through or not. After all, the three of us were each licensed to operate a vehicle. We did have to think about Carly, as she needed to be exercised, fed, and watered. Whatever the discussion prior, we made a valiant attempt to keep her happy. But, after three flat tires, time to fix them, and being stopped by law enforcement four times—we rested at a hostel in Jasper.

Down through Saskatoon to Regina and across to Winnipeg, we finally made it to Thunder Bay and back to our home province. Yes, a long way to go, but it felt like home. Franco's sister Pat and her friend Trudy were driving west at the time, and as if it was meant to be, all of us ended up in Thunder Bay at the same time. Shenanigans ensued. We stayed a couple of days, finally said our goodbyes, and continued homeward. The trip around Lake Superior this time was much different than earlier in the summer. Even though we were again entering some pretty thick wilderness, I still felt safer in the old, beat-up Meteor than I had in the back of that old, beat up GMC.

We arrived home Labour Day weekend. Although it seemed much longer, we were only gone two months. Much was done and seen in that short period of time. Jim and I were exhausted from our cross-country trek, but for all the freedom and adventures experienced, it sure felt good to be back in Sarnia, and I knew I was going to see Nancy again.

Jim and I had previously discussed who was going to take Carly. Although it was not my idea to get the puppy in the first place, I agreed to take her. I had given my parents a heads up about the dog, and they were cool with it. She was accepted as one of the family.

The open road and the freedom to travel had been what I needed. It was a glimpse into the perpetual motion that was quickly becoming my "MO." I came to the conclusion that I wanted more adventure in my life, and so, the decision was made to put my education on hold for the time being. I'm sure this did not come as a surprise to my parents—them knowing my wandering spirit so well. It did, however, set the tone for my lifelong love affair with everything outdoors. The reality now was, I needed a job—a real job. It came soon enough.

13. Promises Fulfilled

It didn't take long for my employment status to change. I was hired in mid-September at Standard Auto Glass on Confederation St. The business was known for installing windshields, vinyl tops for cars, aftermarket trim—just about anything to dress up a new vehicle. Mike Sharon, a young and brash Irishman, was my first actual boss out of school, and a pretty good one at that. He always made time for the new guy—dispensing lots of advice on how to do the job well. I am happy that my first post-school employment experience was a positive one. I learned much about teamwork, a clean work environment, getting along with co-workers—and tardiness. Yes, I was late a few times, and was set straight by Manager Mike. I know his positive attitude helped shape my own administrative style, years later. I continued to see Mike off and on for almost forty years. Sadly, he passed away from a rare form of men's breast cancer in 2018. Until then, I didn't even know that was a thing.

After spending the summer travelling, I had no cash to buy transportation, so I made arrangements with one of the guys to pick me up each morning for work. The fellas I worked with were very talented when it came to anything automotive, so they convinced me to get the old Nomad over to the shop with an eye to restoration. I thought that was a brilliant idea, and I really did try to get into it, but lacking their level of expertise, I just didn't have it in me. The project eventually went by the wayside, with the old car finally shipped off to the junkyard a few months later. As I have said, that is another one I wish I had kept. With its advanced features, it would now be a classic car collector's dream. I worked straight days all that winter—picking up some useful skills and learning to work with my hands.

This, and my father's initial influence, shaped my abilities to be hands-on throughout my working career.

It felt great to be out of school and among the working class. Even though I had graduated, I still had attachments to my alma mater. Jim had decided to go back to school to get his Grade 13 and instantly became the obvious choice for the Captain's role with the St. Pat's Fighting Irish senior football team. St. Pat's hadn't fared well in previous years when it came to the sport of football. As a matter of fact, they ranked pretty well last—most years. The buzz around the team fielded for the fall of 1974 was of quiet hope that they had the skill and talent to take it all the way. Several of my friends were Jim's teammates on that squad, and I wished nothing but the best for everyone involved. I made a commitment to the team that if they won the championship, I would host the victory party. Well, dammit, didn't they win! This was the first City Championship for its organized football program in many years. Mayhem ensued. My mother and father knew of this promise and were keeping tabs on the league standings throughout the season. Dad was well aware the team had secured the championship and knew what was going to happen that evening at the house. He bought two cases of beer, brought them home, and announced that he and Mom were going to stay at a hotel for the night. Now, that shit was cool. They stayed at the house long enough to greet the victorious players coming in, bid us all a fun evening, and then left. I wouldn't be surprised if that party is still talked about today. I know when I get together with old schoolmates, they inevitably bring it up, and we reminisce all over again about how much fun we had.

Back at work, the money started to accumulate, now that I was receiving a regular wage. I finally bought the first car I actually paid for. It was a navy blue 1971 MGB convertible, the same popular British sports car model that my buddy Al Sowinski had talked of owning. He had purchased his shortly after coming home from the west. I loved his so much, I had to get one of my own. Unfortunately, I didn't have the $400 down payment, so I borrowed that sum from a high-interest loans company to cover the upfront costs of the $2,000 loan I had secured from the Bank of Nova Scotia. As I grew older, and wiser, the hard lessons of that initial foray into the world of finance would come in handy.

Perpetual Motion

My big gift to the family that Christmas was a surprise guest. I had made arrangements to pay for my sister Karen's flight home from St. FX University in our home province of Nova Scotia. No one knew she was coming until she arrived at the house. The most satisfactory part of that act was that Karen could not afford the flight home, so her intention was to stay on campus for Christmas. I would have none of that. When she walked through the door, I made sure Elvis Presley's hit, "I'll Be Home for Christmas," was playing on the stereo. This first, simple act of kindness would influence me the rest of my life.

14. Stretching My Horizons

Even though we had continued to see each other often, at some point along the way, Nancy and I sputtered. I'm sure me being out of school had a detrimental effect on our relationship. We had kept in touch throughout my travels and still cared deeply for each other, but things were not the same. As had happened in each of my relationships prior, we finally parted ways—but damn, that one really hurt. Hugs, my old friend.

My sister Karen was getting married in May of 1975. I got time off work to go to Nova Scotia for the wedding. I called Greg and suggested he come with me in my little ragtop. Well, that turned out to be a blast! I picked him up outside his dorm in Toronto, and we drove most of the way with the top down, our long hair blowing in the wind. This trip would prove to be the start of my many trips to the east coast over the years. I've lost count after surpassing the hundredth time making the trip, each more memorable than the last. As will be told, all that love for the east coast would be transformative.

While there, I hooked up with a family friend, Jim Browe, a lobster fisherman from Harvre Boucher, NS. He and I hit the water in his trawler at about four-thirty in the morning and proceeded to fill two very large crates with the spiny crustaceans. We netted a hundred or more lobsters by the end of the run. My payment was a large box of live lobsters, which I took home to Nanny's house in Tracadie. The look on my mother's face was priceless. I don't know if I've ever seen anyone love lobster as much as she. I went down to the ocean to fetch a couple of pails of salt water to cook them in. It was a fabulous meal. Just knowing I had actually harvested them from the ocean with my bare hands made it all the better—an experience I will never forget.

Perpetual Motion

The wedding was a grand affair. You can imagine, with the number of aunts, uncles and cousins we have in Nova Scotia—the party went on for days. Then, finally homeward bound, it was time to get back to work.

I worked at the auto glass shop until September of 1975 when I left to start a job in the repair department of Sears, one of the biggest national retailers of the day. Many drills, lawnmowers, power saws, and such were taken apart, rebuilt, and returned to their rightful owners or sold as a repaired item. Unfortunately, due to the inevitable impact of the future phenomenon known as online shopping, Sears closed the last of its stores in the fall of 2018. I enjoyed that job—adding to my growing set of hands-on skills that would assist me for a lifetime.

Christmas of '75 came and went. My gift to Mom and Dad that year was a floor model console stereo—the likes of which they had never owned before. I got a real charge out of gift giving. My parents didn't make a lot of money and had to support a very large family. I don't recall ever doing without, and still don't know how they did it. I do know that I loved paying it forward then and still do to this day. That stereo remained in the living room on Wellington St. until they packed the house to move many years later.

97

15. Chance Meetings

I was still hanging out with many of my old school friends. My buddy Mike Schauteet asked me to go skiing in Collingwood—a resort town on the banks of Georgian Bay. I had only been skiing ten or fifteen times in my life. I was not real good at the sport but enjoyed the thrill, so I said yes. What an impact that decision made! He informed me the St. Pat's Ski Club would also be there, enjoying their annual trip. As a bonus, it was also to be a trip for the graduating seniors.

I could begin this paragraph with the quote, "And that kids, is how I met your mother." If you don't get the reference, it was a tagline in a comedy series on TV in the early 2000s. After a day on the slopes, Mike and I headed over to the chalet where the group was staying. I walked in and noticed her immediately. She knew who I was, but I didn't recall seeing her at school when I had attended. She introduced herself as Mary. I was smitten—again. She was as cute as a dream, petite, with a little curl on her nose, dark, wavy hair, and an infectious laugh. It seemed she commanded the room at times. What struck me as crazy was when I thought I was seeing double. Standing beside her was her twin, Maureen. It was a fun evening, and everyone got along famously. Mary was affable, and I enjoyed her company a lot.

Back in Sarnia, we began our budding romance. Mary was still in school, and I was working full-time, so we didn't see each other every day, but both felt there was something special between us. I was eager to introduce her to my family, and as expected, they fell in love with her instantly. I, in turn, met Mary's family. Things were certainly headed in the right direction.

Sometimes, the unexpected happens and unfortunately for me, I came down with tonsillitis in late January. It was severe enough to warrant surgery. I hadn't been in a hospital since my hernia, eighteen years earlier, and wasn't looking forward to it. The procedure was scheduled and the operation performed in early February. My good friend Brett Oake visited me in the hospital, gifting me the *Frampton Comes Alive* album and a bottle of Heineken beer. I'm sure bringing alcohol into the hospital was somehow illegal, but we didn't care. For the next week, I laid on the couch in the living room watching the Winter Olympics from Innsbruck, Austria on a little portable TV I had purchased for fifty dollars. I healed nicely from that surgery, even after eating a full pork chop dinner the night I came home. Damn, that was a mistake!

Mary and I picked up where we left off after my recovery. Her senior prom was fast approaching, and she responded in the affirmative when I asked if I could escort her to the gala. The dress she wore was of her own creation—made of peach satin and sewn by her very capable hands. She was radiantly beautiful. I had, in the past, borrowed my parish priest's new Ford Thunderbird on occasion when needing transportation to certain events. Father Sasso again loaned me his car for the night, and Mary and I rode in style over to the Fog Cutter Restaurant in Port Huron, MI for dinner before the dance. We continued to date often, but in hindsight I know I wasn't ready to settle down. I hadn't even given that a thought. We slowly drifted apart and only saw each other a couple of times in the next year.

In March of 1976, I was interviewed for a process operator's job at Dow Chemical of Canada, a world renowned chemical manufacturing company that had established itself in Sarnia in the 1940s. The future was looking bright. I was successful at obtaining employment and was assigned to Block 40, Building 44, the dreaded Caustic Unit. The pay was great. I was making about seventeen thousand dollars a year. Unfortunately, the work was hell. The *Hole* was the worst. While performing in that environment, we were dressed in flame-retardant Nomex coveralls, hard-hat, ear protection, steel-toed boots, goggles, and gloves. We would physically manhandle forty-five-gallon drums of very corrosive Caustic Flake for a solid two hours, filling them, and then, using a fork truck, stacking them in the warehouse. A half-hour break was well warranted, and then we repeated the same ritual all over again. The shift lasted a full twelve hours.

The senior operator didn't have to do the dirty work. They got to sit in the control room, monitor gauges, and read the paper. Twice a shift they had to do their rounds to make sure the unit was running properly. I liked that job description, so, for the first time in my working life, I aspired to get promoted. It wouldn't be the last.

I bought my first brand-new car shortly after landing that job. It was a 1976 Pacer X, equipped with fancy rims, wide tires, and an aftermarket Craig 8-track stereo. I know everyone thought it was a strange-looking vehicle, but it was my strange-looking vehicle. I was getting used to having the first known luxuries in my life. Oh yes, taxes included, the car set me back $4,200.

I also moved out of the house for the first time. That summer, Rob Butler, Bill Plummer, and I moved into a house downriver—south of Sarnia, about a mile past Corunna. I was working, making good coin, and enjoying life. It was at this time I got my first taste of street legal motorcycles. The two guys I lived with both had bikes, and several of my friends bought them too. I knew it was just a matter of time before I bought my own. The first bike available to me was a dirt bike, a 125cc Harley Enduro, which I rode through the fields behind our rental. I started to hone my limited skills on that bike.

I had continued to smoke cigarettes for the last several years and was unfortunately addicted to them. Smoking close to two packs a day is not good for your health. I was starting to feel their adverse effects. The three of us spent an evening at the Campbell St. Station night club and, just prior to leaving for home, I bought a fresh pack—du Maurier being my brand of choice at the time. I woke up in the morning, and as per my usual routine, prior to getting out of bed, I lit one up. That didn't go well. I started hacking and coughing—and was so mad at myself, I threw the new pack of cigarettes out the open window. I swore at that moment I would quit, and I did. It was one of the best decisions of my life.

We certainly had some fun times while living downriver. It seemed most days, there was a house full of friends, mostly partying, and always listening to great music. One album that got lots of play was Robin Trower's *Bridge of Sighs*. I had no idea until recently there is actually a real Bridge of Sighs in Venice, Italy. My life continued on carefree all that summer.

Perpetual Motion

The bar scene across the St. Clair River, in Port Huron MI, was crazy fun. We made it a regular occurrence to cross the Bluewater Bridge—over to the good old USA. The Garage, the Brass Rail, the Roach Bar, and many others were frequent hangouts. However, The Red Fox always made the cut. Cliff Erickson, a young Michigander, was a one-man entertainer, taking the stage every Thursday to Saturday nights. He played an Ovation acoustic guitar with an electric pickup, and even today I can pick one out for its tonal qualities. He was very adept at getting the crowd into each of the songs he would sing. Bob Seger's album *Live Bullet* provided several ballads to sing along with. There was also lots of Neil Diamond's "Sweet Caroline," and so much more. Talk to anyone from my generation growing up in the area, and they will have awesome stories of that cool little bar in the basement of the Harrington Hotel.

One evening, while listening to some great music at the Boardwalk, another downtown Port Huron bar, I ran into my old girlfriend, Linda. I hadn't seen her in several years. We had a great conversation, and as it turned out, we were both currently single. I told her of my upcoming plans to head east for a vacation, and she said she was keen to tag along, so that's what we did. We took two weeks that August and visited many places along the way. My Uncle Eugene was building a home in our little hamlet of Afton, so Linda and I went to visit. We ended up staying for three nights at the old family homestead in Merland, now a hunting lodge that has been in the family for more than two centuries. Some years later, I would make several trips to Nova Scotia each late October to do some hunting with Uncle Eugene. This was the lodge of choice each time.

The drive home from that vacation was a rough one. Linda and I stayed in Fredericton the first night, and then for reasons unknown, we decided to drive straight through to Sarnia. It was a long, tiresome stretch. Just outside the Forest town line, about a half hour from home, I fell asleep—briefly—while driving, only waking up when the wheels hit the gravel. We were very fortunate that evening to get home alive. I learned a great lesson from that harrowing experience. That was the last time I would see Linda for many years. I wonder why?

Dow Chemical was providing me with a great lifestyle. I had the ways and means to do the things I enjoyed without financial constraint. Looking back now, one of the smartest things I did was to buy myself a good film camera. It was the new Canon AE-1 SLR. I would cut my teeth on that state-of-the-art technology. It was also the catalyst for the passion I now have for creative photography—which waned somewhat at different times but was always there in some fashion. Truly humble beginnings.

All good company must part, and our time in the rented house on the St. Clair Parkway ended in late August. It seemed my roommates and I were headed in different directions, so I made the difficult decision to move back to my parents' home, knowing this was only a temporary solution. I would eventually find another place.

My mother and father were about to celebrate their twenty-fifth wedding anniversary. This was going to be a family and friends affair at the house. After much planning by all involved, we had a great evening. I experienced eating fondue for the first time and loved it. I wanted to do something extra-special for my folks, so I mounted five one-hundred-dollar bills and a spare set of my car keys into a shadowbox frame. The note inside instructed them to enjoy my car and the money on their second honeymoon. They again chose Nova Scotia as their holiday destination.

Christmas with family and friends continued to be a great tradition—well past high school. By this time, Karen and her husband Alvin were flying home frequently to be with family. Lorraine and Jerry had made me an uncle for the first time that August, with the birth of Shannon Marie. I took advantage of such a wee subject and photographed her several times over the ensuing months.

Steve Zub had owned several different cars over the course of our early years. The first I can remember was a 1968 Thunderbird with the suicide doors (the back doors swung out from the centre post) and then a 1971 AMC Ambassador, both awesome muscle cars of the day. He and I had driven to Windsor in his AMC to do some shopping. I think he wanted some new leather boots to paint. He purchased what he needed, and we set out for the return drive to Sarnia. Some discussion ensued as to what plans we had for New Year's Eve, happening later that same day. Turns out we didn't, so in a spur-of-the-moment decision, we found a pay phone, called Greg in Toronto, and asked him what his plans were. He informed us of an awesome party taking shape at his place and, of course we were invited. Steve and I abandoned our plans to return home and continued east, arriving in Toronto just after supper. It was one of the more memorable New Year's Eve celebrations I have had. Not having attended college or university, this was a game changer. Without me going into detail, let your imagination experience the social norms of life at a university—in Toronto—on New Year's eve—in the mid-'70s. Yes, it was that much fun!

PART 3

16. Career Choices

1977 would prove to be a very pivotal year. It started with a wedding. No, not my wedding. My good friend Jamie Dillon and I had hung out for most of high school. I considered myself part of his family, as he did mine. In fact, by this time, we had already booked and paid for a two-week vacation on Waikiki Beach in Hawaii for the middle of March. His sister, Robin was getting married that January, and I was invited to the wedding. While seated at a table enjoying one of many beverages that evening, a tall, thick gentlemen sauntered up to the table. I was introduced to Jamie's uncle, Jack Duffield. I had never met Jack before that evening, but this introduction had a significant impact on my path forward.

One question, that's all it took. During my brief time with Jack, I asked him about his occupation. He told me he was a fireman, and in the ensuing conversation informed me his employer—the City of Sarnia—was actively seeking recruits for the department. This news could not have come at a more opportune time. I was disillusioned with my current employer and was looking for some meaningful work I could call a career.

Upon hearing Jack's news, I put a very crude resume together and brought it to City Hall. Shortly after, I received a phone call with a time and date for the written portion of the firefighter's entry exam—to be conducted at the East St. station, the main firehall in Sarnia. Not having ever written an entry exam for a career job before, I really had no idea what to expect. My first three jobs out of high school were a breeze to land. Jobs were plentiful in the '70s. The exam I eventually wrote certainly was not as difficult as the intense recruitment programs that are conducted by today's standards.

Perpetual Motion

I was in the room for no more than two hours. I felt I did well and was excited to tell my family the good news. The two men I admired most, my father and my brother Greg, had two very different reactions to me wanting to join the fire service. My father could not understand why I would leave a stable job like the one I currently had at Dow Chemical—working indoors in a relatively safe environment—to take a lower-paying civil service job with all the hazards that accompanied it. He was rather adamant about me not pursuing this avenue. On the other hand, when I called Greg in Toronto to inform him of the potential career change, he had a classic reaction, and I quote: "If you don't take that job, I will kick your ass." No matter their reactions, I had full intentions of pursuing this newly created opportunity.

In early March, I was asked to come back to the main station to do the physical portion of the testing. I breezed through these routines also. That same day, after I had finished, I was invited into the deputy chief's office. The chief of the department, Clifford Hansen, and the deputy chief, Jim Knight, were conducting initial interviews. After answering the several questions they had asked me, they told me they were impressed and wanted to offer me the full-time position. I was thrilled!

I will never forget the next question. Chief Hansen asked me if I could start work on the following Monday. Without hesitation, I answered him as directly as I could, informing him that I could not start the following Monday because I was flying to Hawaii on Sunday—for two weeks. With a look of puzzlement, he politely suggested I cancel my trip. Well, thinking back now to my twenty-year-old self, cocky, assured, and self-confident, I just as politely refused the offer of employment and thanked them very much for their consideration. I left and went back to my life and my job at Dow. I did have the balls to suggest, however, that if there were any openings in the future to give me a call. Jim Gough, another recruit applicant, filled that vacant spot on the roster. He jokingly thanked me many times for turning down my initial offer, thus allowing him to get hired. Over the years, and especially more recently, when I relay that story to the young firefighter recruits, they can't believe how hiring practices have changed.

Two weeks from our planned trip to Hawaii, Jamie had an unfortunate mishap. He dumped the dirt bike he was riding, broke his right wrist, and ended up in a cast from elbow to knuckles. He and I had bought that 250cc Kawasaki trail bike only a month earlier.

We continued with our vacation plans despite the setback. For the full two weeks we were gone, we didn't dwell on the what ifs. Jamie resorted to using plastic bags to ensure he didn't get the plaster cast wet, making it somewhat inconvenient when splashing around in the surf on Waikiki Beach. He adapted quite well, and we ended up having a fabulous time. Unsure of whether I had sealed my fate in turning down the career firefighter job, I put that whole episode on the back burner for the time being.

While I was on vacation, my father was in a serious car accident—rear ended on London Road. Fortunately, he was not injured, but his pride and joy—his first-ever car, the Custom 500 was destroyed—definitely the end of an era.

My vacation to Hawaii was memorable. It was the first time I had actually planned and paid for a trip to a sunny destination. We had chosen Hawaii because at that time it was one of the cheaper places to go. The two-week trip, including airfare and hotel, cost me just over $500—unheard of in today's market. And obviously I have no regrets in handling the employment situation the way I did. As you already know, and will continue to read about shortly, that decision did not affect my eventual career path.

I returned from Hawaii invigorated and ready to move forward. I had finally ordered my first street-legal motorcycle, a green 1977 Kawasaki KZ650cc. I was to pick up the assembled bike April 5th, but of course it snowed heavily that day. Not to be deterred, I walked over to the shop, paid for my bike, and very gingerly rode it home in the snow. I had previously written the test for my beginners permit, which allowed me three months to master the skills needed to operate the bike. With few restrictions on its use, I rode head-long into the summer.

I went back to work at Dow. Every once in a while, I would have that *what if* moment and wonder if I would ever get the chance to become a career firefighter.

Concerts continued to be a part of my entertainment as they had always been. One of my most memorable ever, happened on April 30th. A group of us made our way to the Pontiac Silverdome on the outskirts of Detroit, MI, to see Led Zeppelin perform—now much more famous than they were back in '69 when I first heard them on that tinny-sounding transistor radio. It was a historic event, with attendance pegged at 76,229, a world record for a solo indoor performance at that time.

The summer laboured on. I started to develop a pattern I was not aware of until several years later. It seemed that I frequently enjoyed trading my current vehicle for the next big thing. I sold the Pacer X and bought a 1976 Dodge Charger Daytona Special, complete with green velour interior—built-in 8-track stereo—power everything, and very fast. I was moving up in luxury, and brand name.

A huge blow to the rock world happened in August with the death of Elvis Presley. He died from an apparent heart attack at the age of forty-two. The world over, mourned his untimely death. His music played a big part in many significant events in my life and I will always enjoy the connection I have to this legend.

Continuing to live at home for the time being—but after being on my own the year before—I found it somewhat troublesome sticking to house rules. I wasn't getting along with my baby sister, Noelle, who was ten at the time and somewhat of a bother to me. I loved her, but in hindsight I was an asshole. I didn't want anything to do with a kid since I was a grown man with a career—currently in the petrochemical industry, and all she wanted was to be loved by her big brother. It pains me deeply to write this paragraph now. If only I had known . . . What a dickhead I was to her. So many regrets.

I was at home on a September afternoon when I got the phone call I'd been anticipating. The head of personnel from City Hall asked me if I was still interested in the position of firefighter recruit. Of course I was! It seemed they had a sudden opening, and if it all worked out, the start date would be October 17th. With a resounding yes for an answer, I immediately gave Dow Chemical my two-week notice and began to plan for my future career. I had just over a month before I had to report for duty, so I took full advantage of the break between jobs. I grew some facial hair—knowing that it would be the last time for many years—and enjoyed the hell out of the time off. There were also papers to sign at City Hall, uniform measurements to have taken, and gear to be fitted for. It was an exciting time.

17. The Real Deal: It's Getting Hot in Here!

Then the big day came—October 17th, 1977, just over two months after my twenty-first birthday. I had no idea what was in store for me, not only that first day but for the next lifetime of achievements and memories. I walked through the front doors at the East St. firehall and stopped at the duty desk. Behind the counter, manning the control room, was dispatcher "Hammy" Hamilton, a veteran smoke eater, who, after spending many years on the rigs, was now fully assigned to answering the phones, and initiating our fire calls. After a brief exchange of greetings, he instructed me to go out to the "apparatus floor" and wait for shift change with the rest of the guys. I was in awe of what was transpiring in that moment. Excited, intimidated, and full of piss and vinegar, I went through the man-door to the apparatus room and was immediately overwhelmed by the sights and smells of the large firetrucks in front of me. The sounds of a dozen or more guys chatting to each other prior to the morning's official roll call drew my gaze away. I introduced myself and they did so in exchange. Each of the guys had a nickname, and that's how they introduced themselves. Grimesy, Egie, Smity, Dutch, Neif, Derf, Rollie the Goalie, and of course, Cap. I had never been subjected to a full-on fraternity of guys with nicknames before. Ironically, when they got wind of my last name, it was "Pittsy" from then on. They didn't know it had been my actual nickname for many years, so it fit perfectly.

That first day was eventful. I was introduced to the day staff. The guys showed me around the hall, and we went through the truck inventories very thoroughly. I was assigned to Ladder #2, which at the time responded to just about every call due to manpower allotment. I couldn't help but just about go out of my mind with anticipation of my very first call as a rookie firefighter. Lunch time was family oriented. Each of us, milling about in the fully-serviced kitchen, would prepare whatever it was we'd brought to eat, and then would gather as one around the two large tables in the dining hall. We ate our meals among the constant chatter of conversation—and the blue haze of cigarette smoke, to the joy of everyone. I couldn't help but remember back to my childhood, standing on that street corner and watching the big red trucks—the guys in their black canvas coats and rubber boots, fighting that fire at St. Paul's Church. I was, at that moment, sitting with some of the same firefighters who were actually on that call. It would be just one of the many times I would be reminded of that scene from my youth—history revisited, and new events to be written.

The sound of "The Hundred"—as it was known—the very loud, and disturbing audible notification of an alarm when dispatched to an emergency, is a unique sound I will never forget.

It happened mid-afternoon. I was going over the inventory of my truck for the umpteenth time when that guttural sound came through the bullhorns in the station. Dave Dicaire and I were dispatched to an apartment complex on Exmouth St. for a potential medical emergency. The caller's description told of an elderly lady who was possibly stuck in the bathtub and couldn't get herself out. Upon arrival, we entered the unit by way of a key supplied by the landlord. What we encountered is vividly etched in my mind. The dear old lady was definitely in the bathtub, engulfed in a cocoon of hot, steamy water. She was quite large in body mass, and it seemed she had filled the tub to near capacity—then got in to soak. Once settled in, she became suctioned to the sides of the tub and could not move at all.

I'm sure I was staring but tried not to show it. Her ample breasts were floating up and over the sides of the tub. I had never seen anything like it before—or since, for that matter. We tried to pull her up by the arms, to no avail. She was suctioned in tight. Dave then asked me to "get the green soap" from the glove compartment of the truck. Whether that soap was some special formula—or just an over-the-counter generic brand, I didn't know, but hopefully it would do the trick. Being the rookie—remember, it was my very first day—I was given the job of pouring the soap all over the areas where her skin was adhering to the sides of the tub—and that was everywhere! I then used my bare hands to lubricate those areas, to lessen the friction caused by the suction—I know, visuals, right? After I finished lubing the lady up—literally—we grabbed her arms again and gently pulled. With a *shlurp*, she came free, finally released from her predicament, and no worse for wear.

More embarrassed than anything, she wrapped a towel around herself to protect the little bit of modesty she still possessed. After Dave's brief questioning as to the particulars for our report, we headed back to the station. My first—and very memorable call—was on the books. Needless to say, as was the custom, my colleagues had a real chuckle at my expense, and it didn't take long for the story to reach the other stations. The rookie had surely been initiated that day.

I had left a very stable job at Dow Chemical, making $17,500 a year, and started at Sarnia Fire Department for a rookie sum of $12,400. Some questioned my wisdom in taking a pay cut of five thousand dollars to work in such a potentially dangerous environment, but after that first day—and the thrill I got going to my first call—it was all worthwhile. I knew I had made the right decision for me, and was hell-bent on proving my naysayers wrong—and prove them wrong I did, in spades!

Over the course of the next few months, I delved deep into fire service training, and concentrated on learning the ropes—literally. Fires during this initial period of service were few and far between for my A-1 Platoon—garbage bins mostly, so I was getting antsy for my first big one.

The first-class exam for all firefighters who were qualified to write it was held on shift, each December. I didn't have to participate in this exercise since I was not a qualified firefighter, and especially because I had only started two months earlier. Even so, I was granted permission to take the knowledge-based test, just to get a feel for what lay ahead. I wrote the exam with the rest of my crew, scored a 77 percent, and was elated. It proved once more that I was doing what I was meant to. It also gave me a confidence boost to continue improving my skills.

Below is an excerpt from my notes, describing in part, my first significant structure fire.

Perpetual Motion

Night shift, Feb 5th, 1978—approximately 2 a.m.—The Hundred rings us out of a dead sleep. The luxury hotel in the downtown core, The Drawbridge Inn, is on fire! Several callers have confirmed the information. This is it, my first real conflagration. I am riding the tailboard of Pump #5. I will be the grunt for this fire. My job will be to pull the hose off the truck and make sure it is in position for the entry crew to safely attack the fire.

We pull up to the building. Sure enough, smoke and flames are seen coming from the lower floor of the structure—which to my limited knowledge, is the bar/restaurant area of the hotel. We spring into action on this very frigid night. The entry crew begins to advance the hose line down the south hallway. I hear shouting through the thick blanket of smoke. It seems the hose is caught on something. It is now my job to figure out what is stopping the forward progress of the crew. With my breathing apparatus donned, and fully dressed out, I begin my own advancement through the thick smoke, along the deployed hose line, as I am taught to—looking for the snag. I am not ten feet past the doorway when I see a wall of flames to my left. I do not have a charged hose line with me, and my crew is thirty or forty feet beyond my location. I stop—frozen—immobile in my tracks.

Now, for most of the world's population, this would have been the time to let out a panicked scream, but—with that thought not yet fully formed—I actually shout out loud to no one, "What the hell am I doing here!" It takes a moment for me to get my bearings. I quickly realize the flames I perceived were around me are actually a light over an ornamental wishing well, built into the side of the corridor. The smoke-filled hallway and the adrenaline coursing through me at this moment has just wreaked havoc on my senses for that brief moment or two—damn.

I quickly recover and continue down the hall to find the hose jammed between a fallen plant stand and the wall. After removing the obstacle, the crew advances to the seat of the fire in the bar area. I retreat—following the hose line in the dark—back the way I came—to once again be ready to assist as needed. I eventually hook up with the interior crew to water down some hot spots. I perform one of my newly acquired skills—mechanical ventilation of the toxic smoke. Wow! What an adrenaline rush!

We were at this fire scene all night—and come morning, it was time for the dayshift to take over. I witnessed for the first time how the crews change equipment, radios, and other essential tools at a working fire.

The building sustained considerable damage, and we were fortunate to come away with no casualties of our own. One sight that stands out vividly to me happened right about daybreak. I was in the charred-out bar area doing some post-fire overhaul when in walked Chief Hansen. The light of daybreak was just starting to penetrate the broken windows on the east side of the building. He stood amid the rubble—hands resting on his hips, embers still smoldering at his feet—in silhouette, drenched in grey wisps of smoke and the god-rays of morning sunshine. This scene, forever etched now in my mind, made him seem larger than life itself. Here was our fearless leader, dressed in full white bunker coat and helmet—large and in charge, surveying the ruins. It was a pivotal moment in my fledgling career. Respect.

I had started shift-work for the first time while employed with Dow Chemical. The shift schedule in the fire service was slightly different—actually somewhat streamlined. We would work four ten-hour days from 7 a.m. until 5 p.m. followed by four days off. On the fifth day, we would reverse that schedule and do four fourteen-hour shifts from 5 p.m. to 7 a.m. At the time, the average work week was forty-two hours long. I quickly became used to the hours, and it would not change for the next twenty-eight years. The beauty of the schedule was that we had lots of time off and, combined with our vacation allotment, had plenty of time to do extra-curricular activities such as travel or part-time work, if we so chose.

Perpetual Motion

I cannot say that doing part-time work was a direct result of notoriously low wages or, because of our scheduling, having plenty of time off to do other activities. Quite possibly, it was a combination of both. As was our nature, firefighters in general are hands-on, get-it-done type personalities, and being in the *helping your fellow man* mode created many opportunities to do just that. It was the same in departments all over. We had guys who were carpenters, electricians, plumbers, brick layers, cement finishers, roofers, painters, and just about every other trade known to exist.

In the early days, my preoccupation when not on shift was painting and wallpapering. I had been taught the craft by my father and had done enough work to feel confident in venturing out on my own. One of my lieutenants, Billy Pounds, had a large clientele base and was kind enough in the beginning to send work my way. It wasn't long before I had my own clientele, my own accounts at the paint stores, and a vehicle full of equipment. Over the next thirty years, I did a myriad of different jobs while still employed as a firefighter. I will touch on these as I continue to recount my tales.

Thom Kingston, a co-worker, was quite the avid biker. He had run motocross most of his young life and was now into street-legal machines. He owned a Kawasaki KZ 1100cc—one of the biggest, baddest bikes on the road—back in the day. During my first year at the department, I continued to enjoy my motorcycle as well, and given the fact Thom worked my same schedule, we started developing a plan for an extended vacation together. The plan we settled on was a June trip to California. This, given the fact that I had never had my bike more than sixty miles from Sarnia, was a huge deal. By the middle of May, seven months into my career, I was ready to take my first real bike trip. I had purchased a used Windjammer fairing from Ruben McMurter, a local motocross racer. Leather side bags and a new low-rise seat completed the preparations. June 1st couldn't come soon enough.

18. Badass Biker—or Crash Test Dummy?

We departed Sarnia early that morning with nothing but blacktop and adventure in front of us. This was surely to equal my adventures hitchhiking to the west coast of Canada with Jim, four years earlier. My trusty Canon AE-1 was along for the ride to document our fun times. We made it as far as Indianapolis, IN the first day—complete with a sore butt, but in a totally good way. I was twenty-one years old and off to see the great nation of the USA. It would be an understatement to say I was excited as to the possibilities for new adventures. We found a cheap motel next to a rowdy bar and enjoyed the first night of many more to come.

We were not ten miles west of Indianapolis that following morning when an old, green Volvo pulled alongside us. Two young starlets in the vehicle waved to us in a very friendly manner. It wasn't long before the four of us were pulled over at a truck stop, having a great conversation about where we were from and where we were headed. Cinda and Trish wanted to take turns riding with us. Thom and I obliged, and it made for a wonderful day. Sometime that afternoon, we decided as a group we would stay in St. Louis. Again, we found a cheap motel—piled all of our worldly possessions in the room, locked up, and went for supper. Needless to say, the drinks flowed, the food was plentiful, and we had a real fun night with our new friends. After breakfast the next day, we parted ways, never to see or hear of them again. As it turned out, the girls were on their way to Topeka, KS to attend Bible College—oh, the irony of it all.

We put many miles on our bikes over the next couple of days. Due to a driving rain, we had to pull off in Springfield for several hours and then eventually made it to Joplin, MO that night. It was then through Oklahoma City to Clinton where some real shenanigans went down:

I tasted moonshine for the first time. We had settled into the KOA and found a local watering hole. After consuming several beers, the conversation turned to the availability of moonshine. We must have looked like trusty souls because we were led into a back room where the bottle of hooch was set on the bar. Damn, it sure burned going down—and all this before supper.

Back at the campground, we noticed a pretty young woman at the pool, so after getting our shit together we walked over to meet her. She was a Southern preacher's daughter, and very flirtatious. I just knew this was going to go bad.

Thom had been gone a good while when I was awakened by him scrambling back into the tent. Things had gone bad, and the preacher was on the hunt for him. We packed up our belongings, and high-tailed it out of the campground at daybreak. So far, we were still in one piece.

We were both a bit hungover that morning, so to cure those ills, we shuffled our belongings around in our saddlebags, filled one with ice, and packed several cans of Coors beer. That seemed to do the trick. Off we went.

Thom just couldn't leave it be. He found out where his date was staying that next night and, you guessed it, that is where we headed. He even suggested at one point he was going to strap her to the back of his ride and take her with us. Finally, more level heads prevailed and we again escaped with our lives.

We continued west through the Texas panhandle. We had some incredible tacos in Santa Rosa, but by this time the bikes were taking a beating from the heat, wind, and road grime. I even had to bandage my cracked battery with duct tape to get me to the next town so I could buy a new one. I wasn't the only one having issues. We were travelling in a pack now, and there were several breakdowns along the way. After breakfast the next day, we were preparing to explore the Petrified Forest National Park when I dropped my camera—damaging it. I was pissed. This, combined with the heat and mechanical failures, had everyone on the edge. Thom and I were no different—it wasn't all bad, though.

We did stand on the corner in Winslow, AZ, and yes, it was a fine sight to see! But that was nothing compared to the fine sights and extraordinary vistas of the Grand Canyon at Flagstaff, AZ. After a hell of a ride through the driving wind to get there, the payoff was worth it. Standing on the precipice of a sheer vertical drop, overlooking the miles of wind and water-etched terrain, had to be the most inspiring vision I had ever witnessed in my entire life. If you haven't been there, mark that on the top of your bucket list of places to visit. You will understand what I'm talking about when you see it. We met some great girls and spent the next couple of days enjoying their company. I was feeling carefree, and Thom started to lighten up somewhat.

We crossed over another marvel of construction in the USA—the Hoover Dam. I was amazed at the enormity of this project. We then headed for Las Vegas. What a treat! I had only seen pictures in movies—the city of lights lived up to its name. We stayed at the Cazbah Motel, a cheap dive off the beaten path—it suited us just fine. Casinos, slot machines, free drinks, and good food—all plentiful, and we took full advantage of it. Two days later—a few dollars short in the wallet, we were off to L.A.

The ride between Flagstaff and Bakersfield, CA, is through the Mojave Desert. We experienced sandstorms that were so strong—at one point we were riding on a forty-five-degree angle, fighting the winds. It was so hot that I almost boiled my MC battery dry again—good thing I had bought a new one.

We came across a welcome oasis by the side of the road—just a pipe and a water tap plumbed into the earth, but what a relief in the dry, desert conditions. We took our helmets off, filled them with the cold liquid, and splashed them back on our heads. We hoped this would cool us down enough to get us through the remainder of the desert landscape. I will never forget saying from that day forward that if I ever had to choose between the extremes of hot and cold, I would choose cold every time. My reasoning was simple—you can always put layers on to warm up, but once you've taken all your layers off, you can't cool down anymore if you don't have the resources to do so. I am still not a fan of extreme heat.

California, here we come! My very good friend, Marilyn Dunn—my future wife's cousin—had finished her nursing degree a year earlier, and was recruited on a two-year contract to work in a Culver City hospital—in the suburbs of Los Angeles. It was our goal to stay with Marilyn and her girlfriend Shelly for about five days while on the Pacific Coast. We enjoyed the time exploring the area. We walked the famous Santa Monica Pier, explored Marina Del Rey, bathed in the surf at Zuma Beach, enjoyed some great food and fine So-Cal weather.

San Jose and San Francisco were two of the next stops, and again we had our fill of fine wine, food, and great weather. The only room available in San Fran was a conference room in a hotel. Of course, we laughed at that, and took it—copped some fine hashish, drank some beer, and went to bed. We toured the city the next day and then continued our ride inland towards Yellowstone National Park.

We stayed in Carson City, NV for a couple of days, just east of Lake Tahoe, a beautiful area to explore. Thom and I met some firefighters from the Lake Tahoe FD, and we hung with them during that time. We rode our bikes to the top of the mountain, its grand vista still blanketed in snow. On to Reno. The Wild West is full of plaques and memorials to the pioneers of the day, a very historical area. Old *Bonanza* reruns played on a continuous loop in my head. The TV family, the Cartwrights, lived on the Ponderosa Ranch, and were forever riding into Carson City and Reno on the show. We rode by the Ponderosa Ranch on our way to Reno, Winnemucca, and Twin Falls.

The next big adventure was very unexpected. After missing a couple of turns, we rode into Yellowstone National Park and by the grace of God got a cabin directly across from Old Faithful. What an incredible sight, to witness the geyser shooting skyward. I had studied this phenomenon in school but never thought I would see it in person.

The next day was perfect for our planned itinerary. Our intentions were to ride the perimeter of the park from right to left—and be back in time for supper. Off we went. My first encounter with a moose in the wild happened about a half hour into the drive. The majestic bull was standing in a field about 150 yards away—just like the postcard images for sale back at the cabin office. We stopped by the edge of the road, tried to snap some photos with limited luck, and then continued on. Halfway around the park circuit, on the north tip of the trail, we stopped for lunch at Mammoth Springs for burgers and a beer. After food and fuel, we headed back to the cabin. So far, it had been a fine day.

We had done about three quarters of the ring loop when it happened. Thom was out in front—about a hundred yards or so. We were rounding a bend when I noticed his bike start to hop. It all happened so fast I really didn't have time to process the scene playing out ahead. Thom, being quite adept at motocross riding, realized right away what was happening and took charge of his machine. With precision skill, he navigated through the late June frost-heaves that had damaged the road. Unfortunately, all of this sudden movement, and witnessing Thom's bike somewhat out of control, startled me. Before I could defensively react, I hit the broken pavement also. Fortunately for me, I don't recall the next many seconds of my life— that's a good thing. There was a very steep embankment to my left and a very steep vertical rise to my right. If I had been tossed left, I would have tumbled down into the ravine and would not have survived. As it was, my motorcycle bounced through the damaged pavement, and as I lost control, I found myself on the dirt shoulder, aimed directly at a stand of pines just beyond the grade of the road. What I believe happened is this: The front end of the bike hit a large granite boulder, which in turn, catapulted me over the handlebars—my head taking a glancing blow off a tree—and I was deposited on the forest floor. Thankfully, I was wearing a helmet. There was bark wedged into the binding around the face piece. By the sheer weighted force of my body's forward motion, I tore the fairing completely off the bike. The contents within, including my previously damaged camera, were all but destroyed.

Thom, meanwhile, had managed to keep his bike upright. He stole a quick glance back just as he was entering the next bend only to see me smash like a rag doll into the tree line—witnessing with a sinking feeling, all the debris flying around. His first thought was that there was no way I was going to live through that. What he did see, after what must have seemed like an eternity getting his bike turned facing the opposite direction of our previous travel, was me sitting on my helmet just beyond the road's edge, dazed, and repeating the words "I'm alive! I'm alive!"

I was hurt, but yes, I was alive. I didn't know the extent of my injuries until much later because of the trauma and shock. The front end of my bike took the brunt of the impact and was severely bent out of shape and alignment. My handlebars were in the shape of an S. My beautiful Windjammer fairing was destroyed—scattered in several pieces across the forest floor, contents and all. Weirdly enough, the cap over my timing solenoid was blown apart, but my bike still ran.

Traffic had begun to back up, and a white Toyota Land Cruiser was the first on scene. They had witnessed the crash and wanted to check on my well-being. I have no idea why we did what we did next. It was probably because of the shock. Thom and I discussed whether I was capable of riding the bike the last ten miles to the cabin. Of course, the adrenaline was pumping through me, and I said I was quite capable. Before we could discuss it any further, we threw the debris, chunks of fairing and all, into the back of the Land Cruiser, and proceeded to slowly make our way back to our rental. I was actually riding my damaged bike. It must have looked very unusual to anyone who witnessed that sight. The right handlebar and throttle mechanism were sticking straight up at a ninety-degree angle to their original position. I do recall, during those last ten miles, laughing along with Thom as to the absurdity of it all. We had done a quick medical assessment of my physical condition at the scene. The only visible injury was a cut under my chin. I thought I had escaped major damage. I was so wrong.

Back at the cabin, once the bikes were secure, I started to shake. I knew I had to lie down because I was beginning to feel pain. The adrenaline was definitely wearing off. Thom knew I needed medical attention and so, after assuring him I was okay, he went to a nearby clinic in search of a doctor. I believe I fell asleep while he was gone. Next, as if in a dream, I heard him trying to wake me. After coming to, I tried to sit up but couldn't move—as if frozen to the bed. That scared the shit out of me. I was paralyzed from the neck down. Of this I was certain. When my head, still in the helmet, hit the tree, I had jammed my spine and my neck muscles rather severely. I just knew I was in deep trouble. Fortunately, standing beside Thom was a very tall man in cowboy boots and hat, hovering over me. Thom had found a doctor. After a quick assessment, the diagnosis was not as bad as it could've been. Yes, my muscles were all seized up. I was going to hurt for days, but he couldn't find anything broken, so he prescribed muscle relaxants and painkillers. I was in rough shape, but my bike fared much worse.

The next twenty-four hours were a blur. I drifted in and out of consciousness, awake just enough to attempt to eat, take more drugs, and pass out. I'm sure Thom and I talked about his next moves, but during that time of recovery, he was busy figuring out the logistics of what to do with me, my motorcycle, and most importantly, how I was going to get home.

He did a great job of setting everything in motion. The first order of business was to find a buyer for my damaged bike. I certainly wasn't going to repair it and ride it home, so after some digging, he managed to find a motorcycle shop willing to buy it. He even arranged for them to pick it up and bring it to their shop.

Thom then arranged my flight home on Frontier Airlines, through Denver to Detroit. Prior to leaving, he took me over to the bike shop so I could have one last look at my damaged scoot. He also did very well in negotiating a price. I signed the ownership over to them in exchange for two thousand dollars. I will always be indebted to him for taking such good care of me during those few days of craziness. Thanks, Thom.

The flight home was painful. I had been fitted for a temporary neck brace and could not turn my head left or right. The first leg into Denver was rocked with turbulence, and I suffered with every bounce. To make matters worse, the kid next to me was airsick; it couldn't get any worse. The flight to Detroit was much better, and my father was waiting for me upon arrival. Dad was never one to show much outward affection at that time but when he saw me, he gave me a big hug and told me he loved me, with a tear in his eye. We certainly grew much closer after that scare.

It took a few days of convalescing at home, but I mended well and was ready to get back to work. About a week after the crash, I was at Canatara Park, hanging with some friends. The comment was made that I would probably never ride again. Well, I took that as a challenge, grabbed Rob Butler's bike, and took off around the park. It felt good to be back in the saddle.

Since that time, I have owned several street machines and have never so much as dropped any of them. I sold my last bike in August of 2018 after riding for forty-five years. I do miss the thrill but am happily moved on from the ever-increasing danger to all bikers on the overcrowded roads of North America.

19. Not Quite Ready to Grow Up

The crazy adventures of the last several weeks had imparted a feeling of invincibility on me, the likes of which I had never felt in the past. I had wandered across the country, survived a near-fatal crash, and now had my equally adventurous career to sustain me. My next issue to deal with was my living arrangements. The fact that I was gainfully employed, independent, and mobile only served to create a need for me to find my own place to live—and soon.

Before, and especially after my sojourn to the southwest, I seemed to be at odds socially with my siblings, and Noelle as the youngest, bore the brunt of my self-induced stress. My father, the ever-quiet but keenly observant patriarch of our family, sensed that things were getting out of hand and not going to improve. As much as it probably pained him to do so, he politely suggested I find a place of my own. Yes, he'd had enough of the bickering and fighting. It was time to move on, and deep down, we both knew it was the right thing to do. I just needed that push.

He was right of course—it turned out to be the best move for everybody. I found a house on Davis Street and moved in with my good friend, George Gottfried in September of 1978. My relationship with Noelle and the rest of my siblings improved quickly. I found out years later that Noelle had struggled greatly with the guilt she felt about me leaving. She put the blame squarely on her own shoulders, which was not necessary at all. As per usual, I was the dickhead. She wrote me a beautiful letter explaining her feelings, and I still have that letter today; given future tragedy, it's a treasured keepsake for sure.

I still had a couple of weeks' vacation time left, so my buddy, Mike Shauteet and I decided a road trip in the Charger was in order. We headed east in early October and spent two weeks visiting family, travelling the eastern provinces and the northeastern United States. Mike loved that car so much that when we returned to Sarnia, he bought it from me. He had decided to move west and wanted a reliable vehicle. This created an opportunity for me to go car shopping. What I found was a sweet, candy-apple red 1968 Chevrolet Impala Super Sport. It was a fastback, and very quick out of the gate. I loved that car.

Firefighting was my career, but photography was still a big part of my life, so I set up a dark room in an upstairs bedroom at Davis St. so I could develop my own film. I never got any good at it, but it was a progressive step in my creative journey. Upon my return from the west, I had sent my damaged camera in for repairs and was surprised they fixed it up good as new. I continued to use it for several more years.

The rookie pay scale in the fire department at the time was pretty low, and I continued to supplement my income by doing several part-time jobs. One such job was actually a lot of fun. I became a driver for Veteran's Taxi—working on my time off from the firehall. I made some decent money and continued for about a year. We had to get fingerprinted at the police station as part of employment with the cab company—that being the only reason my prints remain on file today.

George and I had some great times in that house on Davis St. It became a drop-in centre just as my parents' house on Wellington St. had. We partied the year away to some great music. Pink Floyd's *The Wall* got played until it was scratched beyond repair. Artists such as Frank Zappa and The Mothers of Invention and Billy Joel saw heavy rotation—I know, diversity in musical tastes was all the rage then.

My buddy Jeff Zierler was attending OSU (Ohio State University), and several times during those years, I had gone to Columbus to see him. One day, his dad approached me offering his big Cadillac Fleetwood to use if I would take Jeff's little brother Robbie along for the ride. That was a no-brainer! Jeff was thrilled. We couldn't let all that space in the big car go to waste, so we devised a plan to bring some Canadian beer with us to OSU. Jeff had a buddy who lived just over the border in Port Huron, so for the next couple of weeks, we stashed a total of twenty-seven cases of beer in his garage until it was time to go to Ohio. The day Rob and I left, we crossed the border, went to the garage, picked up the beer, and headed on down the highway.

What a reception we got as we entered the parking lot outside of Jeff's dorm. He was straddling the open window ledge, seven storeys up, one leg dangling in the air, waiting for us to arrive. Within seconds, an army of his closest buds came out to greet us, providing the help needed to carry the loot upstairs. We actually constructed a throne in Jeff's room out of the beer cases, and made good use of it during the ensuing parties all that weekend. I was also introduced to the music of Jimmy Buffett that weekend and he continues to be a true favourite all these years later. Robbie's indoctrination into university life was epic! We have reminisced about those days many times since.

I met some wonderful friends during those trips. Lynn Kool, a stunningly beautiful young coed, really caught my eye. She was a tiny thing, pure blonde, edgy and playful, and was definitely all that for me. We hit it off really well. Well enough that I drove to Shaker Heights, OH that fall to spend time with her and her family. But, I'm sure you guessed it, that didn't last either. I do, after all these years, wonder what ever became of her.

20. Meet the Missus

I was starting to make some serious coin with a couple of raises we had achieved at work. The future was looking up. Then something happened that would again redirect my energies. I ran into Mary Brown—my prom date from a year earlier—one day that fall, and sparks flew! It seemed so different this time. We started hanging out more often and all seemed right with the world. This progressed to dating more frequently, and we spent a wonderful New Year's Eve at a dance at the Air Force Club with my whole family. She sat on my lap most of the night and when she wasn't doing that, we were dancing the night away. She and I could really cut a rug! We just got each other—as we moved so well together. That, very clearly, is the day I knew I was truly in love with her. I also knew then I would ask her to marry me. It was a magical time with many cherished memories.

The winter of '78/'79 came and went. Spring was upon us and Mary and I were heading in the right direction. I could feel the love and just knew she was the one. She fit in well with my family and soon became very good friends with Joan and Valerie. Mom and Dad loved her and were extremely happy I was growing into a more caring and loving person. I got along well with Mary's family also. Her brother Tim and I became quite close.

At that time, I didn't own a motorcycle, but Tim did. He had a Kawasaki 440cc LTD and I loved taking it for rides. Of course, Mary didn't care for it or for bikes in general, feeling that they were dangerous. This fact proved to be the main reason I didn't own a ride again for about twelve years.

The highlight of the summer, not yet known to anyone, was that I was planning an engagement. I had been working on the logistics for months. After saving some serious coin, I went to Nash Jewellers in London, Ont.

and purchased a diamond cluster ring, set in a beautiful band of gold. The surprise was planned for the weekend of July 28th.

My soon-to-be fiancée, it seemed, had other things in mind. She had planned a surprise party for my twenty-third birthday that same weekend. Of course, I didn't suspect anything—it being a week before the actual date. We both had no idea what was in store for us, but both knew it would be a fun weekend.

Mary and I had a recent conversation in which she filled in some of the details. She reminded me that we were going to go out for supper (where I was planning to propose), and when she came to the house to meet me, she noticed peach roses on the table—her favourite. We had made a pact that the only time she would get peach roses would be on very special occasions. Well, this turned out to be a real special occasion. She must have informed her friends of the significance of the flowers, because when we came back to the house after supper and were greeted by a huge crowd—all there for my surprise party—they had suspected something was up. Of course, they were thrilled for us, and the surprise birthday party turned into a celebration of our engagement also.

Life on Davis St. ran its course. It was time to move up in the world, so George and I parted ways when I moved into a townhouse at 626 Indian Road #11 with my good friend, Steve Zub. We knew Steve's tenure at the townhouse was temporary because the wedding date had been set for a year later, on August 9th, 1980. Mary and I were going to live there after we got married.

A few memories come to mind from that following year. Steve and I thoroughly enjoyed living there and got along famously—so much so that I asked him to be my best man. I bought my first big cabinet-style TV so we could watch the Super Bowl in January. The Steelers beat the Rams, becoming the first team in NFL history to win four Super Bowls. It was worth the purchase. Work was awesome, and I was months away from becoming a first-class firefighter, which meant a huge raise. Soon, it was time for a wedding—and yes, this time it was mine. First course of action: the stag. A drunken affair for sure.

We also had a joint wedding shower. Its theme: booze. Every attendee had to bring some type of alcohol, complete with an explanation as to why they picked that particular kind. We came away with a great variety of liquor, enough to last quite some time.

We had done everything to prepare for this day. The engagement shoot had gone well. The planning details, which included securing the hall, liquor permits, tux rentals, and every other nuance, were all taken care of, and now it was finally happening.

Mary and I planned and paid for our own wedding. Both families had contributed in different ways, but in the end it was us who would foot the bill. I know it seems like a paltry sum today, but back in 1980, the grand total of $4500 was huge! Of course, that did not include the honeymoon.

The day started off well. The groomsmen and I went to my sister Lorraine's house for a swim. It was hot and sunny with plenty of time to chill. The 2 p.m. ceremony was being held at St. Joseph's Parish on Stuart St.—the church I had attended as a child. I remember being quite relaxed despite the fact I was getting married in a few hours.

I will never forget seeing Mary as she walked down the aisle. She was beaming with a radiance unparalleled. The church ceremony was beautiful, attended by many friends and family.

After its conclusion, we drove over to the Germain Gardens next to the firehall for wedding photos. It was unfortunate that we had picked a day when my co-workers were on shift, but it couldn't be avoided. This issue was somewhat tempered when the crew brought a fire truck over to the gardens to use as a photo prop. It was a great way to include my workmates.

The reception was held at the Sarnia Township Arena on Wellington St., with the upstairs hall decorated beautifully. In order to recoup some of our costs, we held a Toonie Bar where all drinks were two dollars. This eased the financial burden somewhat. The night was magical. We danced until midnight, then changed, said our goodbyes, and left.

The honeymoon was fabulous. We took Mary's new Honda Civic for a leisurely drive to the East Coast. Having many relatives in that area who could not make the wedding made for a perfect excuse to continue the celebrations.

We were back in Sarnia by Labour Day, ready to start our new life. The condo was set up nicely with new furniture. Work was going well for both of us. Life was good.

Perpetual Motion

Mary and I did enjoy a couple of evening soap operas. The TV show *Dallas*, and its spinoff *Dynasty*, were very popular. After all, this was the season we were going to find out "who shot JR." If you don't get the reference, google it, you'll find it.

It was Monday, December 8th, and we were just settling in to watch *Dallas*. A breaking news bulletin interrupted programming to inform the world that John Lennon had been murdered outside the Dakota Apartments complex in New York City. I was heartbroken. Being such a big Beatles fan, the news was devastating. Generations of fans had always hoped the group would get back together to record and tour, but this was now an impossibility. I had been subjected to other world news disasters in my life, but the death of this musical icon hit me hard. I bought Lennon's newly released album, *Double Fantasy*, the one the killer, Mark David Chapman, got autographed by the singer just prior to the murder. It is still one of my favourite albums.

I was becoming more interested in American politics. Ronald Reagan, a character actor from Hollywood turned California governor, was elected President of the United States. He had defeated one-term democrat Jimmy Carter for the oval office and would go on to become a very strong Republican president.

The biggest political issue of the day was the crisis in Iran. Fifty-two American diplomats were held hostage for 444 days in the American Embassy in Tehran. The hostages were released only after Reagan was inaugurated on January 20th, 1981. It remains to this day the longest hostage situation in modern recorded history.

Prior to this political crisis, I had not delved into world affairs much at all. This, again, changed me. I believe it also changed the world. Our planet just did not seem to be as Utopian or generally as safe any longer. Until that time, the word "terrorist" was used very sparingly in conversation. There had been some terrorist incidents in the world prior to this savage act, but Tehran opened my eyes to a new world order. Maybe it was because I was maturing as a person, married, contemplating children, and holding down a responsible job. Life just seemed more important. As discussed further on, the political landscape would grow even more dire in years to come.

21. Work Hard, Play Hard, Never Stop Learning

Two of the biggest news items in 1981 couldn't have been more different. The first was the marriage of Lady Diana Spencer to Prince Charles of England. This charming lady would go on to do great things, and, as tragedy would have it, died in a car crash in August 1997. Like other milestones that for whatever reason have played a significant role in my life, I remember fully where I was and what I was doing when the marriage took place, and also when tragedy struck. I was not a Royal watcher per se, just enamoured with Diana's strength and beauty. The other event, something you are much more familiar with, was the birth of the Internet. Yes, this old guy did a lot of living before the Internet was unleashed upon the world. I don't need to tell you how important that fact has become.

I mentioned previously my love for my home province of Nova Scotia. Having found out this particular summer was designated *Old Home Summer,* (basically a province wide Celtic party, all summer long), I decided to go back east, and enjoy some of the scheduled festivities. Mary was busy working and couldn't get time off, so I headed cross-country, and stayed two weeks. Karen's house was used as my base for travel. Celebratory events were held throughout the province, and when I stayed in Afton, there were several impromptu field parties I attended with Uncle Eugene. I had a spectacular time. It helped to further cement my love for the East Coast and also allowed me to nurture relationships with my extended family.

A huge tradition, which started in '81, was an annual guys' fishing trip. Mark LaBrasceur, Brad Taylor, Steve Faulkner, Steve McCann, and several others would get together each of the next dozen years and make time to do some fishing, and bonding over some great food, bonfires, and song. We tried several different places, but Rice Lake in central Ontario became the go-to destination. We even wrote a song about it titled, "The Rice Lake Ditty." I still have the original, handwritten lyrics.

Back home, work continued to go well. I had achieved my first-class firefighter's status, and along with that, my raise in pay. I had also been encouraged by my older colleagues to attend the union meetings held by the Sarnia Professional Firefighters' Association (SPFFA). These meetings were held monthly at the main hall, and were designed to inform the membership of the goings on in the fire service—things that would or could affect our careers now, and into the future. This sounded like something I should be interested in, so I started to attend the meetings regularly.

One example of information worth knowing was the constant discussion of our pension plan. At the time, being on the job approximately four years, and knowing I had thirty or more years ahead of me, I took little interest in the pension issue or more specifically, the pension requirements, and how they would change several times prior to me being eligible to collect it. I wondered aloud to my colleagues as to why I should be interested in it at all so early in my career. Wow, did I get an earful. I was so naïve. The pension plan did change approximately five times, all for the better of course, and if the more experienced members had had the same attitude I did, then it most likely would not have improved. I had a lot of learning to do, not only in my fledgling career as a firefighter but in the political arena too. This conversation became a wake-up call to me, and my interest in making the fire service a better place to work became a passion.

One of the advantages of attaining first-class wages was the ability to afford a winter vacation. I had not ever been south in winter. Shortly after the new year, Mary and I, along with our friends Brad and Vicki Taylor, went to Florida. We stayed in a condo on Hollywood Beach owned by my neighbours, Bob and Marg Barnes. During our vacation, we went to Disney World for the first time and enjoyed the magic.

Another event with a completely different outcome was our deep-sea fishing adventure. The four of us set out on a charter early one morning, and after spending an hour or so travelling to a good fishing hole, we set our lines and waited to catch fish. Unfortunately for my poor wife, the waves were too much, and seasickness prevailed the whole time out on the water. She was too proud to be seen getting sick over the side of the boat, so she insisted on me helping her down into the galley so she could vomit in private. This went on for quite some time. Mary was green around the gills. Finally, the captain had enough and returned to shore. The moment Mary's feet hit the dock, she was perfectly fine, and the first words out of her mouth were "I'm starving, let's eat!"

That vacation was where I first enjoyed a good gin and tonic. Brad would mix a pitcher of the tart elixir every day to take to the pool. Overall, despite the setback on the boat, we had a wonderful time.

Back at work, I had expressed my opinion on association matters over the course of time. It must have resonated with some of my fellow firefighters because soon enough, I was encouraged by past president Jim Fritzley to run for a position on the executive board of the Sarnia Professional Firefighters' Association. I was duly elected treasurer of our local association in the fall of 1982. This would culminate in a sixteen-year run on the SPFFA executive board. I would eventually hold positions as treasurer (two different terms of three years), secretary (seven years), and president (three years) over the course of that time. There is no doubt these extracurricular activities played a huge role in the advancement of my career, but I see now how they may have also contributed to future issues in my life, as explored in depth in later chapters.

Things did not start out smoothly at the beginning of my political career. It was shortly after I took over the treasurer's position that I discovered some mismanagement of funds attributed, most likely, to a former board member. Over the course of the next two years, we would see criminal charges laid against this firefighter, and subsequently a conviction on civil charges of misappropriation of association funds. This episode would mark the first time I was required to testify at a criminal trial. It was a nerve-wracking experience, but I learned much, and by doing so, it helped me in future court case testimonies. The firefighter in question, after being mandated to pay the association the money he'd misappropriated, left the employ of the fire service, and I have not seen him since.

22. My Little Peanut

The world became a better place to live in September of 1982. It was then I found out my wife was pregnant with our first child. I was beyond thrilled we were starting a family and was so ready for fatherhood. Although Mary and I had no idea how to be parents, we had a loving and supportive family circle and just knew we had all the help we needed.

Mary and I discussed much in those next months. Long talks about how we were going to raise our child, and what type of parenting style we wanted to convey. It didn't matter to us whether our child was male or female, and to that fact, we discussed many names for boys and girls. What we settled on, ironically, was something rather simple. If our child was female with blonde hair, she would be Stephanie, and if she had dark hair she would be Jennifer. If our child was a boy with dark hair, he would be Joel, and if he had blond hair he would be Shaun. I'm not sure how we arrived at that solution, but it seemed to have worked.

Mary was due in late May of 1983. Through much of our discussions over the course of her pregnancy, one of the feelings she expressed was that she was going to deliver our child early. She never gave me a scientific reason for thinking that way, but sometimes there doesn't need to be one. The best she could come up with was that her girlfriend, a co-worker, had delivered her child six weeks early, just a short time before, and Mary just had a feeling the same was going to happen to her. I of course, dismissed those notions as raging hormones during pregnancy. What did I know!

There was a baby shower scheduled the weekend of April 9th. We were thrilled with the gifts and the love received. Mary still had seven weeks to go to full term. Sticking to my schedule, I left the following day for Niagara Falls to attend a firefighters' seminar, an event held in that city twice a year. It had been an easy decision to go, because I knew Mary still had over a month until her due date. As we now know, babies have a way of feeling what their mother feels while in the womb. This baby must have been listening to all the conversations about premature birth and decided that we needed the challenge. Mary started having contractions on April 13th while I was in Niagara Falls. She called me and quietly informed me that I needed to come home—immediately. I made it from downtown Niagara Falls to Sarnia in two hours flat, the fastest I would ever drive that route.

Contractions and labour pains settled down that afternoon, but during the early hours of the following morning they intensified, and we knew it was time to go. I was still in a little bit of shock trying to figure out why things were happening so early. I will admit that I was concerned, but I couldn't show it because I didn't want to worry Mary any more than she already was.

We arrived at the hospital around 6:30 a.m., and our beautiful baby daughter Stephanie Rose-Anne was born at 9:38 a.m., approximately six weeks premature. She weighed in at a whopping four pounds, four ounces at birth. She was the tiniest little baby I have ever seen. She fit into the crux of my forearm.

After the initial euphoria of childbirth, it was immediately apparent this little child needed extra care. The medical staff were concerned that being premature, her lungs were not fully developed, so more testing was needed. For the next short while, we waited—scared shitless, actually. Sometime later, we were informed she would be in an incubator for the foreseeable future, to help with the completion of her growth to full term. No, we were not taking this child home with us any time soon.

Mary was released from the hospital a couple of days later. One of the hardest things we had to do was leave the hospital without our bundle of joy, but we knew she was in good hands. So, for the next six weeks, we went to the hospital every day to spend time feeding, bathing, and cuddling our precious child.

In the beginning, Stephanie lost just about a pound of weight—falling at her lowest to three pounds, eight ounces before starting to rally in the weeks to come. Finally, after six weeks of the intense hospital stay, and topping out at five pounds, nine ounces, we took Stephanie home on Mother's Day. What a beautiful Mother's Day present it was.

We walked into our townhouse with our precious bundle wrapped up tight, and I will never forget those initial feelings. From that day forward, my life would take on a completely different meaning. Fatherhood changes you, and now I had two women to protect. I was ready for the challenge.

My little peanut—as I so affectionately called her—was growing and maturing at a normal rate. We had been told there could be some developmental challenges with her because she was a preemie, but having had her assessed several times that first year, we were quite satisfied she was as normal a child as anyone else. Stephanie was walking at eleven months and understanding speech quite well.

Noelle was especially fond of Stephanie. She would visit often to hang out with us, and if we were going out, she would babysit Stephanie for as long as we needed her. Those two had an amazing bond.

In the spring of 1984, Mary and I were contemplating buying our first home. We had discussed our likes and dislikes and were bound and determined to find the right one. I was driving down Wellington St. in the central part of the city one day when I saw a *For Sale* sign on a cute, two-storey, vinyl-sided house not far from the firehall. Knowing my firefighter friend Jack Popowich was also selling real estate, I called him, asking for details. He had bad news. There was an offer just presented on the house, conditioned on finance. Mary and I were rather disappointed because we really liked what we saw. Two days later, Jack called with a different story. The offer by the initial purchasers had fallen through because of those same financing issues. I immediately instructed Jack to put an offer in to the owners for the exact same amount of money—with no conditions—to see if they would accept it. Without hesitation, they did! Because there were no conditions, and we didn't have a previous house to sell, the papers were quickly signed. We became first-time homeowners at 557 Wellington St.

We were damn proud of that house. A selling feature was the sixteen by thirty-two-foot in-ground pool in the backyard—beautiful, but in need of repair. The first chore on my to-do list was a drive to London for a new pool liner. I wanted it up and running. By the middle of June, we were swimming. Now that we had the backyard functioning, it was time to concentrate on the interior. We painted, wallpapered, carpeted, and did all the necessary things to make this house our home.

The nursery was on the main floor—equipped with a two-way monitor to hear any movement and sound from within. This allowed us to enjoy being poolside and still have an ear to our child. The kitchen, formal dining room, and living room made up the rest of the main floor.

The rec-room, as it was known to us, had a wood-burning fireplace which we used often. There was a bar already built, and in need of some updating, so I added a wood top, and railings for more function. Off to one side was an alcove we made into a play area for Stephanie. The laundry room and furnace room were combined to finish the space.

The upper level had two bedrooms and a full bath. A unique feature of this upper space was the built-in drawers in each room, and the hallway. Overall, I have to say it was one of my favourite homes I've owned, and I'm very fond of the many memories made there.

Not long after moving, we attended my brother Greg's wedding in Toronto. He and his beautiful bride, Wendy, got married on the paddle-wheel tour boat, Mariposa Bell. We sailed all through Toronto Harbour, enjoying the festivities with the whole family. Greg had asked me to be the official photographer for his wedding—the only reason being that I owned a nice camera. I certainly didn't know what I was doing, and fortunately they did get some decent pictures as keepsakes.

23. Time To Go Home

Shortly after we got home, Mary, Stephanie, and I were asked to come to Mom and Dad's for supper. This didn't happen often, but at the time, it was nothing out of the ordinary. What transpired that evening would change our family dynamics forever. We were informed that they were selling the house on Wellington St., the house they had lived in for over twenty years, and were moving back to Nova Scotia. This was to take place sometime the following summer.

At the time I remember feeling angry. I believe it stemmed from the fact that I had been so happy to have my parents so close by for Stephanie. I wanted her to know her grandparents, and I couldn't see my way through the clouds of confusion surrounding the news. It took some time for it to sink in, and after months of processing this future event, I warmed to the idea. Mom and Dad had always said that after the last child graduated, they were going to move back east. At the time, most of us siblings thought it was just conversation.

Several family socials happened over the next few months and each time we got together, I couldn't help but think it was the last time we would be doing this. We had a couple of grand pool parties at our place with several of our friends in attendance. One such party was held in August for my 28th birthday. I still cherish the pictures of Mom and Dad being there, sitting comfortably in the backyard along with Mary's mom and siblings.

That Christmas of 1984 was especially hard for me, and I'm quite certain it was for Mary too, knowing it was the last festive season with Mom and Dad in Sarnia. What I didn't know then was that I would never spend Christmas holidays with my parents ever again.

Another tradition we had on Wellington St. during the time my parents owned the property was a winter barbecue. Back in 1967, my father had built a brick barbecue in the backyard for a centennial project, it being Canada's one-hundredth birthday. We used that barbecue in summer and winter. What made this particular event special was again the fact it would be the last. There is a picture of Martin and me barbecuing—shirtless—in the winter—while drinking beer. The grins on our faces tell the story. They were special times.

Spring 1985 arrived and with it a promotion to the rank of Acting Lieutenant within the fire service. My career was moving in a very positive direction. It was also a time of happiness and hope for my parents' successful move to the East Coast. The house had sold. It was purchased in 1964 for $11,300 and sold in June of 1985 for $49,000. A departure date was chosen. July 1st, it seemed, was as good a time as any to embark on this new adventure. Much was to be done before then—a house to pack, and lots of stuff to purge. I was asked, when the time came, if I would drive the rental truck containing the contents of their life to Nova Scotia. Their belongings were to be stored in a building owned by family in Afton. Of course, I agreed to this, thinking it was going to be an adventure for me also.

Stephanie turned two on April 14th. We had a wonderful birthday party at our house attended by many family and friends. In the recent past, the fire department had taken possession of a state-of-the-art VHS video camcorder. I had borrowed it on a couple of occasions, and this birthday party was no exception. It would turn out to be a huge memory maker. I have thought for years to get those tapes digitally remastered and now as I write this, it has started to happen.

Mom and Dad had always been very social people. The fact of their imminent departure created the need for several farewell parties. One such party was held at the Navy club. It was billed as *Maurice and Helen's farewell/going away party combined with mom's retirement party from Woolco Department Store*. Oh, what a party it was. They were so well loved by so many people that the hall was packed beyond capacity. You must be able to imagine, us eight siblings, many of our friends, Mom and Dad and all of their friends, all not wanting to miss the party of the year. Mark Armstrong and Terry Liebelt, friends for many years, were the DJs, as they had been for many of the benefit (Benny-Foot) dances Mom and Dad held at the Air Force Club over the years. It certainly was a night to remember.

The next psychological hurdle for me to get over was that Noelle had decided after graduation from St. Pat's in June, she was going to make the journey with Mom and Dad to start a new life in Nova Scotia. She was seventeen years old and very independent. I was proud of her adventurous spirit for making this decision and just knew it would be the right thing for her to do.

Two significant things happened in rapid succession. Firstly, Noelle was voted valedictorian of her graduating year, proving how popular and well-loved she was. She wrote a beautiful speech and asked me to proofread it prior to her having to deliver it. I was honoured. The next was that Noelle was voted Prom Queen by her peers at her senior prom. We were never so proud of her as we were in that month prior to her departure for the east.

Joyous memories still flood my thoughts when thinking of the afternoon of Noelle's prom. She and her date, Joe Malongat, along with Martin, Anita, and several other couples came to our house for drinks and pictures. Noelle was stunning in her spring-yellow dress, the rest of the gang also sharply outfitted. I really don't recall seeing her as happy as she was that day.

Of all my siblings whom I love dearly, I just knew she was going to change peoples lives. I just didn't know in what way.

In late June, the possessions of the little house on Wellington St. were packed into a rental truck as I prepared to leave with my parents' worldly belongings for the trip to Nova Scotia. Mom, Dad, and Noelle were to leave July 1st and take a leisurely trip to their new home province. It was a sad day in many ways, knowing our family unit in Sarnia would never be the same, but conversely it was a joyous occasion whereby a new life, new adventures, and the great unknown lay ahead.

For my part in this adventure, the responsibility in getting a house full of furniture to Nova Scotia was no big deal. I obviously had experience handling large vehicles through my experience driving fire trucks, so I was comfortable doing what I needed to do. By this time, Martin had decided to come along for the drive. Having him as company definitely made the drive more pleasurable. It was an uneventful trip, and upon arrival in Afton, there was plenty of help from my many relatives in the area. We unloaded their belongings into the old wooden structure, praying it was somewhat weatherproof. Martin and I stayed at Uncle Eugene's house for a few days and, after loading up several coolers full of fresh lobster, we headed back west.

On July 1st, 1985, Mom and Dad, along with their youngest daughter Noelle, left Sarnia for good. Their first stop was with Greg and Wendy in Toronto. They had a wonderful visit and departed the next day to continue the journey. They stayed in Québec City for an evening, finally arriving in Nova Scotia, at Karen's house in Lower Sackville on July 8th.

There was much to do. The prospects of looking for a forever home was first and foremost on their mind. After settling in, they started the search. Of course, Mom had criteria. She wanted a large piece of property with room for her gardens, and as much nature surrounding them as possible. As far as the ideal house was concerned, they wanted something large enough to accommodate anyone who came to visit, or more importantly, when everyone came to visit, and they well knew this was a real possibility at any given time.

It was only a few days searching when they came upon 133 Rosley Rd., out the Beaverbank Rd., to the west of Lower Sackville. Everything about this property was ideal. The house was large enough, with five bedrooms, two baths, and ample living space. The property was almost an acre in size—plenty of room for gardens and an eventual garage for Dad. The biggest selling feature by far was a beautiful brook running through the back of the property. It was about thirty feet across with varying depths. Mom took her time absorbing this feature. She wanted to make sure the property was the right fit. Noelle was not with them when they initially looked at the house. The offer went in, was accepted, and finally they had their little piece of heaven.

A couple of days later, although they weren't able to get into the house, they took Noelle out to see her new home. As they stood on the front lawn describing the interior, Noelle picked the small, yellow bedroom in the corner as hers. She would never get to step foot in that bedroom.

24. Cross-Country Tragedy

Meanwhile, Martin and I had arrived back in Sarnia—again, a very uneventful trip home. I did have dozens of lobsters with me, which made for some very happy people who had ordered them, none happier than my platoon chief Owen Forsythe, who had requested the majority of my haul. He was originally from Kentville, NS, and upon hearing I was bringing a large truck home empty, was instrumental in me getting him some delicious crustaceans.

The most tragic news of my life accosted me at about 11:20 p.m. the evening of July 18th, 1985. Mary and I were asleep when the phone on the nightstand rang. I answered and was greeted by a male voice I didn't initially recognize. He introduced himself as Father McAllister, who I knew to be the pastor of St. Benedict's Church, the parish that my family had belonged to for years. He went on to explain that he had received a call from my father a short time earlier with the news that my dear baby sister Noelle had been in a very serious car accident. The trauma to her body was devastating, and the doctors had determined there was no hope for recovery. She had been taken off life support and passed away a short time later.

Well, fuck.

I had talked to Noelle on the phone two nights earlier. She was happy with life, and now, no more.

I was shaking my head, hoping this was a dream. I wanted to wake up from the nightmare, but tragically, it was all too real. Father McAllister went on to explain that my father could not make the phone call himself because he too, was traumatized. The priest instructed me as to my father's wishes, which was to be the bearer of this news to Lorraine and Martin. I assume, in my father's mind, because of my profession in the fire service, he deemed me most capable of delivering the devastating news. After a quick prayer and a blessing for peace, we ended the call. By this time Mary was awake and crying, having heard the one-sided conversation.

The rest of the night was surreal. I called Martin and gave him the news. I explained Dad's wishes, then picked him up so we could go to Lorraine's. I needed the emotional support. We all ended up at my house, hugging, crying, and trying to make sense of how our lives had just changed forever. For the next couple of hours we talked and began to formulate the necessary arrangements for getting to the East Coast as soon as possible. Plans were finalized. Flights were scheduled to Halifax for later in the day. I was, by then, exhausted. I needed a moment alone with my thoughts, so I went to the backyard, sat on the picnic table, head in my hands crying, trying to understand my present reality.

Sometimes things happen that are unexplainable. As I sat under the weight of the trauma enveloping me, I suddenly felt a great pressure on my shoulders, as if somebody was sitting on me. Surprised, I looked up. There, directly above me in the clear night sky, was a huge star—more brilliant than anything I had ever seen before. It twinkled, and shone so brightly, reminding me of the Biblical stories of the Star of the East, which guided the Magi to the manger, the cradle of Jesus, the night of his birth. I was overwhelmed. This had to be a sign my dearly, departed sister had made it to Heaven! I spoke her name out loud. "Hi, Noelle." I sat there for what seemed an eternity but was probably no more than a brief few minutes. Gathering my thoughts, I went back inside to share with my siblings what had just happened. Upon hearing the details of my encounter with that celestial body, we went into the yard to see for ourselves. The star was no longer there.

I will never forget the feeling of peace that had come over me in those few minutes after witnessing such a miracle. From that day, the sight of that star lives with me in my heart. Mary and I lived in that same house for another three years, and each July 18th at approximately midnight, I would go out to the backyard to see if that star was shining brightly. It was not. It never came back to sit on my shoulder ever again, thus cementing my belief that it was Noelle, letting me know she was in Heaven, and all was well.

Perpetual Motion

That morning, prior to leaving for the airport, I went to the firehall and had a quick meeting with Deputy Chief Knight. I informed him of my circumstances, and his words were of such comfort to me. He told me to go and only come back when I was ready. His kindness, generosity, and understanding of what I was going through shone through that day. During my later years in the fire service as a member of the management team, I paid this same act forward several times.

The next ten days are a bit of a blur. We had the wake at the Atlantic Funeral Home in Halifax, and the burial at Mount Pleasant Cemetery on Sackville Dr. in Lower Sackville. Directly across the street from the burial site was a farm with horses running in the meadow. Noelle loved horses, and we all saw this as another positive sign. Many of Noelle's friends made the trip along with aunts, uncles, and cousins from all over the province. That evening, we had a full-blown Irish get-together at Karen and Al's house. We laughed, cried, and hugged each other until the wee hours of the morning.

25. Vulnerabilities

Time for a reality check. We made it back to Sarnia, and moving forward, tried to put the events of the last two weeks behind us. We had our toddler Stephanie to keep us in line, and I threw myself into work harder than ever. I really don't know if I ever properly grieved Noelle's death. In hindsight, I can tell you I didn't deal with her tragic demise the way I should have, given that it started to adversely affect me in many ways, including my home life. I loved my wife dearly and would do nothing to hurt her, but inside I was hurting, and, not realizing it, started my initial spiral into the rabbit hole that is PTSD. To be clear, little was known about Post Traumatic Stress Disorder then. At any time, we as firefighters felt the pangs of anxiety because of different traumas we witnessed—we would bury it deep inside, laugh it off, create off-colour jokes about it, and move on. So, keeping true to what I knew, I soldiered on.

One thing I knew would take my mind off the experiences that affected my mental attitude was to read, a passion if you recall, I didn't pick up until after high school. At the time I was enjoying Clive Cussler, a great adventure-style author. His third book starring the venerable Dirk Pitt was called *Raise the Titanic*. The plot was rather far-fetched, in that the actual *Titanic*, which sank to the bottom of the North Atlantic in 1912, had not been located at the time Cussler penned his tale. In the fictional book, the ship was found in one piece, and through the miraculous use of airbags and such, was raised to the surface and sailed into New York Harbor. In actuality, the *Titanic* was discovered by Robert Ballard that early fall, September 1st, 1985, resting two miles below the waves. Surrounded by a giant debris field, the mighty ship was discovered to have broken into two large pieces during her descent to the depths. They were strewn about a quarter mile apart, laying to rest any dream of recovering that ship for whatever purpose lurked in the hearts of the discoverers. I remember contemplating that historic event because of the significance of its ties to my home province, and especially to Halifax, where many of the deceased passengers and crew were laid to rest after the tragedy. It would be many years later, I would finally get to visit the *Titanic* grave site with my daughter and her children.

Still needing to fill the hurt within my heart, I bought a new Yamaha L-35 left-handed acoustic guitar. I had always wanted to learn how to play, and it seemed this was the time to do it. It would take my mind off the shit happening in my life.

No one really knows how or why certain noteworthy events affect us to the degree they do. After going through a fairly severe rough patch in the past several months with Noelle's passing, I was hoping to put the demons to bed and start fresh in the new year.

Mary had her twenty-eighth birthday on January 26th, and we celebrated with cake and gifts. Things had seemed to be good as of late. On the morning of January 28th, being a NASA space-junky nerd, I was looking forward to watching the launch of the space shuttle, *Challenger*. The significance of this historic flight was that Christa McAuliffe, a civilian schoolteacher from Concord, NH, was part of the crew and was going to broadcast her incredible journey to the millions of school children below over the course of the next week. This was not meant to be. Due to a faulty o-ring seal, *Challenger* blew up at the seventy-three-second mark after launch.

I, along with millions of other viewers, both at Cape Canaveral and around the world, watching through our television sets, were in shock. It was hard to imagine and to comprehend what we were seeing. Even the announcers were doing their best to make sense of what was being viewed in real-time. In the end, seven astronauts perished in what was the most tragic incident and loss of life in NASA's long, storied history. Looking back, it was another traumatic event that I didn't know was adding to the cumulative effect of my PTSD.

Unfortunately, for those of us who are adversely affected by tragic events, we never seem to find a shortage of them. A scant ten weeks later, the worst nuclear disaster in history happened in Ukraine. The nuclear power plant at Chernobyl suffered a catastrophic meltdown on April 26th. You might wonder why something that happened on the other side of the world would affect somebody in such ways. All I can tell you is that once you start spiraling down that hole, it doesn't have to be just worldwide catastrophic events that trigger you. Triggers can be the slightest things, like witnessing a car accident with minor injuries. Because of the nature of my job, this shit occurred on a regular basis. We all develop coping mechanisms, and some develop stronger abilities to cope than others. This nuclear incident affected me inwardly. It just added another layer to the accumulation of crap and devastation in my head. It will become clear to you in subsequent chapters why I am telling you about these things now. You will soon see how it's all connected.

I was, by this time, becoming adept at finding medicinal things to take the edge off. Although I didn't abuse it at any time in my life, alcohol was a clear and present crutch to get myself, and most of my co-workers, through the hard times. Besides enjoying drinks on occasion to help with the mind games, things that certainly helped during this period were the good news stories. It always lifted our spirits when we saved some property from the ravages of flames, or performed a successful rescue, even when it was a little cat up a tree.

26. My Everything's

Great news stories, on the other hand, can also affect you for the rest of your life. I could not have dreamed up a better feel-good story than finding out Mary was pregnant again. We found out a short while after returning from Nova Scotia, and even through all the triggering events of the last few months, I had held on tight to the knowledge that my family was growing. I wanted nothing more than to move on to this new chapter in our lives.

This miracle of birth would change everything. Our son, Shaun Patrick, was born April 3rd, 1986. Of course, I was ecstatic that we now had a son. It completed the perfect family dynamics. He was born two weeks early, but healthy, and cute as could be. When all of this happened, Mary and I wondered if we would be repeating the same routine as we had done with Stephanie three years earlier. Shaun was a strong one and got to come home with us without delay. We were over the moon with joy. All seemed right with the world, and as I had been accustomed to doing so often in the past, I subconsciously buried further any difficult thoughts or feelings that hammered around in my head.

Shaun was one handsome lad. From the day he was born, he had blond hair, which in time turned really curly. He was a happy child and gave us so much joy. As he grew a little older, we let his hair grow out quite long. This boy was the hit of the party. I can still to this day hear him do his Pee-Wee Herman impression (forever etched on video)—one of the best memories ever! My children were my world. My shift at the firehall allowed me four days off in a row, and I spent as much time with Stephanie and Shaun as possible.

Mary was well established in her career, just as I was in the fire service and the extra curricular things I did for the Treasury board for the Firefighters' Association. When we both needed to be away, we had MaryAnne Ellis, our young babysitter from across the street. She was the best little helper in the world. She loved our kids like they were her own, and we all loved her too. We employed her regularly for several years, and she didn't mind a bit. MaryAnne eventually moved on, but to this day I consider her part of our family. One of the highlights of my life was when both kids were in her wedding party, and I was asked to deliver the toast to the bride at her reception. I wrote the toast in the form of a nursery rhyme and pasted it into a large nursery rhyme book so it appeared I was reading my words from the book. It was such a hit, and I know MaryAnne treasured that moment.

Mary and I took such pleasure watching the two little ones grow up. We would splash around in the pool all summer with family and friends, go for walks around the neighbourhood often, and love our children like there was no tomorrow. I just can't imagine what my life would have been like without my babies.

27. On The Brighter Side

Despite lingering trauma, the year continued through some good times. My sister Valerie was still living in Nova Scotia at that time, and, so it seemed, had met a man. She and Rob had met at the car dealership where they had both purchased vehicles, and it wasn't long until they were engaged to be married that September. Our little family planned to venture to the East Coast for the wedding, but just before we were to leave, Shaun came down with the measles. The poor little guy was only five months old. We eventually flew to Halifax when he was deemed healthy enough to travel, and enjoyed a beautiful week with family celebrating the love of Rob and Val. The dealership even supplied them with a brand-new Buick to use for their wedding and honeymoon. It was another memorable vacation to the East Coast.

Back home, I continued to be extremely busy with family commitments, my fire service career, the extra duties of being on the executive board, and my painting business. Being engaged helped to take my mind off the tragic events of the last year.

Work continued to go well into 1987, with some successful moves of my own. Elections were held for positions on the executive board of the SPFFA, and I decided to run for the position of secretary. I was successful in attaining that position. With it came much more work than I was used to as treasurer, but I was loving the learning curve. I now had a voice on the grievance and negotiations committees, along with much more responsibility for the daily running of the association.

Martin was living with us at Wellington St., which meant he could take full advantage of the pool facilities. Several notable parties with his friends still bring a smile to my face. I was introduced to a musician on CD named David Wilcox, and the rest, they say, is history. He is to this day, one of my favourite artists. I also met a young blond-haired local rocker, Doug Stewart. At the time, we had no idea that over thirty-six years later, we would still be listening to great music from his band CDDC. Love ya, brother! Cheers!

My project for the summer was to build a wood-slat fence around our property. There had been a chain-link fence dividing the yards for many years, and I wanted to upgrade the aesthetics. I had never built a fence before and enjoyed designing it and seeing the job through to fruition. Mary bought me an awesome birthday present in August. I received a cool Sony Walkman, which was very much appreciated and came in handy while doing my yard work. I used it daily for years after, and now am pretty sure you can find a similar device permanently on display at the Smithsonian Institute. True story!

By January of 1988, our first home on Wellington St. had been completely renovated, inside and out. Both Mary and I were making decent money, and somehow the idea crept into our heads to buy a newer place. We put our first home on the market, and it wasn't long before the offers started to come in. Our agent was on the ball and presented two offers to us in one evening. We accepted a cash offer from a young woman, Karen Mills, who was absolutely thrilled when she found out she had won the bid. It was cool that Karen worked for Sarnia Police Services as a dispatcher. As I write this over thirty years later, Karen still lives in that house, and we became friends. Karen is now retired, and as far as I know, has no intentions of moving. It is very obvious that she loves her home as we did for the years we lived there. I'm so happy for you, Karen!

It was time for us to find a new place to call home. We looked at many but settled on a custom, four-year-old home on Thames Crescent, east of Murphy Rd. Ironically, this subdivision was built in the exact same area as where Jamie broke his arm riding our dirt bike so long ago. Other than some paint and wallpaper, the house was move-in ready. It didn't take long for us to feel comfortable in our new surroundings.

The neighbourhood itself was relatively new, the homes having only been built in the last five years. We had definitely moved up in the world. Looking back, probably the only thing I didn't like about the house was that it didn't have a back door to the yard, except through the garage. Of course, the backyard was where we kept the barbecue, making it somewhat inconvenient when wanting to cook outdoors. I splurged on some unique landscaping, planting a triple-stem birch tree in the front yard, mainly because I just liked birch trees. I would go on to plant the same type of tree in each of the subsequent homes I owned. Mary and I looked forward to many happy years in our new home.

28. Resumé Building

There was much going on in our lives at this time. I ran for and was awarded the president's position for the SPFFA after having served as treasurer and secretary for the last several years. I believed I was ready for the challenges to be faced and looked forward to putting my stamp on the continued success of the association. It was politically tough times for Sarnia, and the fire service. This extracurricular activity took up much of my free time.

Many contentious issues faced the fire service in Sarnia during my tenure. As president, I had to respond to this ever-growing litany of problems, and the willingness of City Council to cut overall fire protection to the city. They wanted to slash our operating budget—reduce first-responder manpower, and dragged their feet on a much needed replacement program for our aging fleet of vehicles. I was frequently in touch with the chief, the mayor, the director of personnel, and the many other bureaucrats who needed to hear what I had to say—and believe me, I had a lot to say! I was in front of City Council several times, and spoke my mind to the press, giving them the truth of the matter—that being dire consequences, and even death, if council didn't wake up and see the need to increase the ways and means of the fire service. This constant battle certainly played a huge role in my stress levels at that time.

The fourth bedroom in the lower level of our new home was converted into an office so I could do my union work comfortably. To help facilitate that, I bought my first personal computer. It was the recently released Mac Classic with a whopping two kb of RAM. When purchased, it was state-of-the-art and allowed me to do things for the fire service thought previously impossible. I had just, singlehandedly ushered in the computer era for the SPFFA.

Perpetual Motion

Sarnia, and the recently created town of Clearwater, were going through an amalgamation of the two jurisdictions. At midnight, on December 31st, 1990, the two became one. I, as chief negotiator for the union, and our team, had the daunting task of attempting to combine our two separate and distinct firefighter contracts into one. I used that little Mac to meticulously manipulate the legalities contained in the existing contractual language from both agreements—each clause, each phrase, all reworded, prepared, and printed for the next marathon face-to-face meeting. This exercise took approximately eighteen months to complete. At the outset, given the huge, seemingly impossible task that lay ahead, not many gave us a fighting chance to pull this off. There was constant talk of having to eventually present many of the unresolved issues to a provincial arbitrator. I would have none of that. I never gave up hope of a successfully negotiated merger of the Sarnia and Clearwater firefighters' collective agreements. In the end, we managed the impossible. It did come together, and that little Mac worked flawlessly to help accomplish what had never been done previously in Ontario.

In early 1991, I was promoted to lieutenant after thirteen years on the job. In and of itself, that certainly was a milestone in my life. My career was progressing at the perfect pace, and each challenge was met with enthusiasm and passion. The historic thing about the promotion was that it became the first time in the history of Sarnia Fire that the sitting president of the Firefighters' Association was officially promoted to an officer's rank. I must have been doing something right!

The office I had set up in the house was painted a Hunter Green, which was all the rage at the time. Some IKEA shelving and a new Sony stereo completed the room. I also signed onto Columbia records, their CD division, and proceeded to start my collection of great music. Just for the record—no pun intended—my first CD purchase was Motley Crue's *Girls, Girls, Girls*—how ironic, given the way my story unfolds. Over the years, I amassed hundreds of CDs, most of which, after making digital copies, I have now given away.

29. Nope! Didn't See That One Coming

Mary and I loved to entertain and frequently had dinner parties with one or two couples. Although we were both comfortable in the kitchen, we certainly had a lot to learn. Mary was the more adventurous chef. I don't recall ever thinking that what she had prepared for supper was anything but delicious. For that matter, I did pretty well too. The only thing I ever made that Mary absolutely did not like was a lamb stew with caraway. Who knew? She didn't like caraway!

One of the things Mary loved to do then, and still today, is to keep her home spotless. Greg came to visit us for a weekend, and while sitting on the living room couch, suddenly lifted his feet off the carpet with a big grin on his face. After inquiring as to what he was doing, he laughed and then commented on how sterile the place was—he didn't want to leave his footprints on the carpet. Yes, it had been vacuumed with the pile all running in the same direction. I look back on that incident with fond memories. I really did learn to appreciate the cleanliness of our home and give kudos to Mary for keeping it so.

The kids also settled in nicely. I had again borrowed the video recorder from the firehall and filmed the house and grounds shortly after we moved in. I wanted Mom and Dad, now comfortably nestled in their home back east, to see our new purchase. It was also our good fortune to be able to commit to video, Stephanie and Shaun running around while I was filming, treasures to be kept forever. The irony of this is not lost, remembering my father had done the same with his old Super-8.

Shaun was playing in the rec room one day and face planted into the fireplace, splitting the skin on his forehead. It's a good thing he had a hard head because other than the blood all over, he came away with only a remembrance scar. He would go on to do this twice, the second time opening up the old wound.

Life, it turns out, was not all wine and roses—and it pains me to commit this to print. Like many married couples, we felt the monetary pinch due to the crazy interest rates of the late '80s. They had risen to 19.5 percent and subsequently dropped to 13.5 percent when we purchased Thames Crescent—a tough go, knowing we were mortgaged at 7 percent previously. I truly believe this was at least partially responsible for the decline in the strength of our union. We were working too much, struggling financially, and not communicating properly—rough times emotionally, for both of us.

Without belabouring the point or getting into any of the personal details, we drifted apart. Yes, we still lived together, but it wasn't easy. For the most part, we put on a good front for the outside world. In the end, there seemed not to be enough to hang on to. After much soul-searching, and an intimate review of our life paths, we parted ways in May 1992—adding more fodder to my fragile state of mind. In retrospect, I wish we had tried harder—I am so very sorry, Mary, I truly am.

Until then, I honestly don't recall ever being depressed. I had suffered from anxiety in the past, but this shit was traumatic—an extremely difficult time for all of us. I thank God the kids were as young as they were, and after all they have been through, both Mary and I are blessed that Stephanie and Shaun have weathered the storm. Our dear children are healthy, well-adjusted individuals.

30. Learning To Fly, But I Ain't Got Wings

The next seven years would hold some excruciatingly painful experiences, the likes of which I had never felt before. I would also experience some of my favourite times ever.

I left. I needed a place to stay. Where to go? What to do? How was I going to live? The answers to these questions were a long way off, but at the time, I needed to put one foot forward. I rented a room from my friend and co-worker, Phil Walsh. The house was dark and dingy—so was my mood. It was a perfect fit. I think I lasted two months.

The other staple in my life was gone for good also. Our annual fishing trips were cancelled, or more to the point, I was cancelled from them. In times of uncertainty, we tend to choose sides in a dispute, and as history played out over the next several years, I was on the outside looking in when it came to my friendships with those same guys I had been fishing with for years. Even though I don't see much of them today, thankfully, we have all had a chance to clear the air. All is well with our mutual friendships.

My next move was more upbeat. We had hired a young firefighter, Chris McGrath about a year earlier. He owned a large home on Bright St., so I asked "Tug" if I could rent a room. He was happy to oblige. It was probably the best thing that had happened to me in a long time. The arrangement worked because we were on opposite shifts. With the pressures of the separation, the political climate at work, and trying to make ends meet, it was the escape I needed at a very low point in my life. Not that it was a wise thing to do, but I did hit the bottle pretty hard for a few months. Tug's house was like a drop-in centre, and there were plenty of great social times, music, and new friendships to be made. Most of the people who came into my life at that point were ten years younger than me, so it was a fairly new lifestyle for sure. One of my early favourite memories from Bright St. was the fully equipped bar in the rec room, complete with a beer keg, and taps—and yes, we drained a few.

Tug had gone to school at Seneca College for commercial diving and when I met him, he had already started a company with his friend, Terry Dolbear. Terry would join the fire service a short time later. I do believe knowing these two gentlemen is the reason I became interested in the sport of scuba diving. It had always been on my bucket list, ever since watching *Sea Hunt* and *Jacques Cousteau* on TV. We talked extensively about the thrills of diving in general, those conversations driving my interests further. Several co-workers and I decided it was time. We were going to get certified. Soon enough, we had completed the course—classroom time, pool work, and open-water testing included, all within a few short weeks. My efforts culminated in me obtaining my open-water certification under PADI. For me, the moment my head was immersed below the waves, I was at peace. I had never known a feeling quite like that. It was as close to a Utopian world as I had ever come, before or since. I continued to dive for years after and have many recorded dives to my credit. Some of the most beautiful moments these eyes have beheld came from the depths of blue.

I eventually felt comfortable enough to call Bright St. home. I had settled into a routine that included work for the most part, and with limited access to my children, continued to struggle mentally. At that time, "limited access" meant that I could not have Stephanie and Shaun stay with me overnight. I struggled with that fact way more than I let on. Eventually, leveller heads prevailed and I was allowed overnight access. My life and mental state improved immeasurably when the kids and I spent time together.

Over the course of time, Tug and I became good friends. Our social lives meshed and I enjoyed getting to know some of the significant women in his life. It was during this period that I was introduced to Carole Legere. She and "Tuggie" as she called him, were inseparable for quite some time, but in hindsight, being young, they were like oil and water. I liked Carole and we got along great. She was so much fun, energetic and driven. Years later, Carole and I started to hang out more and became quite close—so much so that to this day, I consider her my best female friend. And now, even though we reside in different provinces, we still speak or FaceTime on a regular basis—love you, Carole!

The other young lady who took up most of Tug's time was Dix. Sue Dixon was herself young, fun, beautiful, and energetic also. They got along great, and fortunately for me, fit in nicely with my newfound friends.

Dix had a sister—Pam. She and Dix lived together on Devine St. with Pam's two young daughters, Apryl and Becky. I met them while doing some painting at the house. Pam was a frequent attendee at many of our social gatherings, and over time, we started hanging out—often. It slowly became more—we started dating. Pam, being an early childhood education teacher at the YMCA, took to my kids easily. Many a Saturday morning, she would be seen making Play-doh, or spending time with the four children at the kitchen table, colouring. She was good to Stephanie and Shaun, and they, in turn, got along very well with her and her girls. I was grateful for the companionship and feelings of normalcy as I struggled with the dissolution of my marriage.

That first Christmas alone in December 1992 could have been disastrous for me mentally, but two things happened to help alleviate those fears. Pam presented me with one of the best Christmas gifts I had ever received—a personalized license plate for my car that sported my nickname: "PITTSY." It was the feel-good lift I truly needed. I had carried that handle since childhood and it was the name I was known by, to most of my friends and acquaintances. I tagged those plates proudly on several future vehicles and only stopped using them when I moved out of province years later.

The other reason for keeping my shit together was an invite to the Dixon family winter home in Florida where her family would be spending the upcoming Christmas holidays. After arranging for some time off, I drove straight through to Sarasota in twenty-two hours. Arriving about 3:30 a.m., I began an incredible ten-day vacation in the sun—something I sorely needed. Siesta Key Beach is still the nicest beach I've ever stepped foot on. The sand is the consistency of flour and so cool to walk on, even in the midday sun.

Perpetual Motion

On New Year's Eve, we went to the Outback Steakhouse for a great supper, and then to a couple of pubs for the evening. I was in heaven. It seemed that all the stressors in my life were gone for the time being. I can say without a doubt I was truly happy.

When it was all over, I drove the gang to the airport and said some tearful goodbyes. I was going to stay at the trailer for two more days and had agreed to close it up so that Pam's dad, Dave, wouldn't have to do it. After such a fabulous vacation, those two days—now without Pam around, felt like the longest "year" of my life, and I still had to manage the drive north. In hindsight, I sure didn't plan that very well.

Sometime later, as I was struggling mentally, and financially, Pam and I discussed me moving in with her on Devine St. We talked it over with Sue and all came to an agreement. Even though this is just a short mention in my memoir, the significance of this move was huge. Sue became my guardian angel. I was able to live rent-free at a time when I needed that help the most. I contributed as best I could, including buying groceries, providing transportation and excelling in the role of live-in handyman. Again, thank you, Dix!

Pam took great interest in my life, my career, and my adventures—eventually wanting to become a certified diver also—the irony being that she was also a certified lifeguard. You can imagine, given that specialized training, that she was all about preventing people from drowning, or at the very least, keeping their head above water. She struggled for a bit with the concept of breathing while underwater. We finally completed her certification with no complications, and I've never seen a girl more proud of her accomplishments than she was that day. It would lead to several years of fun, diving together in different locales.

Speaking of transportation, it was time to upgrade. I traded my Mercury Topaz for a new vehicle—a blue 1993 GMC Safari minivan—the first of several leased vehicles over the next few years. There were several reasons for getting this van, the main one being the number of bodies now needing transportation. With our four kids in tow most days, we obviously needed something roomier than a car or truck. This vehicle seemed to fit the bill perfectly. The second reason, and one that I thoroughly enjoyed, was that it was—well, a van! The back seats were removable—providing plenty of room for cargo, or as we soon discovered, a makeshift home on wheels when Pam and I decided to drive to Florida.

What a trip that was. We outfitted the van with a mattress, loaded all of our dive gear, suitcases, and other paraphernalia we needed, and took off south. There were just over five hundred kilometres on the van when we left.

Three highlights stand out on that trip south. The first is diving at Ginnie Springs, FL. The water in the natural cave-springs was a constant 72 degrees Fahrenheit and visibility was just about infinite. It was certainly the best diving I had done to date.

We had also rented a cabin at a dive resort in Key Largo, Kelly's Aquanaut Divers. Shortly after arriving, I made one of the most significant purchases I had in years. I bought my own personal diving regulator and BCD (Buoyancy Compensating Device). They would serve me well my whole diving career. We dove several times in and around the famous marine reserve, John Pennekamp Park, off the east coast of Florida. Beautiful shipwrecks, coral reefs, and of course, the Christ of the Abyss statue—a famous dive spot many tourists flock to every year—all became part of my dive log. I eventually wrote a travel article about this spot for our local newspaper, *The Sarnia Observer*. It became the first published, and paid for work of my fledgling writing career and can still be found in a google search, quite easily.

We continued south, spending a fair amount of time in Key West just as their annual Mardi Gras celebrations got underway. Little did I know, this southern town was actually where Mardi Gras had originated—not New Orleans, where many believe it started. We needed a home base so had parked the van in a regular parking lot near the south end of town—and paid dearly for the privilege. We spent each evening touring Duvall St., witnessing the festivities that went on throughout the night. Voices from a loudspeaker woke us up just before noon the next morning. The bar next door was gifting the first twenty-five people in the door free drinks of Mount Gay rum, all day. Hungover as we were, we quickly got dressed and headed to the bar. We scored the passes. Needless to say, it was another wild day and evening in Key West. If you ever get the chance, it is worth the cash to get there for Mardi Gras. It's something I won't soon forget.

Perpetual Motion

There were more moves towards a bright future in 1993. Pam and I had settled into a comfortable relationship and our four children got along well. That year also saw a return to my motorcycling days. I purchased a used 1980 Yamaha Maxim 650cc from a young guy on Lakeshore Road and kept it for five years. I had no intention of selling it, but years later a knock on the door changed all that. A young gentleman was inquiring about the bike in the driveway. It turns out he was the same guy I bought my Yamaha from five years earlier. He wanted it back so I sold it to him for what I had originally paid—eight hundred dollars. In the long run, it had been a good deal. I wish all transactions in life were that easy.

Early that following spring, I got a call from the car dealership, asking if I wanted to upgrade my vehicle at no additional cost. Well, that was a no-brainer, so I did just that. The new vehicle was a 1994 Safari van, this one tan and brown in colour, with pin-striping to match. We took possession just in time to take another trip to Florida—accompanied this time by our four children. This marked a major milestone in the improvement of my relationship with Mary. Yes, we still struggled at times as most separated couples do, but were on the right path to civility.

We left for Sarasota, and eventually arrived at what we referred to as base camp—the family mobile home we had stayed in the previous year. It was a wonderful vacation with many good times had by all. The highlight was our time at Disney World. I had been there with Mary twelve years earlier, but it was a first for Pam and the children. The excitement on all their faces and the memories made are precious to me.

Back at the trailer, we lounged by the pool, enjoyed the sun, and Pam taught Shaun how to swim. I will never forget the first time he jumped into the pool without his water wings—what a thrill. I cherished the ability to make memories with my children like that.

Back home, life continued with edged turmoil. The political firestorm between City Hall and the association raged on. Some decisions were made for the betterment of future working conditions for the bargaining unit but were perceived as unpopular by that same group. Those decisions cost me my re-election to a fourth term as president. It took me all of two minutes to realize the weight that had been lifted from my shoulders. I hadn't realized how much stress I was under. The ongoing political fight during the last three years had exacted a toll. I also continued to deal with deep wounds and personal issues.

That fall, more memories were to be made. It saw the addition of our first fur-baby. Kato was a beautiful kitten—white with black markings. We had been gifted him by friends. Although I had owned dogs before, I have never owned a feline. Kato was very affectionate and even though he started life in a barn, we decided that he was going to be an indoor kitty. He would go on to live a long life—I believe it was almost eighteen years. A brief explanation of the cat's handle: He was named after Kato Kaelin of O.J. Simpson lore, a very big news story that year. The kids thought Mr. Kaelin was handsome, so they chose his moniker—it was certainly fine with us!

Wanting to move forward, we turned the conversation to home buying. Pam and I discussed the features and ideas we liked and came to a conclusion that the most important feature necessary at that time in our lives was a "beer drinking front porch." I know, priorities right?

We again enlisted the help of our friend Gary and proceeded to view several houses—none of which attracted us to the point of putting in an offer. Gary called me one day and suggested we look at a house in Point Edward. This piqued my interest, knowing that the Village of Point Edward was engulfed by the shores of Lake Huron and Canatara Park, two very desirable features in the area.

We pulled curbside to 29 Alfred St., and before I even got out of the car, I said matter-of-factly, "I'll take it." It had a covered front porch, ten feet deep by twenty feet long. Perfect! As a formality, we toured the house. All the while I knew I would make an offer. I discussed the purchase with Pam and we both agreed the property was desirable for several reasons. The asking price was $99,900, but we purchased it for $92,000, including all appliances and draperies.

Moving date was January 25th, 1995, a very happy moment in our lives. There was room enough for the children and it didn't take long to make this house a home. The first thing we did was buy a case of beer, sit on the front porch, and consume several. It was still quite chilly weather-wise, but we had to honour the reason we purchased the house in the first place. Once settled, the next event was to rent a portable hot tub for Valentine's Day weekend. We were going to celebrate our new home in style, and we did. Our friends, Andy and Denise, spent the night, and helped us celebrate. It was a fabulous weekend, of which many more were to come.

That first summer in the house, two very important things happened. The first was my promotion to captain at Sarnia Fire Rescue Services (SFRS), again a huge milestone in my life, and next was the addition of our second fur-baby. Harley was a purebred golden retriever. I may be prejudiced, but he just may have been the greatest dog ever born. One of Pam's friends had been successful in having her male golden bred with a beautiful female out Petrolia way and was offered the pick of the litter in return. She, in turn, offered this pick to us—knowing we were interested in getting this breed of dog, our favourite. It was an exciting time. Once the litter of six was born, we had first dibs. After our second visit to the kennel, we decided on a rambunctious little ball of fur and named him Harley. It would be several weeks before we could take him home.

The day finally came and we were like two little kids—so excited as we drove to the farm to get our puppy. It was great to see the joy on Apryl and Becky's faces when they got to hold him on the way home. Oh, the joys that dog brought to us going forward.

My kids couldn't wait to meet their new puppy. It was, again, a joyous occasion, with everyone feeling the love of our newest member of the family. The joy wasn't felt as strongly the first few nights when the poor dog would whine and cry all night while being locked in his cage. It was going to take him some time to get used to it, and as all puppies do, so did Harley.

Those first six months went by quickly. I was surprised to realize it was time to get the boy fixed. He was becoming quite the unruly child and bolted from the house on several occasions, only to be chased down the street, captured, and returned to the yard. He did lose a bit of that spark after surgery but remained a loyal companion.

Our first year on Alfred St. saw the start of many structural changes to the place, the first being a full removal and replacement of the man-door in the kitchen. Mark Stephenson, a co-worker, did the work in one day. I had never seen that type of job done before and put my full faith in him to get it right. Over the years following, I employed Mark's skills many times to handle the renovations I was uncomfortable doing—learning much from him in the process. We too, remain great friends today. Cheers, brother!

With the family unit now forged, we settled into an easy, fun routine. It was nice to finally have a place to call home, having been quite unsettled for the last three years. Memories of music, laughter, great food, and the occasional party come to mind. But, with changing family dynamics, there is always the possibility of drama—and drama we got.

It was during these rather tumultuous times that I was not getting on with my parents at all. To put it bluntly, they were still not over the breakup of my marriage, and definitely not happy with my relationship with Pam. It got so bad at times we were not even on speaking terms, and this had been going on for many months. Truth be known, it was one of the darkest periods of my life. I chose not to show it and outwardly was as charismatic and extroverted as I always was—inside, another story. The only blessing in it all was that they were in Nova Scotia and I was in Sarnia. I could escape the drama to a certain extent, but being who I am, and having had such a loving relationship with them for almost my entire life, this was eating me up. The only recourse I could muster was a very long letter to Mom and Dad. In it, I spilled my guts and did everything possible to explain how I got to where I was in the moment. I did not ask for their forgiveness because there was nothing to be forgiven for. I needed them to know it was my life, and I had to live it my way. My priorities were my children, my relationship, and my job. There was enough shit on my plate, and I didn't need any more. I only wished at that time that they would come around to my way of seeing things and put the past to rest. It remained to be seen if that, in fact, would come true—again, just more fuel for the PTSD bandwagon.

It was shortly after we moved to Alfred St. that I started to hang around an acquaintance from down the street. Lorne Bourrie and his wife Laurie became good friends and as fate would have it, he was also an avid diver. It didn't take long before we were making plans to dive the Florida Keys. This trip was scheduled for late January of 1996, so preparations started right away. We dove Lake Huron and several of the shipwrecks lost in the violent Great Lakes storm of November, 1913. We dove the St. Clair River and a couple of the known shipwrecks in that stretch of very fast-moving water. By the time of our departure for the Keys, I was a confident diver and had amassed many dives to my credit.

Perpetual Motion

Prior to leaving, Pam and I attended a get-together at Andy and Denise's house. We spent the evening consuming some great wine and a delicious roast beef dinner. After the meal was over, Andy got the idea he wanted his wife to shave his head, an act she had performed on several occasions prior. Once that act was complete, it became my turn. I'm still not sure why, but there I was, faceplanted in Denise's rather ample bosom, getting my mullet shaved to the scalp. It was the first time I had ever done anything like that, and when it was all over, it felt amazing. My locks lay strewn on the kitchen floor and Pam had the foresight to seal some hair in an envelope for posterity. I know today, if I looked hard enough, I would find that envelope of historical importance somewhere in my worldly possessions.

So, in true *Jeopardy* fashion, here goes:
Category: Memoirs—for one thousand, Alex.
Answer: Early January, 1996.
Question: What month and year did Dana first shave his mullet?
I am laughing while I write this—can't help it.
It should have been a double-jeopardy question.
Ok, I'm done!

The adventures in the Keys were priceless. We dove every day, and because of our dive history in the fast currents of the world-renowned St. Clair River, we were treated with respect and even a little reverence by the Divemasters and the patrons alike. I dove the deepest dive of my career, down one hundred and two feet to the deck of the sunken coastguard cutter *Duane*, and as an exclamation point, went over the side, down another twenty-eight feet to the sand bottom of John Pennekamp Park, at a full recreational dive-depth of one hundred and thirty feet. It was a short-lived thrill, having only about a fourteen-minute bottom time, but a thrill nonetheless. We also dove the Christ of the Abyss statue, several coral reefs, and several other shipwrecks while there. I would go on to dive many more times before finally selling my gear and moving on to other adventures.

That spring, we decided to build a large wood deck off the back of the house. It was to replace the dilapidated one that barely existed now. Our goal was to add a hot tub to the finished product. I took my time designing it alongside Mark Stevenson, and construction started just after the last snowfall in April. My dive buddy, Lorne, was an electrician, so he secured the proper length, and gauge of cable to run for the hot tub power supply. The deck was huge—three tiers with steps on the two exposed sides. When the project was completed the following month, we purchased a seven-person hot tub and had it installed in time for the long weekend. We anticipated several years of great times would follow.

A small miracle happened during construction of the deck. Mom and Dad had come to Sarnia for a visit with family and I was fortunate enough to have them over for supper. We had done much healing in the past few months and I was very relieved to know they were letting things go. I also knew it would never be perfect, but we were moving past the issues. I can still see my mom now, standing on the half-finished deck surface, the sun shining down on her face. We had a good visit and I finally felt like I could heal somewhat from previous aggressions.

These were the good moments. The kids were getting along great, Pam and I were settled into our home environment and the dog was growing to a hefty weight of over one hundred pounds. The cat was—well, a cat, what more can I say.

Pam was a very social human. She had solidified friends and acquaintances from all walks of life. We also enjoyed many activities together, with one such event a priority: *The Corporate Challenge*. Simply put, teams were formed by the different companies who wanted to be a part of the day. We would all participate in several games of fun and exercise, all the while raising a boatload of money for charity. It was quite well attended and many cities around the province held their own version of the same. So it was that during one of these events in mid-July of 1996, I came to know John Kinchen and his wife Kathy, a chance meeting that would again alter my career path.

During a random conversation with John that day, he asked if I would be interested in assisting him in selling a line of Canadian-made bunker gear. It seemed like an odd question, one I didn't see coming. Bunker gear, in case you are not familiar, is part of the PPE (personal protective equipment) that a firefighter wears while conducting hazardous operations in and around a structure fire. My first inclination was to answer a resounding no to his initial question, on the grounds I had no desire to sell anything, ever. He persisted, explaining the benefits of this particular style of gear and extolling the virtues of the company he was working for. I listened politely—said no again, and we left it at that. I expressed to Pam my thoughts on the subject, about having no intention of taking on any more outside work. I was quite happy hanging out with my beautiful family unit and doing a little interior house painting on the side, for a buck or two. It would not be the last I'd hear from John.

In the very early part of 1997, John and I were in deep conversation again, regarding his ventures. I think to appease him, I agreed to meet him for a demonstration of the features and saleability of this wonder product he was peddling. After spending some time listening to his sales pitch, I was intrigued. The phone rang in early February, with an invitation to try my hand at selling a set or two of this Securitex gear. I was invited to meet the chief of Tilbury Township, a small town near Windsor, Ont. He was interested in two sets of gear. This I agreed to, knowing it was a trial to see if I liked the selling concept or not.

Everything went smoothly and I got the sale, complete with a hearty commission attached. Now I was hooked. Sales continued to come rather easily to me. I started to develop a style, and my own clientele. It was quite a thrill to actually set up a home office in our main floor bedroom, outfitted with a fax machine, computer, and any supplies I might need to run such an operation. Oh yes, it was also Shaun's bedroom, so there was the matter of a pull-out futon on the far wall—we somehow made it work.

After two months in the bunker gear business, I found that my little gig was not interfering with my fire service career at all. John and I flew to Montreal—the headquarters and manufacturing facility for Securitex Inc. This would be my first company sales meeting, and the first time meeting and interacting with the owners, Ross and Claude, my sale manager, Sam Watts, and the other staff. I was nervous at best. An airport limo picked us up and drove us to the Marriott Hotel in downtown Montreal, our home away for the week. I thought to myself, *I could get used to this kind of living*, and I guess I did—that little gig lasted seven years.

Several months after that initial sales meeting in Montreal, and some success behind me, I was informed that in late August the bosses were coming to Sarnia to meet with John and me. We assumed it was to give us some clear direction on where the company was headed. The meeting was to be held at the Holiday Inn in Point Edward at 9:30 a.m. I arrived on time, only to be greeted by Ross and Claude—and no one else. My first reaction was of surprise, as I didn't see John anywhere. Was he late? I soon found out the real reason behind the meeting. John had been let go from his position as salesman for the company earlier that morning, and the owners were there to offer me his position outright. I was taken aback somewhat but thought I would roll with the punches and see what was on the table. I eventually accepted their offer and began what I had mentioned earlier as a seven-year gig with a fantastic company, all the while maintaining my career in the fire service.

John and I remained friends, understanding that the decision to let him go was made by the company executives and had nothing to do with me. He continued to work in sales for the automotive industry until his untimely death several years later.

We, as a family, continued to enjoy a very comfortable routine. All four kids were getting older and more active with their friends. The house on Alfred St. became a drop-in and a safe haven for all the neighbourhood kids, including several who were now schoolmates. Over the ensuing years, there were many house parties with gaggles of young kids from all over. Our home was filled with song, the stereo blasting lots of great music well into the night. It was during this time that the sounds of the guitar, borrowed from his sister, could be heard coming from Shaun's bedroom. He was a newbie, but I could tell there was something in his willingness to learn. I will never forget the look on his face the first time I played some marque songs off a Led Zeppelin album as he crouched on the floor in front of the speakers. That simple act was a game changer for Shaun and me. We bonded that evening as father and son more than we had ever before. Music has become a lifelong passion between us, which I would not change for the world. To this day, I love getting together with him and playing many varied styles and genres of music we both love.

Pam continued to work at the YMCA, and I had my two jobs as a captain at SFRS and as a salesman for Securitex Inc. Some of the best times to come out of that era were our frequent excursions to the neighbourhood bar, Brittany Arms, owned by Jerry Horner, a friend from Point Edward.

Perpetual Motion

The bar was within walking distance, and several times, feeling very much at home there, we arrived with our slippers on. Damn, they had good wings and really cold beer. Life rolled on.

Christmas came and went with many good celebrations with family. We spoiled the kids as per usual and all had a fabulous holiday.

With the onset of winter came the need for a new vehicle. I chose a red, four-wheel-drive Jeep Cherokee Sport, a first for me. I definitely needed the extra safety features of that vehicle for travel to the many locations I needed to go.

If I'm being honest in the writing of this book, I would be remiss not to mention what I wish I'd seen in myself back then. I now know, after taking a hard look at my life choices over the years, that I had a very destructive pattern of immersing myself so deeply into whatever was occupying my time that I neglected most everything else around me. The drive to succeed was at times all consuming, and the fear of failure, and the need to prove myself—constant. It seems I was never satisfied with the status quo. This was very evident in my relationships. The years of my involvement on the executive board of the SPFFA, had a profound effect on my marriage to Mary. I admit that. Just as my involvement with Securitex, and the frequent trips out of town for days—sometimes weeks, seriously damaged my—at one time, very stable relationship with Pam. I again take ownership of that. This fact will be proven again and again throughout these passages, with every partner I've ever been involved with.

As much as I hate the saying "all good things must end," it again rang true. Pam and I were struggling in our relationship, and it seemed we needed to figure this out or call it quits. We had for some time, been planning a trip to the East Coast. My extended family was hosting the first Boyle Family Reunion on the farm in Afton, NS at the beginning of August. We, as a family, rented a camper van and made our way east for what I hoped would be a great family adventure. Looking back now, I believe Pam had checked out already. I think she made the commitment to come east with me to see if there was anything left to work on. We did have a fabulous time the four days we were at the farm. I have recently seen photos of a smiling Pam enjoying herself with my sisters and extended family.

Arriving home, the signs of a failed relationship were all pretty much out in the open, but I was oblivious to them. We were cohabitating at best. I just didn't see those signs—until I did. We finally talked about it, and the decision was made to split. As in the past, after some soul-searching conversation between us, we parted ways in September of 1999. The kids were devastated. They were now old enough to understand what was happening and that just produced more feelings of guilt. Pam, I am truly sorry, I surely didn't want or intend any of that to happen, ever.

The next few weeks were a blur. I can tell you now, this was the incident that finally triggered an all-out, lying-on-the-floor, curled-in-a-ball, wanting-to-die anxiety attack, followed by months of debilitating depression, the likes of which I had never before experienced, and a full bloodletting of my PTSD symptoms. My world was crashing down around me, and it became another very low point in my life. It was also the first time I asked my family physician for some medicinal help in coping with my new reality. I am not ashamed to admit it, I was desperate. The drugs helped immensely. It wouldn't be the last time I would need to rely on medicine to help me cope with my ills.

31. Tunnel Lights, Brighter Days

Thank God for friends. Lorne dragged me off the couch several times to hang out. Dan Cadieux got me out golfing. It couldn't have been much fun because I remember walking down the fourth fairway at Greenwood Golf Course, crying like a little baby. I had no control over my emotions. But that's what friends are for. They stuck by me when I needed it most.

I mentioned earlier that I had sold my grey Yamaha to the kid who previously owned it. It was now time for a new ride. I chose a new, larger model of the same make. This time it was a pearl and red Yamaha V-Star 1100cc. I outfitted it with leather saddlebags, and I was off to the races. That made me feel better.

Slowly, life became more tolerable. I had taken some time off work to recuperate, and it was time to get back to the present. In early October, I ran into an acquaintance, Gayle, while she was visiting her friend, Bonnie, our admin assistant, at the fire station. Gayle was a fit young lady, very much at home in the firehall setting. She was a volunteer firefighter in Clearwater and we had crossed paths on numerous occasions. Bonnie suggested I ask Gayle out on a date. I know now, I might not have been ready for that but, as explained, my destructive pattern had me believing I needed to be in a relationship, in order to provide validation to my life. So, picking up the charge, I did just that. I believed it was the best thing I could do for me, at the time. We got along famously and things got serious pretty fast.

Gayle was a motorcycle rider and owned a Honda Shadow 750cc. She had been riding for years. That was definitely an added attraction to our budding relationship and we enjoyed many outings together.

She also had two young daughters, Ciara, and Kiana—the baby, not quite two years old. I was enjoying my new surroundings. Within a month of our first date, Gayle, her kids, and I were off to spend the day at Sloan's Christmas Tree farm in rural Lambton County. We had a fabulous day harvesting our first tree and tying it to the roof of the Jeep for the ride home. We all got into the Christmas spirit by decorating the tree in grand style. Yes, all this was starting to make me feel whole again.

New Year's 2000 was fast approaching, and the world was hung up on Y2K. In essence, this was a perceived issue with the millions of computers that were basically running every known program in the world on a daily basis. The problem, as described, was with the date setting on each device. The readout for the date had not been programmed to turn over to the year 2000. It had been 19___ since the computer was invented, and only recently had the powers that be become concerned that all those computers would just—stop working. The major concern of course, was the shutdown of the world's power grid, the wheels of commerce coming to a grinding halt, and pretty much the globe, as we knew it, self-destructing. The doomsdayers were having a field day. At the firehall, in order to counteract all that potential destruction, we installed a very powerful generator on a cement pad outside of the main station on East St. The only thing we could do was wait with bated breath and fingers crossed and hope that January 1st, 2000 would dawn as it should.

Before that could happen, there was the matter of celebrating the end of the twentieth century and the beginning of a new millennium. To that end, Gayle and I had invited Bonnie and a guest over to my house for an evening of drinks and a good soak in the hot tub. I had prepared some snacks and we were all looking forward to riding out the computer-glitch storm in style. It was about 6 p.m. when Gayle arrived at the house with five dozen roses. It was one of the most beautiful gestures I had ever been on the receiving end of. She just wanted me to know how much she cared for me, and this was her way of showing it. I was truly impressed.

We poured ourselves our first drink of the evening and waited for company to arrive. I was standing beside the dining room table admiring the multicoloured display of roses, all arranged nicely in several vases, when my stomach flipped. In an instant, I was on my knees in the bathroom, vomiting everything I had eaten for what seemed like the last year. I had never experienced such a sudden and violent attack of sickness, and to

Perpetual Motion

this day I have no idea what caused it. I'm assuming it was food poisoning, but Gayle had consumed the same snacks I had, and she was ok. Off to bed I went to stop the world from spinning. For the next several hours, I was delirious with the sweats, and I don't remember the several times I retched into a nearby pail. Company did arrive and proceeded to enjoy the evening without me. I was in no shape to even converse. And then, just as suddenly as it came on, I started to feel better—well enough to actually interact with our guests for a spell. I didn't get in the hot tub, but thankfully Gayle and her friends enjoyed themselves.

Midnight was fast approaching, so I turned on the computer and waited until the time changed over to the new year, holding our breath in the last few seconds of the century. It was a relief to see there were no issues after the clock clicked over to 2000, at least on the surface. We took one last good sniff of the roses and got a good night's sleep. A new century was awaiting at dawn.

Physically, I was feeling better, and with Gayle's help, I got back to the gym—we started working out together. She had been a fitness buff all her life—had competed in bodybuilding competitions in the past and had, at one point, owned the gym we were attending. Over the course of the next couple of years, I became a regular at Ironworks Gym, just down the street from me. With Gayle's guidance, I got into the best shape of my life. We did a program called Body for Life and I became a lean mass of human for quite a while.

My children were growing up. Stephanie was approaching her seventeenth birthday, and Shaun was playing his guitar faithfully, enjoying his early teen years. Life was good again.

Come this time, I was in my fourth year at Securitex, making some serious coin and doing lots of travelling all over North America. I was promoted to market manager, in charge of different areas of the continent, at different times. Some of those assignments were in SW Ontario region, All Ontario region, Eastern Canada region, Midwest USA region, and West Coast USA region, some of them overlapping at times. We continued to grow as a company and became the third largest bunker gear manufacturer in the world. I was putting about forty to sixty hours a week into that aspect of my life, not including the forty-two hours a week at the fire hall. Sales meetings became quite the adventure. The company started scheduling these week-long meetings at different locations around the country. It was nothing for us to end up in Napa Valley CA, Dallas TX, the French Quarter in New Orleans, Great Monument Park in Utah, or Mont Tremblant in Quebec for a ski/conference—just to name a few.

The talk at the Dallas sales meeting was of a new device coming to market later in the year. It was called the Blackberry. This device, we were told, was revolutionary and would allow us to actually email each other from a little portable device we carried on our hip. The kicker was—it was a phone too! Being in the sales field, this was almost too good to be true. Oh, how naive we were about the rapid advancement of technology and where it would lead.

As mentioned, all of this was happening while maintaining my twenty-three-year career at the firehall. I had written my acting platoon chief's exam and passed. This would allow me to gain experience running the shift when my platoon chief Bob Burns was on holidays. I enjoyed that development and felt like my career was headed in the right direction. Retiring as a PC would be a noble goal to attain.

In order to juggle the two seemingly conflicting schedules, I devised a plan to pay my brother firefighters to come in and cover my shift while I was away for Securitex business. Looking back now, it may not have been ethical, and I probably wouldn't get away with a similar arrangement today, but it worked at the time. The other issue I would have in today's world would be selling my brand of gear to my own department. Again, back in 2000, it was not a problem, and I ended up outfitting the whole department in Securitex gear, for several years.

32. Local Causes, Local Effects

As noted in several chapters previous, I did—and still do—like to drive new vehicles. The year 2000 would be no different. Being the start of the new Millennium, I decided I wanted a car built at the beginning of the new century, knowing it would only happen once in my life. I settled on a black Pontiac Grand Prix Sport. It was much different than my Jeep, but hey, it was new. When purchased, it was the coolest car I owned to date—with its orange-coloured instrument cluster and sleek styling.

Firefighting professionals in general are a very giving group, and the Sarnia Professional Firefighters' Association was no different. We were always coming up with new ways to raise money for different charitable causes in and around the area. For many years, we participated in different functions supporting an issue near and dear to the profession: muscular dystrophy. Our big fundraiser to support this cause was known as boot tolls. Organized at different spots around the city each year, we would hold out a firefighters' rubber boot and solicit donations from passing motorists. We would very successfully bring in ten thousand dollars or more in small bills and coins for just one day's efforts. All of this culminated in myself, Graham Emslie, and a few others appearing several times on the Canadian segment of the Jerry Lewis Muscular Dystrophy Telethon, staged every Labour Day weekend in Toronto.

Realizing the success of such ventures, a core group of us got together to brainstorm other ways to raise charitable funds for causes closer to home. We organized and then created what became known as the Community Benefits Fund, of which I became the founding treasurer.

Our first venture was a firefighters calendar, which was a wildly successful start. We had a Girls Night Out, held at a popular nightclub, and several of the guys strutted their stuff to the delight of the crowd. A bit of a talent show ensued and votes were cast to see who would end up being photographed for each of the twelve months of the year. I didn't physically participate in this inaugural effort but worked behind the scenes and came out to support the shenanigans wholeheartedly. We would end up doing two calendars, in 2000 and 2001, and raised many thousands of dollars to bolster our fledgling coffers for the fund.

Our efforts, and the ability to draw a crowd for fundraising, didn't go unnoticed. Not long after the first calendar came out, our group was contacted by the Big Sisters Organization. They were, as always, trying to come up with new ways to raise funds for their own cause. The latest idea was a fashion show, supported by many local merchants displaying their wares—modelled by a group of firefighters, escorted by several of the Big Sisters themselves. After attending a couple of meetings, we agreed to help them with their effort. None of us were models, and we had no idea how to walk a runway, but in true fashion, we were willing to learn. And learn we did. Big Sisters recruited a former model, makeup artist, and all-around awesome lady to whip us into shape. Julie Chamberlain, married with a small child at home, had been involved with the community in different capacities over the years. Her training and skills from the modelling world made her the perfect person to tackle the almost impossible task of getting us guys to figure out our left foot from our right. It was going to be a challenge for this young mother, but Julie proved she was up to the task.

A dozen guys volunteered for this event and now had six weeks to get our routines down pat. We practiced sometimes twice a week to polish our newfound skills. It all came together in the end. The first Big Sisters' Fashion Show was a sell-out and a huge success. As expected, planning for the next year's event started almost immediately. This wouldn't be the last time Julie and I found ourselves in each other's company.

A local highlight, each of the summers between 1999 and 2013, was an annual event called Bayfest. This was an outdoor, multi-day concert produced by two Sarnia entrepreneurs, Jim and Michele Stokley. It was held at Centennial Park on the waterfront, and although it started rather small, with mostly local talent, a rented stage, and a big band or two thrown in, it grew into the premier Canadian venue for multi-genre musicians to play.

Jim and Michele eventually designed and erected their own professional stage, the likes that rivaled any outdoor venue in the country, with the appearance of Alanis Morrisette in the early years, to a full slate with the likes of Aerosmith, Collective Soul, George Thorogood, Bon Jovi, ZZ Top, and The Hip. In the later years, the country groups Dwight Yokam, Toby Keith, Rascal Flatts, Big & Rich, Alan Jackson, Keith Urban, and more, graced the stage. Not only was this the place to be in July, in Canada, but it was also a huge charitable event, raising hundreds of thousands of dollars each year for very noble causes.

During one of these early events, the stage became available on the Thursday night before the weekend of big-name acts. The firefighters were told of this opening and proceeded to put together a talent show, performed by any firefighter who wanted to hang out on stage for a few minutes. It was even advertised and promoted by the Stokley's. I, in my infinite wisdom, decided I was going to lip-sync the Commitments' version of "Mustang Sally," in my bunker pants—shirtless—gawd! And that is exactly what I did, to over a thousand members of the screaming public. Nailed it! From that day forward, my fifteen minutes of fame on that stage has parlayed into hours of hilarious fun, in many venues, and on many stages, in several different provinces—so damn much fun!

33. World Events and 9/11 Effects

As we age and mature and navigate the path we ourselves create, we experience many different events that will shape our lives for the better—or for naught. Some are remembered as being symbolic of happy times, while others—totally out of our control—can change us deeply. You have read about some of the events that affected my growth in previous chapters. Other events, as you will learn, would affect me years later. The events of September 11th, 2001 will always be remembered as the latter. The proof in that statement is steeped in irony. I write these paragraphs nineteen years to the day after those horrific events took place—with a clarity like it happened this morning. It was such a traumatic shock to the world, and especially to all of us in the first-responder community. Our lives, and our professions, changed that day—forever.

I was enjoying my scheduled days off from the firehall. This day promised to be sunny, with perfect fall temperatures bringing me some continued peace and joy after a long hot summer. September has always been my favourite month—the marked changes of the season, the cooler temperatures, the leaves starting their presentation of a kaleidoscope of colours to look forward to.

My phone rang at about 8:50 a.m. I was sitting at my desk in my home office, preparing to do some of my scheduled work for Securitex. I answered on the second ring and heard the familiar voice of Chris Palmer, a brother firefighter from my squad. There was no hello or pleasant greetings from his end of the line, which was definitely out of character for Chris. He simply said, "Are you watching TV?"

"No," I said.

"Turn it on," Chris said and hung up.

Perpetual Motion

Figuring something was amiss, I headed to the rec room to turn on the TV. It was already tuned to the CNN network.

My world slowed to a crawl. I can honestly admit today that in the first minutes of the news coverage, I didn't grasp the severity of what the world was witnessing. The news anchors on CNN were talking. That's all they could do. What they were saying didn't make any sense. They were reporting that a plane had hit the south tower of the World Trade Center, in New York City. *Ok*, I thought, *A small commuter plane hit one of the buildings.* That had happened before. But no, that is not what I was hearing—this was a bigger incident. This was a passenger plane, a large one. I sat, mesmerized by the images playing out on the screen.

Then, on national TV, while the world watched, a second plane slammed into the north tower of the WTC buildings. I looked at the screen, bewildered. A shudder ran through me. The talking heads at the networks were also trying to make sense of the carnage raining down on the streets of New York.

Soon there were videos of the brave men and women of the New York Fire Department (NYFD) looking up at the burning structures. More images began to air of the many pieces of fire apparatus heading towards the fireball in the sky. I think it was then, seeing actual footage of the personnel of the NYFD, that the magnitude of this incident finally started to sink in. At this point in my career, I was almost twenty-four years in, and trained in high-rise operations. I knew without a doubt that these brave men and women had a life-or-death firefight on their hands.

The news worsened. New reports, sketchy at best, of a third plane crashing into the Pentagon Building, many miles away from the towers, was put out over the air waves. The thought on everyone's mind: *What the hell is going on?*

It continued. With total disbelief in what I was witnessing, the south tower of these massive structures actually collapsed in on itself, and just . . . dropped to the ground, as if in slow motion, cement, steel, glass, and so much more, raining down on the streets below. My mind was protecting me, letting me know this could not really be happening. It just had to be a staged scene—they were filming a movie—right? I don't remember ever feeling so disconnected from my own thoughts as I did right that second.

Even in seeing that moment of catastrophe, I was not mentally prepared to understand the immense loss of life that was happening before my eyes, in real time, for all the planet to witness.

There were reports of a plane crash somewhere in rural Pennsylvania. Was it in any way connected to the unimaginable events of the last hour? We would learn in days to come that it was. We would also learn of the heroism of the brave passengers of Flight 93 who, taking matters into their own hands, managed to overwhelm the hijackers, and although unsuccessful in their attempts to retake the plane itself, certainly saved many more lives by making sure, even in a sure-death situation, the plane was not going to be used as the terrorists had intended. It is believed the actual target was the seat of government in the United States, the Capitol Building. They did not make it.

Could it get any worse? By this time, the whole of North America was glued to any news outlet they could get to, hoping for some clarification on what was happening that morning.

It did get worse. Like a mirror image of the first tower collapse, the north tower was felled—in real time—on live TV. The news anchors were literally speechless as they, along with the rest of the world, watched the mind-numbing devastation.

I knew by then, understanding the tactics used by firefighters at high-rise building fires, that I was witnessing a historical event of Biblical proportions. It would become the greatest loss of life ever inflicted on the emergency services field, at any one single incident, the world over.

There has always been a saying in the fire service: "We are running in when you are running out." It was no different that day. Three hundred and forty-three firefighters—New York's bravest of the brave—were in those buildings when they collapsed, every one of them killed instantly. An unthinkable, inconceivable, unimaginable tragedy.

Yes, my chosen profession changed that day—and so did I.

We would also learn of the tragic deaths of many of the other first responder disciplines. Several police, port authority, and paramedic personnel succumbed to the terror that morning, along with almost three thousand civilians. God bless them all.

Perpetual Motion

I basically sat in front of my TV for the next thirty days, watching the aftermath of these events unfold. I don't remember communicating with anyone, even Gayle. I didn't realize how all-consuming it had become. I also didn't realize how it was affecting me mentally and physically. I know it contributed to my bouts of severe depression and anxiety—and because of all that, the continual and worsening PTSD.

Somewhere about the 12th of October 2001, I turned off my TV—and never turned it on again for close to ten years. True story.

34. Pharmaceuticals and Freedom

Gayle saw the change in me. She recognized the symptoms of depression rearing its ugly head and tried to come to my rescue. She was in for an uphill battle. Travel had resumed over the skies of North America in time, even allowing my own parents to finally leave Vancouver and fly back to Halifax, after being stranded for two weeks. The airline industry had suffered catastrophic losses, as did the whole travel industry, due to the shutdown of airspace over the continent. Knowing I needed a break, and suspecting rightly that this would be a good time to find travel deals, I did some research, eventually settling on a week's vacation for two at the couples all-inclusive Sandals Resort in Montego Bay, Jamaica. I surprised Gayle with the tickets. It was the best decision I had made all year.

On top of all of this, and out of the blue, came a new creation of my own doing. Just prior to us departing for the south, Gayle and I went to a nightclub for dinner and drinks. While there, we ran into some very good friends, including some fellow firefighters. During the evening—without forewarning—an incident occurred that sent me into a jealous rage. What the hell was this? Inwardly, I was seething. Outwardly—as calm as I could be. It wasn't long before I suggested we needed to leave, because we had a big day of travel ahead of us. What bothered me more than the incident itself was the fact that I could never remember feeling jealous before. This debilitating sensation was totally new to me, and I was baffled as to where it had come from. I know now. Unfortunately, it would not be the last time this new malady would happen. Because of these unbridled emotions emanating from the "damaged" me, and the inability to suppress them, my jealousy festered, and I most assuredly went on to ruin this, and several future relationships because of it. It would eventually take years, and much personal work, to rid myself of this cursed demon.

I would love to tell you the dream vacation we had that week was perfect. Parts of it were. As much as we both had a fabulous time in the sun, those demons inside me had taken hold and were too much to overcome at times. To function, I jumped all over the bottle. Of course, it didn't help that there was an endless supply of free booze—as much as I could consume—all week long. The only saviour—the authentic jerk chicken—just fabulous.

Back home, I needed to get myself back on solid ground. After seeing my doctor to again receive some medicinal help, things did turn around—thank God for pharmaceuticals. I have no recall as to how I dealt with work, children, and my social life during that horrid time. I eventually got back to the gym and came to the slow realization that exercising was really good for me. From that day forward, each time I felt like I was heading in the wrong direction mentally, I would exercise. Even going for a walk or a run was enough to completely change my mood. I can't run like I used to, but a brisk walk still works today.

The year 2002 looked more promising. Valerie and Rob were doing well after relocating to Sarnia from Nova Scotia in the spring of 1998. After some discussion over the past winter, they decided to fulfill a dream and buy a boat. They settled on a new 24.5' Rinker, purchased from Maple City Marine in Chatham. What a thrill for them.

In February, Gayle and I took another mini vacation together. We flew to Quebec City for a magical time at the Quebec Winter Carnival. She had attended this event once before and was a great guide to all things winter. I had never done anything such as this and had a great time in the cold outdoors of Quebec. Feeling better physically, and mentally, I trudged on.

After securing a mooring slip in the Lagoon area at the Point Edward Yacht Club, Rob and Val's boat was delivered in early April. It was still rather chilly weather-wise, but Rob couldn't wait to take it for its inaugural run, and so, bundled in layers of winter wear, Rob, Martin, and I headed onto the St. Clair River. What a fabulous feeling of freedom—seeing someone you care about, over the moon with excitement for his new toy. Over the course of the summer, we spent several days plying the waters of the St. Clair River and lower Lake Huron in that fine craft. It also got me thinking about owning just such a gem someday.

Life again began to stabilize around me. Stephanie was finishing high school, and Shaun was in the throes of it. They were both enjoying all that came with that special time in their lives. Their lifelong friends had been solidified, and many times over the course of those years I entertained a houseful of teenagers, most times just prior to them heading out for the evening or just after they would return from the bars. It's amazing how life comes full circle. I remember consciously trying to emulate how my own parents treated my friends during our high school days. I know my kids appreciated their freedom, just as I had in the '70s.

Yes, freedom in the '70s—always there for the taking. I was never restricted or held back by my parents for doing anything I felt was reasonable, or safe. In that time and space, they trusted us to do the right thing based on the way we were brought up. They trusted in their good teachings. But now, the world had lost its innocence. It had changed, and the issue of terrorism was fast becoming more prevalent on the world stage after the unconscionable acts of September 11th, 2001.

Please indulge me a small rant. It won't take long. I promise you, it has relevance to my story. I was reading a lot—it had become one of my passions—and I was very interested in societal history. American politics, especially the lives of the presidents, had all the intrigue of a good spy novel. The love for this genre stemmed from the reams of printed words on the assassination of JFK—I read twenty-two books on that one subject alone. Other subject matter I found psychologically fascinating included the act of war, and its consequences, the rise of Hitler, Fascism, and the Nazi party—all of which had the elements of new ideals and redefined actions, surrounding the word *democracy*. It was hard to comprehend that back in the 1930s and '40s, one man could hold sway over so many seemingly intelligent people, both here and abroad. How could we ever let this happen again?

Well, in an interesting twist to history, and only a short time ago, it happened—again. We are seeing a renewed awakening of societal fanaticism and far-right views—all encompassing, and, at one point reaching all the way to the highest office in the land, south of the border. The violent rhetoric still continues to this day.

But I digress. As had been done since the Vietnam War, all of this diatribe was being piped into our homes via radio and TV, by the talking heads at the now established cable news networks. The world was becoming more unstable, and being a father, the fear for my children's safety was real. I needed to tune it out for, at times, I could feel myself spiralling down, and I began to learn every trick in the book to bring me back to centre. It still boggles the mind how history is inevitably doomed to repeat itself. Ok, rant over.

This is important. I write these comments so you may hopefully understand and relate to how post-traumatic stress manifests itself. It is not just one incident that causes someone to feel unwell. It is an accumulation of untold numbers of seemingly unrelated incidents and actions, some happening years apart, that exact their toll on a person's physical and psychological well-being—and don't—for one minute, think it can't happen to you.

For the record, I was outwardly showing the world my smile and my charm. I could have won an Oscar for my performance. Most thought I had the world by the tail—inwardly, I was in a dark place. I was still working as an active firefighter, and with that came new incidents, adding to my affliction. Even though I was not watching the endless reels of news on TV, it still managed to penetrate my defenses. Constant news cycles had become unavoidable in the age of social media. Unfortunately, it was also taking a major toll on my relationship with Gayle.

35. Dock Life

Time for some good news! Rob and Valerie came over to the house for a visit one night and brought with them some colour glossy brochures of a new 27' Rinker power cruiser. They had just decided to upgrade from the smaller craft they had bought in the spring. The kicker was, they wanted to offer me the opportunity to purchase it before they had to trade it in. Well, hell ya! Of course I wanted to own that boat. I had been out with it several times, and knew it was perfect for me. So, in January of 2003, Rob and I went to the boat show in London and met with Rob Rule from Maple City Marine. I was happy to sign the deal for the purchase of my dream machine. Until that day, I really didn't think I would ever own a new boat. Life was yet again balancing back to centre.

Rob had the boat stored indoors, in a hanger at the municipal airport, so it wasn't long before Gayle and I went to visit our new toy. The feeling of euphoria, stepping up that ship's ladder, is one I will never forget. We got to work cleaning it up really well and even pulled out a flask of rye to toast our good fortunes. Now all we needed to do was wait for the weather to break. Our opportunity came, and the boat went in the water on April 15th. Damn, fingers crossed, it was going to be a good year.

Tradition has it that when purchasing a boat, it must be named and christened with champagne, or bad omens happen. So, what to name my sweet vessel? I have had the nickname Pittsy since I was a child, but I didn't want that to be the vessel's name. It was too easy to stick with the obvious so I continued to think about the name change for days—always drawing a blank. Sitting on some lawn chairs at Tug's house one afternoon discussing my dilemma, he suddenly jumped up, flailing his arms like a madman. He was yelling my nickname, Pittsy, over and over. He said, "I've got it!" I was about to say no again, when he stopped me and yelled, "Pitt-sea." Then he proceeded to spell it out: "P-I-T-T-S-E-A!!" Damn! If it wasn't perfect! So again, Tug, thanks for naming my new vessel! And who would have thought that years later—long after I had sold that boat—the name would be revived in the form of a photography business.

Even though *PittSea* was a single screw, it had lots of pep in its 350 hp Mercruiser engine, and I became fairly adept at piloting her. Prior to the marina getting busy, I took the boat out to the lake a few times to get used to its handling characteristics.

Gayle and I decided to get away for one last weekend before the summer fun began. We chose Niagara-on-the-Lake as our B&B destination. It was only a weekend jaunt, but the time away was needed. While en route to our destination, I got a phone call from my friend and fellow firefighter, Brad Raymer. He and his wife Marty had just booked a Caribbean cruise on Carnival Cruise Lines. He explained the great deal and asked if Gayle and I would be interested in tagging along. It took us all of a moment to decide it was something we definitely would be interested in. Brad booked our berth, and once we got home, I took care of the details. Wow, we're going on a cruise in November! It would be the first time cruising for both of us and we talked about it constantly.

Back home, it wasn't long before vessels of all shapes and sizes started to arrive back to their assigned berths, and I was seeing new faces and rekindling old friendships. Life would never be the same.

I made the tough decision to sell my bike. My reasoning was simple. I planned on spending all my time dockside and on the water, so I wouldn't have any free time to ride. I also sold my TaylorMade golf clubs. No worries—I wasn't any good at that sport anyways.

The boating lifestyle, and with it, dock life, came real easy. Being a very social person, it was not long before I counted many of my boating neighbours as good friends. I still feel that way with many of them today. Gayle enjoyed the change in her routine also. It quickly became a habit to spend every weekend at the marina, and for me specifically, many weeknights also. It was a great day when Rob and Valerie berthed their new *Robin's Nest*. Having family so close, and to enjoy the same activities, made for wonderful times. I count this time as some of my favourite activities ever.

In the meantime, there was work-life to handle. I was going full tilt at my "part-time" job at Securitex, and if truth be known, it was getting a little out of hand. The little Mom and Pop operation I had committed to in 1998 had been sold the previous year to a huge multi-national firm called Bacou-Dalloz—the exact thing I feared and didn't want, right from the beginning of this venture. I didn't want to become just a number. I had enjoyed the years of true camaraderie and friendships with all my colleagues, but things were starting to unravel. Pressure was being put on all of us to do more, sell more, and make more money for the top brass. I wasn't happy but kept my feelings to myself for the time being.

There was a family to support. Stephanie and Shaun had grown up so much and were both great kids. I will admit, I spoiled both of them most of the time, but certainly at Christmas. Shaun was now an accomplished guitarist and I made sure he was well-equipped for moving his craft forward. Stephanie had recently bought her first car, so I made sure she had the best stereo equipment for it, including huge trunk-mounted woofers, which were all the rage back then. Neither of them had ever given me a lick of trouble, and I was very grateful for that.

I also had another Big Sisters fashion show to prepare for. For this second go 'round, Julie Chamberlain was back at the helm, and most of us were pretty aware of the requirements for the choreography. I think she found it easier getting us to learn the new routines. There were some new faces, so she still had to contend with the two left feet of a few. She put us all at ease, and we had another very successful fundraising adventure with Big Sisters.

My first summer with the boat was over in a flash. It was a fabulous time with new friends. I had met Dan Fisher at a party years earlier. We didn't know each other well, but when we both ended up on B-Dock with our vessels, the friendship was rekindled and has remained strong ever since. Dan is a real comedian and has kept us in laughter many times over the years. I could regale you with several funny stories, but the Chocolate Chip Cookie story I think best describes the character of my funny friend.

A group of us decided to bring our boats to Lakeside Marina on Lake St. Clair, near Tilbury, for the weekend. We planned this getaway to take in the Jimmy Buffet tribute concert that was happening on the Saturday.

Six watercraft made the trek, and my shipmate for this trip was Dan. The weekend weather was perfect, and after the boats were tied up, we got into party mode pretty quickly. Boat-drinks flowed, the music was great, and we let loose into the wee hours of the morning. After the music had ended on the big stage, we were all to meet at the bar. Dan had to make a quick stop below deck and had been in the galley fussing about for a few minutes. I was soon to find out what he was scheming.

He walked into the bar with an open Ziploc baggie filled with chocolate chip cookies, about four in total. This baggie was trussed up with a string and placed around his neck so it sat right about chest high. I immediately took notice, but before I could say anything, he grinned and said, "Watch the master." Were we in for a show!

As Dan walked along the bar rail, near a group of young ladies enjoying the festivities, he opened the baggie and gently began to blow into it. Instantly, the delicious, sweet cookie smell wafted from the package. As he had planned, the ladies turned around and made several comments about the great smell of the cookies—the question, "What the hell are you doing?" being the main one. Not to be deterred, he started to chat them up, as he did often when out at a nightclub. All this time, the rest of us were standing back a few feet, witnessing this display of surefire peacockedness, and laughing so hard our sides hurt. As the entertainment continued, Dan could sense the conversation moving in the direction he had hoped. He then asked one of the girls he was most notably interested in, a question to the effect of "So, are you single?"—to which she replied, pointing to the girl next to her, "No, I'm with her!"

Dan had hit on a group of lesbians! I'm pretty sure most of us spit our drinks through our noses at the irony of all that. From that day forward, the standing joke between us was the symbolic gesture of blowing the cookie smell any time we saw a group of pretty girls at a bar. Anyone who witnessed that hilarity still laughs at it today.

Soon it was November—the Rinker put in storage, and time to cruise. I truly didn't know what to expect, having never taken part in this type of activity before, so I asked around and got some worthy tips for a successful vacation. The ship, the *Carnival Inspiration*, was a floating palace in my eyes. We spent the week travelling from port to port, enjoying ship life, and when we went ashore the excursions were fabulous. My first time having an authentic Mexican taco at a little roadside stand in Costa Maya is something I won't soon forget. I enjoyed all aspects of the cruise and swore it wouldn't be the last.

Alas, hindsight is all knowing, and as much as there were many times a cruise would have been a great vacation, I never did take another. Actually, I'm still not convinced it is again, a safe way to travel. In all honesty, I am just not inclined to subject myself to its maladies. Maybe someday.

36. Endings and Beginnings

In February of 2004, the world-wide sales team from Bacou-Dalloz had been invited to their annual meeting. It was to be held in Florida at the Orlando Convention Centre and Suites—surely the swankiest place I had ever stayed. The highlight of the week was that the company had rented out a large bar/restaurant for our private party, inside the Universal Orlando Resort Park. It was a full evening of fun and entertainment. A professional cigar roller had been hired to continuously hand-roll cigars for us, the whole night long. Damn, I felt special. Unfortunately, nothing could shake the overwhelming feeling of me not wanting to be involved with this company any longer. I played along for the week, and why shouldn't I?—it was a great time as far as the extra-curricular activities scheduled. By the time Friday came, I had had enough. I didn't attend the last morning's meeting or the closing ceremonies. I was on a plane back to Ontario—and noticeably missed.

It wasn't long before my boss, Jean Drolet, called me with questions. I could have told him the truth, but a little white lie sufficed. I told him I wasn't feeling well and had made the decision to come home a few hours early. In my mind, I was in the process of checking out of this line of work for good.

The next week was a blur of travel and sales meetings around the province. We had in the recent past, taken on a new line of gear with the launch of a program to sell this well-established line of breathing apparatus to the Ontario fire services. I had already been to Orange County CA, to the manufacturers facility, for extensive training on the product and was by now quite familiar with it. I had confidence in my ability to sell it but just didn't want to take on any more responsibility.

Looking at my travel schedule, I just knew those meetings were not going to stop. It was about the third week of March by this time, and I was exhausted. I remember sitting at my office desk that morning, becoming so overwhelmed with everything I saw in front of me. I needed out. The moment of truth came when I pushed myself away from my desk and said quite loudly to no one, "I quit." To hear it come out of my mouth was such a relief. I meant it, and now had to do something about it.

I dialed into head office and got John on the phone. After brief pleasantries, John started into the week's itinerary. "So, tomorrow you have to be in Vaughn for a BA meeting with the safety committee. Next day you have to go to Cornwall for a repeat of the same presentation. From there, you—"

I tuned him out. He kept talking, but I was not listening. I spoke very plainly into the receiver: "John, I quit."

He continued to talk.

Again, I articulated, "John, I quit."

Once more he continued to explain the week's schedule, and then he paused. "You what?" he said.

Finally—I now had his attention, and he listened. By the time the conversation was done, he understood my point of view and reluctantly accepted it. We agreed to speak again the next day after he had some time to absorb the loss and discuss the future of my territory with the bosses.

The next day's conversation was pleasant and to the point. He accepted my resignation—me agreeing to put it in writing. He also asked me if I knew of anyone in Ontario who was looking for the kind of job I was walking away from. I replied in the affirmative. I definitely knew of a few who would fit the bill. I reached out to a colleague I had worked with on several occasions—he was between jobs, and very interested in my position.

John was pleased I had found someone. It was going to make his job much easier. He then proposed that I train the new guy. We came to terms—me having until the end of April to have him fully trained. What John didn't know was that I had already spent many hours with this prospect and his co-workers at the distributorship level. He was already familiar with our product line. Training him was going to be a snap. I had him up to speed in about eight hours—his truck fully loaded with all of my samples, sizing gear, equipment, and such, and he was on his way. I was through! I had just spent the last seven years in a sales position I didn't even want in the first place. I was going to celebrate the end of my tenure as a fire products salesman. Spring was just around the corner, and I needed to get the boat ready!

The weather was warming up beautifully and soon the boat was back in the water. It didn't take long for each berth to fill up once again. All the regulars were back, along with a few newbies. Sitting with some of the crew that Saturday morning, I was told that the new guy down the dock was a cop. The joke was that now we were going to have to behave ourselves. Nothing could have been further from the truth. I strolled towards his boat, noticing him kneeling on the swim platform doing some maintenance. As I was about to pass, I commented, "So, I hear you're a cop." His reply: "So, I hear you're a firefighter."

That was the beginning of a very long friendship with Paul Dow. We had just about everything in common, and from experience, I knew it was not often you meet someone in your late forties who becomes your best friend. We did much together over the next fifteen years—some of which you will read about in the following pages. I don't see Paul anymore for reasons which, again, will be explained later. I can honestly say though, no matter what shit happened between us, I do miss his friendship and the close bond we shared. Cheers, Paul.

The summer of 2004 is a bit of a blur. Gayle and I ventured out to the lake many times over those months. The boating lifestyle was one I really embraced, and now with such a great group of friends, life was bordering on enjoyable. Paul Dow, Andy Toulouse, Garrett Rocca, Dan Fisher, Norma and Jimmy, Deb and Jay, Greg and Linda, Lynn and Leslee, Rick and Barb, Rob and Val, Joe and Lisa, John and Becky, and so many others, were all one big family back then. A typical Friday night saw all of us arrive at the marina by about suppertime and the shenanigans would commence. Greg Goldsmith had the biggest boat, so it wasn't unusual for all of us to gather in and around his yacht. After a night of tequila, the next day started rough, but by late morning we had shaken the Saturday morning hangover. A flotilla would form by about noon, and we would head off to one of the beaches in the area to raft off and start the festivities all over again. This scene would repeat itself many times over the next couple of years.

At least twice a summer, we would plan a boating trip to another marina somewhere between Grand Bend, up the coast on Lake Huron, and Put-In-Bay, an island in Lake Erie. Depending how far it was, we usually had no less than three boats and sometimes as many as eight.

Put-In-Bay is a little island town about ten miles off the coast of Sandusky, Ohio, known for some pretty wild nightlife. In my years of boating, I frequented the place three times with each being a totally different experience. My best island story stems from my first trip to Put-In-Bay prior to me owning my own vessel. It goes like this:

Todd Gladwish owned a 35' Fountain, a long cigarette-style boat—for those not familiar with the brand name. He invited a few of the gang along for a weekend trip to this island oasis. I wasn't familiar with the destination or what to expect. I just wanted to go for the experience. Tug, Todd, Connor Lynch, and I left from Todd's boathouse on the St. Clair River. It was a Friday, and a fine summer morning. Todd's toy was a *go-fast* boat, and it didn't take us long to cover the miles to the island—at one point travelling over sixty-five miles per hour on the water, through the Detroit cut.

Friday night was typical with much too much to drink at the famed Round House Bar. Saturday dawned to a torrent of rain, and Connor, having slept on the back bench of the open cockpit, got drenched, sleeping bag and all. It was not a great way to wake up. After a slow start, we figured on finding a restaurant for some breakfast. The four of us, hung to the nines, trudging through the mud, must have been a sight. Connor, still chilled from the deluge the night before, had his wet sleeping bag wrapped around him. We got to the eatery and started plying ourselves with coffee and man-sized plates of breakfast foods. The lady sitting next to us, showing concern and feeling quite sorry for us, struck up a conversation. As it turns out, she was the owner of the Round House Bar where we had imbibed the evening before. She was an interesting character, and before long, the two tables were moved together, with beers laid out. Showing concern for our sopping wet sleeping bags and clothes, she offered us the use of her dryers, back at the bar. We were ever so grateful. After another round or two had taken the edge off, we were feeling better. Our benefactor said she needed to get back to the bar to make preparations for that evening's onslaught of patrons, but before she left she wrote a note and handed it to us. We were shocked to read that it was a free pass, all the booze we could drink, all night long! All we had to do was present the chit to the bartender, and we were off to the races.

Wow! This only happens in the movies. Of course, we were skeptical. We did use the drying facilities and got all our wet gear back to usable condition. Once cleaned up, we were ready to test the validity of our proverbial "golden goose." The four of us sauntered up to the bar as if we owned the place—and that night, we just might. Handing the note to the barkeep, we waited—for several tense moments. He looked at us across the bar, then said, "Looks like you gentlemen are in for a great night. What'll you have?" That was it, the gauntlet had been laid before us. It was up to us to see how far we could push this act. And push it we did! We drank for about seven hours, and near the end, just before being finally cut off, we were supplying drinks for several young ladies who had latched on for the free ride.

It was about midnight when the word was passed that we were done, no more freebies. Well, no shit, Sherlock! We were done in more ways than one. Now back to the boat to sleep it off. Tomorrow was going to be a rough ride home. We talked about that trip for a long time. It is still one of my favourite stories to tell.

Gayle and I had finally reached our endgame when, one evening in late August, during a massive get together on "A" Dock, words were exchanged between us, and she left the marina in a huff. Without a doubt, it was something I said. I will own that. My raging jealousy, ever present just below the surface, must have reacted to a trigger. It just reiterates my previous comments—outward smiles don't aways equate to happiness. I want you to know, dear Gayle, I am so sorry that an affliction of my own making, destroyed such a loving relationship.

Boating season was winding down. It was September, and I was single again. The month of September in Sarnia was always beautiful, and despite the fact that I had many of my low times happen during that particular month, I still love it as one of my favourite times of the year. It was time to get on with some other activities.

Stephanie had finished high school, and having had some time off, decided to enroll in Lambton College. This was the beginning of her higher education. She still wasn't sure what she wanted to study or where, so this was the best option for the time being.

The Big Sisters organization was in full swing with preparations for their upcoming annual show being held in a new location, the Dante Club on London Rd. I don't recall why, but I was not a participant in that year's event. I did go that evening to support the cast of characters as best I could. Besides, I wanted to see Julie again. She and I had hit it off as friends over the last couple of events, and privately, in my own mind, I kinda had a thing for her. We did have time to chat over drinks at the after party at Paddy Flaherty's pub, and I got to know her just a little bit better.

I did run into another acquaintance that evening. Shelley worked at the municipal offices in Point Edward, and she and I had spoken on occasion. I always enjoyed seeing this little spark-plug of a thing, and I did notice each time we talked that there was some chemistry there. In the right place and the right time, who knows what would transpire. I would eventually find out.

I set my intentions for 2005. It was going to be a great year. By now, my children were busy with her own affairs, Stephanie continuing her education and recently having met her future husband at the last Big Sisters event, and Shaun figuring out the logistics of attending the University of Guelph in the Psychology Program for the fall semester. All of this was somewhat difficult for me considering my children had been beside me every step of their lives so far. They were growing up too fast, and now off to make a life for themselves.

Summer arrived, and the boat went back to "B" Dock. Finally, some normalcy back in my life. By this time, I had become pretty good friends with Coach T, aka Andy Toulouse. Andy owned a small craft docked a few slips over. I sat with him several times after the crowds had dispersed for the night—us enjoying some great conversations about his career as a teacher and basketball coach. We discussed plans to take my boat to Put-In-Bay later in the summer. He also introduced me to several of his friends. My world was expanding.

Perpetual Motion

Sarnia during the summer months meant great music. The success of our local concert series, Bayfest, spawned other events that attracted huge talent. It was mid-July and first up was the band 54-40 at Ribfest. I was walking through the crowd when I noticed a group of girls just ahead of me. One of them stuck her head out of the group and looked right at me, mouthing my name—"Dana?" It was Julie Chamberlain. We struck up a lively conversation and she eventually confided in me that she and her husband had split. Ok, that was an interesting turn of events. We made plans to meet the following week for a boat ride. I was excited to say the least.

That get-together couldn't come soon enough. Julie met me on the dock that following Saturday morning, and after some preliminary introductions to a few other boaters, we headed out. It was a fabulous cruise down river on a beautiful day. We drifted for hours, just talking and getting to know each other. There were no expectations of what any future might hold—but man, it held a lot! That evening, after more visiting, and drinks with the gang, we retired to my v-berth to continue the conversation. I was enamoured by this time—I cannot lie. We talked until the wee hours of the morning—sharing snippets of our lives—fell asleep in each other's arms, and awoke with a renewed wonder as to where this was headed. All I knew was I really liked her, and I was going to pursue her until she told me to stop.

The next couple of months passed with sporadic contact with Julie. She was just newly separated and didn't want to jump into a full-time relationship, so she did everything she could to keep me at bay. We had many great talks and I totally understood where she was coming from. The initial infatuation began to wear off after being stymied at every turn. Still, I couldn't put her out of my mind.

I did go to Put-In-Bay with Andy. Two events made that trip memorable. The first was the great phone conversation I had with Julie quite late into the night as I sat on the boat waiting for Andy to return with our pizza. I wanted nothing more than to have this relationship move forward, and we still spoke often. The other was the life and death struggle to get back to Leamington Marina and the safety of the harbour on the Sunday return trip. Lake Erie is very shallow, and when the weather turns, the water gets angry. My small craft was no match for its fury. Having no choice, we made sure our life jackets were on tight and plowed through the storm. We had trailered the boat from Sarnia to Leamington Harbour and set out for the island in fine July weather. Then, needing to return to the same harbour to get our vehicle and trailer, the back trip became the scariest twenty-three miles I had ever put on the boat. We were physically exhausted when we set foot on land and I think I even kissed the dock for good measure.

Back at work, all was well. I was comfortable in my role as the captain of B-1 squad and was filling in as platoon chief quite often. PC Bob Burns was our senior man with lots of vacation, so it allowed me some quality acting time. At this point in my career, I was most likely next in line for a promotion to platoon chief. It was just a matter of time.

There had been some movement in the top ranks at SFRS the last several months with Chief Boyes going to Oakville, and Pat Cayen, our DC, moving up to chief. Pat had finally received permission from City Hall to hire a new deputy, a position not filled since he had been promoted. Postings were put out in October and several qualified candidates had put their names forward. I saw myself as a qualified PC and was quite happy to wait for my shot at that position, so I didn't apply. The DC position did not interest me.

Life went on. It was now late fall, and with Julie mostly absent, I finally got up the nerve to ask Shelley to come over for a drink. I didn't know it was her birthday, but the timing could not have been better. We started seeing each other on a fairly regular basis. I had basically given up on Julie and me being anything more than friends. She was consumed with getting her life on track and raising her young son, Jonathan. I couldn't begrudge her that needed time, and let it go.

The next year, 2006, started with a wedding in the Dominican Republic. Again, not mine! My great friend Tug had met a young lady several years prior while they were both separately vacationing in Florida. Mariella was from Argentina, and couldn't speak a lick of English, but somehow, they continued to communicate—she even made a visit to Sarnia at one point. After several years of on and off times, they decided to commit, and eighteen of his friends made the trip south to witness their nuptials. Shelley couldn't go, so again, Dan Fisher was my wingman. It was a fabulous getaway—sun, sand, great friends, and a wedding on the beach. It has been eighteen years since that wedding and both are doing just great with their two sons now in their teens.

37. Be Careful What You Wish For

For the last couple of years, a group of firefighters, including myself, had taken on the huge project of restoring Sarnia's first motorized fire truck, a 1921 LaFrance Foamite Pumper, originally built in Toronto. Each week we would get together and work on that project. It was at this point about three quarters finished, and as more guys got interested in what we were doing, they would volunteer their time also.

One night in early April, about eight of us were working on the rig when brother firefighter Glen Harding came into the shop. We were very happy to see him, knowing he had been chosen as the new DC for SFRS. Out of the many who applied, Glen was a great choice, given his solid career and his attention to detail. He was well schooled after having taken several management courses at different colleges, including Ryerson in Toronto. There were congratulatory comments all around. What happened next was completely unexpected and set me on a different life path, again!

Glen called me off to the side and informed me he hadn't yet made up his mind whether to take the promotion or not. He and I had become quite good friends over the years and I knew he trusted my judgement, so I was assuming at this point, he wanted to hear my advice on the matter. I was curious and asked him why he was hesitating. He then said, "Because the job is yours."

I wasn't sure I was following his logic and reminded him I had not applied for the job in the first place—that I was quite happy in my present position, and so no, the job was not for me. I then began to give him all the reasons many of us thought he was the best candidate for the position. He listened and thanked me for the advice. He also repeated his affirmation as to the suitability of me for the job instead of him.

A couple of days later, word came that Glen had turned the job down. It was a strange turn of events. I ran into Chief Cayen that day and we had a short sit-down in his office. Chief Cayen and I were rather close also. I had met him while he was the chief in Malahide, Ont. during my Securitex days. He felt he could confide in me, and he bared his soul as to his disappointment in Glen not accepting the job. Pat had worked for almost fifteen months straight without a vacation or any break at all. There had been no one to take over for him and he had been looking forward to having Glen step into the role so he could take a bit of time off. I felt for the guy.

The following Friday, I was at home, thinking about Pat and the struggles he was going through. I thought a phone call would cheer him up. We spoke for a few minutes about his options and what he was going to do to try and fill the vacancy. After about ten minutes, we were finishing the conversation—just saying our goodbyes when, out of the blue—and to this day, I have no idea where it came from—as Pat was putting the receiver down, I spoke loudly. "Pat?" That stopped him from hanging up. When he acknowledged me, I spoke those famous last words: "What about me?"

His reply shocked me, and I quote: "You son-of-a-bitch, if you had applied for the job in the first place, we wouldn't be having this conversation." He told me I was always his first choice, but since I didn't apply for the job, there was nothing he could do about it. We made plans to meet at Tim Hortons on Sunday for a real serious conversation. Wow, what the hell did I just do?

When that meeting was over, he decided to re-post the job internally, and I committed to apply. The posting would be for one week only and, depending on how many candidates came forward, interviews would be conducted on Friday, April 28th. Three new applications were submitted—all very much qualified for the position.

My interview was held at 2 p.m. that Friday—the last of the three candidates to go before the board. It lasted about an hour and I was confident in what I had presented. Once it was over, I was told to head home and wait for the possibility of a phone call. It was either going to be "thanks but no thanks," or "come in for a second interview." I wasn't home twenty minutes when I was called back for a second round—now this shit was getting real. The second interview was more casual, and near its conclusion, I was asked formally if I would accept the position of Deputy Chief of SFRS. Damn right, I would! I said yes!

We spent a brief time discussing salaries, benefits, and other particulars, but what surprised me was the request for a doctor's note of health and fitness needing to be presented to HR before any announcement could be made.

I had just been offered and accepted the greatest promotion in my life to second-in-command at SFRS, and I couldn't tell anyone, or celebrate, until I got in to see my doctor? Damn. I was not deterred. It was just after 4 p.m., and in desperation, I made the suggestion that if I could get in to see my doctor ASAP, have him issue a proper medical clearance and get it back to HR by 5:15 p.m. latest, could I then make the announcement and celebrate the great news? Kathy Meade gave me permission to do just that. Ten minutes later, I was standing before the receptionist, pleading to see the doctor for a very important reason. It worked. My blood pressure was through the roof. After a brief conversation, Dr. Stoesser made me promise to come back early next week for a physical, in exchange for the note he would write today. I readily agreed. Off I went—back to City Hall with my medical clearance in hand.

Kathy actually laughed at me when I returned with the note by the suggested deadline. I was so pumped; I just knew I wouldn't be able to keep the news a secret for the weekend.

That evening, Shelly, myself, and several friends went to Lola's Lounge for a wonderful celebration. Yes, my world had just changed greatly, and it was all due to hard work and the choices I had made in my life, getting to this point. Even today, it stands as one of my finest achievements.

My last shift as a front-line, active-duty firefighter was April 26th, 2006. As fate would have it, the evening was anything but quiet. We had a couple of small calls early in the shift, but around 8 p.m. we were toned out to a structure fire at the corner of Mitton and Confederation Ave. I had always been a hands-on captain, and this fire was no different. I recall being on the roof of the home, swinging an axe to get at several hotspots that had been stubborn to extinguish; it was a nostalgic moment. This could be the last time I would ever perform these tasks—honed skills I had been using for almost thirty years. Truth be known, I wasn't getting any younger and found myself somewhat winded from the exertion. I had earned my stripes and felt now was a perfect time to put my skills and knowledge to work for the betterment of the fire service.

We were not done yet. After sucking dry two bottles of breathing air at that fire, I was in need of some rehab. Sitting on the tailboard of the truck around 11 p.m., my radio squawked again. We were dispatched to St. Joseph's Hospital for a carbon monoxide call. Normally not a big deal, and most times a false alarm, we entered the building with our CO detectors, ready to find the source of the leak—if there was one. What we found was alarming—readings of over 400 ppm in several areas of the complex. Just for stats sake, anything over 35 ppm is a serious issue and evacuation is recommended. Needless to say, it was one hell of a long night. The crews finally found the leak, a plugged furnace flue-stack caused by debris falling into it during previous renovations of the building. For patient safety, we moved them to other areas of the hospital deemed safe from exposure. The entire crew was exhausted by end of shift at 7 a.m. I had breathed through three more bottles of air during the remediation of the toxic leak. If I had to put a stamp on the active responder part of my career, that surely did it!

Do you recall in my back story the comments my father and brother made to me when I suggested me joining the ranks of the Sarnia Fire Department? I had defied my father's counsel and made good on my career path. Both of them were now very proud of my fire service achievements.

I started my new position as Deputy Chief on May 1st, 2006. Priorities that day included the physical I had promised my doctor I would get done, and a lengthy meeting at City Hall to get all the necessary paperwork completed for my transfer out of the bargaining unit and into management. The physical went well, and the meeting at City Hall was the first of many in the years to come.

Chief Cayen was thrilled to finally have someone who could take the reins of the day-to-day workings of the department so he could have a vacation. I hadn't been on the job two weeks when, returning from a district meeting in Chatham, he informed me he was taking some time off to see his brother in the west. I was thrilled he had the confidence in me to do that but was anxious about it still.

Perpetual Motion

Not surprisingly, while he was gone, the department fought one of the largest fires ever to hit a Sarnia business. The very toxic and suspicious Abbott Boat Works fire on London Rd. consumed three buildings and destroyed a viable business, all while injuring several first responders who attended the scene. The toxic smoke from the burning chemicals stored on site was a health and safety risk to all who were in the immediate vicinity—the effects of which still linger for some first responders today.

On August 5th, I turned fifty. Shelley organized a massive surprise birthday party for me on our local cruise ship, the *Duc d' Orleans*. It was a jam-packed affair that saw my good friend, Doug Stewart and CDDC perform live for the sell-out crowd. I had been enjoying some relative calm in my life the last few months, and it felt good.

Unfortunately, that was not to last more than a couple more days. Shelley, all the while, was planning her exit from our fledgling relationship for reasons I discovered a short time later. Yes, that godforsaken jealous streak of mine had reared its ugly head a few weeks earlier and she had had enough. Not wanting to cancel the birthday surprise, she forged ahead with the cruise, and to her credit, she smiled all the way through it. I had no idea what was to come—but come it did. It was over.

I was certainly disappointed about the break-up, but in hindsight, it was inevitable, and I don't blame her one bit—again, totally my fault. I desperately needed some help in getting my shit together, so I could stop sabotaging my relationships. Unfortunately, there were still more lessons to learn. I am truly sorry, dear Shelley. Damn.

Not for the first time in my life, I attended counselling—and finally, did start to listen—baby steps. I know now those sessions were what I needed to eventually get healthy—mentally and physically.

38. I'm Taking Control Of My Life

The dog days of August. I had just left the drive-through at Tim Hortons on London Rd. when a major idea came to me. Right there and then, I decided that I wanted to build a house. Yes, I had entertained the thought before, but this time was different. It suddenly . . . felt right. This project was exactly what I needed to get me back to centre. It would be personal—for me, and me alone. I was so ready to commit that I called my realtor and talked for about a half hour. He explained the roadmap I would follow to make my dream a reality.

Valerie and Rob had moved back to Sarnia some years earlier, and after enjoying a couple of pre-owned homes, bought a newly built one on Heritage Park Dr. in the SE quadrant of Sarnia. I knew there were plenty of lots available for sale in and around that immediate area. After some negotiations, I chose the lot directly across from their home. I was really going through with this. I took a shovel and a bottle of beer with me to the empty lot. After excavating the first scoop of dirt, I poured most of the beer into the hole—christening the lot as I did: *Chez Pittsy*. I drank the last swallow as a toast to me and my future accommodations.

Martin was working retail at Home Hardware at the time. I called him with a simple question, knowing he would give me an honest answer. "If you were to build a house in Sarnia today, which builder would you choose, and why?" He didn't hesitate to tell me that Rino of Ritiac Construction would be his choice and proceeded to convince me on the spot that this company was the one for me. I had an initial meeting with Rino, and we were off to the races. This was the second time I had asked one of my brothers for major advice and had yet to be steered wrong.

Perpetual Motion

The next eleven months were dedicated to everything "new build." I spent time designing a home exclusively for me—with the features I truly desired. I meticulously selected paint colours, flooring, cabinetry, colour of granite, appliances, and fixtures needed throughout the house. It was a very busy but hugely rewarding time to be alive. I did have some very valuable help with many of my choices. Julie and I had rekindled our friendship in the last while and, with her flair for interior design, I would have been a fool not to take her advice.

My recreational time on the water, however, was starting to suffer. It was time to consider putting the *PittSea* in dry dock and slapping a *"For Sale"* sign on her. I wasn't sure how serious I was about that act, but I was going to find out. If someone offered me the right price, it was gone. It would sit like that for about fifteen months.

The start date for new home construction was March 11th, 2007. It was going to be a four-month build, and I patiently anticipated the backhoe arriving that early morning. How satisfying it was to see the huge buckets of clay being loaded into several dump trucks as the day progressed.

What I did need to do was sell my house in Point Edward. I hadn't worried too much about this part of the equation because homes in the Point usually sold pretty fast—and for top-dollar too. To that end, I went about sprucing the place up—fixing the minor issues that come with a century home. By mid-April, I was ready to put Alfred St. on the market. I had already decided to sell privately and secured the help of my realtor who agreed to review and write up any potential offers.

It was a Friday, about 4 p.m., when I pounded the *"For Sale"* sign into the grass. I hadn't even gotten the thing secured yet when a car stopped curbside, asking the price. I was actually taken aback, not having given a final thought to what I wanted to get out of this sale. I thought I still had time. I remember blurting out a ridiculous figure and was surprised when the gentleman smiled, nodded, and drove on. I was not sure how to take that reaction, but it was a sign of things to come in short order.

The following day, I had my Rinker in the driveway to do some spring maintenance, prepping it for upcoming showings to interested buyers. My neighbour, Donna, was having a garage sale when she suddenly appeared beside the boat. She had just talked to a couple who had noticed the sign and had expressed an interest in looking through the house. Donna asked me if they could drop by. Even though I was somewhat prepared, this first private showing was going to be a big deal to me—I agreed and waited on their arrival.

They were at the door a minute later. Usually I can read people and get a sense as to what they are feeling—I had no idea with this couple. They were young, quiet, reserved, and most of all, unemotional, in and gone in about twenty minutes. We exchanged pleasantries as they were leaving and I would have bet money that they were just tire kickers. Oh well, I would just keep at it until the right buyer came along.

Two hours later, I received a phone call. The female on the other end of the line, I sensed, was having a difficult time speaking. I immediately had concerns that my children, or some other member of my family was in distress. She was finally able to explain that she and her husband were the ones who had come to see the house earlier that day. "We want to make you an offer on the property," she said, breathlessly. Remembering the couple and my first impressions of their stoic attitude, I was surprised and braced myself for a ridiculous offer—I imagined being low-balled at best. I asked her what they were willing to pay. Between gulps of air, and without hesitation, she told me they were willing to give me full asking price—with absolutely no conditions of inspection, or anything else for that matter. She also said they could come by within the hour with a deposit, to secure the sale. Wow—what the hell just happened?

Once the transaction was completed—the deposit now in my possession—they couldn't contain themselves. They explained why they were so happy to be getting this home. Brad revealed that he'd been born and raised in Point Edward and always wanted to move back to the village. The problem they'd encountered was the lack of housing inventory in their price range—until mine came along. We made arrangements to meet the next day to sign the legal papers. When I called my realtor friend and told him how it all went down, and what I got for the house, he was shocked and very impressed at my negotiating skills—if only he knew! Papers signed, the house was taken off the market forty-eight hours after I put the sign in the ground. The closing date was set for July 1st. I needed to get packing. It all happened that fast.

Perpetual Motion

Time seemed to crawl by during the construction phase. Satisfaction came from attending the property on an almost daily basis. Some builders don't allow their customers anywhere near the site for many reasons, but Rino was great. The workers got used to me being around and everything went quite smoothly. I ended up having a front row seat to all the action after July 1st also. That was the day I moved in with Val and Rob for the six weeks left of the build. It was the perfect arrangement.

August 20th, 2007—another fine day in the annals of achievements in my life. It was moving day. 1621 Heritage Park Dr. was mine. It was a beautiful home of my own design, appointed well by me, and I hadn't skimped on a thing. As it had been with me years ago, being the first member of the family to get my licence, it was now a first also, for new-home construction. I was proud of my accomplishments.

The one thing I had wanted more than anything in this home was a dream kitchen. I certainly got that, and so much more. The granite-covered island was twelve feet in length and encompassed a six-burner gas stovetop, a stand-alone range hood, a prep sink, and a raised bar on the far end. I had ordered all stainless-steel appliances—including double ovens built into the cabinetry. My sixty-bottle capacity wine fridge was dual-zone controlled and built into the design, next to the ovens. I even had a huge walk-in pantry for my dry goods. It was right out of a magazine. Christmas dinner that first year was finally held at my house. I had the space and the facilities to host a great family gathering. I would go on to entertain many guests at *Chez Pittsy*, all of them enjoying my ever-developing culinary skills. Oh, the good old days.

A surprise even to me, was completing the build under budget. Rino actually laughed as he cut me a cheque for overpayment—not ever having had done that before.

Living in Heritage Park, and across the street from my sister, was a dream. The neighbours welcomed me with open arms, and to this day many still remain great friends. The home I had built was everything I had dreamed of, and it continued to provide me with shelter and security that first winter.

Spring was just around the corner, and with that, I made a plan to finish the lower level of the house by myself. With the fine handyman skills I had inherited from my father, I was not afraid to tackle any project. The builder had given me a blank canvas to work with. The only thing done to the basement area during construction was some mandatory main wall supports, and insulation. It was up to me to design the rooms I wanted. The initial list included, two bedrooms, a rec room, a bathroom, and a wine cellar—I had to start somewhere.

I got a phone call in early April. A couple from central Ontario, up Lake Simcoe way, were interested in purchasing the Rinker. I was ecstatic. After a minor repair to some seals in the outdrive, the deal was completed and the boat was on the way to its new home—the end of an era.

This was a good omen. I had been entertaining the idea of getting back into the motorcycle scene since a few of my co-workers and friends had bikes. Now that I had the cash, I went shopping. I purchased a 2008 Kawasaki Vulcan Nomad—a 1600cc touring machine, and by God, touring is what I intended to do. It was like a big comfy couch. I named her Big Blue. It felt so good to be back in the saddle. I immediately started planning a road trip to the east coast for another Boyle family reunion—scheduled for early August.

The solo bike trip east was memorable for many reasons. It was to be my first long-distance sojourn on a two-wheeled vehicle since my unfortunate mishap back in 1978. I was making a grand stop in Quebec City to see a historic concert by none other than Sir Paul McCartney of Beatles fame. I planned a visit with my high school buddy Steve Zub at his house outside of Montreal—finally making my way "home" to the farm in Afton.

Martin and his daughter Shelby were heading east and to the concert also. We booked two rooms at a motel about fifteen minutes from the outdoor venue. I had always wanted to see Sir Paul in concert, having missed my chance way back in '73, when he had played in Toronto. Being in a crowd of over one hundred thousand fans, and sharing the experience with family, really made the experience surreal. Some of the best moments of the evening were when the band struck up the chords to the iconic song "Hey Jude." I immediately took out my phone and called Julie. I didn't say a word but just let her listen to that song in its entirety. It is a shared moment we still treasure.

Hanging with Steve was so much fun! I hadn't seen him in some time, and it was good to catch up. I met his wife and children and was treated royally by all. I only wish I could have bottled that couple of days with him. We haven't seen each other in years, and I do regret that. Hope you are doing well, my old friend.

Big Blue performed admirably. It really was turning into the trip of a lifetime. The only adverse weather I happened upon was when entering Nova Scotia. It steadily rained the three hours it took to get to my parent's home in Beaverbank. I made it, drenched to the bone, but very happy to have landed safely.

The reunion in Afton was filled with love and family. During the opening ceremonies, I had the privilege of introducing my mother, and of course, saying some very kind words about her, when it came time to single out each of the first-generation Boyles—a very special moment for me. It was also that time I met a fellow named Dave Brosha. It wouldn't be the last.

I spent some quality time on two wheels, travelling some of the finest roads in Nova Scotia. The bike was a dream to ride, and I racked up hundreds of kilometres in the ten days I was there. The ride back to Ontario was adventurous with no real agenda mapped out, save for an awesome ride on the *CAT* ferry from Yarmouth, NS to Bar Harbour, ME.

I stayed in Lake Placid, NY, the sight of the 1980 Winter Olympics. What a beautiful village it was. From there I detoured north to Canada for an overnight visit with my boss, Pat Cayen—he was visiting his lady friend in Prescott, Ont. After a night of revelry, I ran through the great state of New York, over to Buffalo, crossed the Peace Bridge at the Canadian border, and on to Welland. It had been a great ride. I finally rested at Stephanie's place before returning home.

Having such a close-knit group of neighbours created its share of good times. Rob and Val decided they were going to start an annual pig roast and Ed and Mary, my neighbours, were going to host it in their large back yard. There were no fences dividing our properties—allowing me to accommodate the live band I had hired to perform. Rick Steeves was a very talented local musician. It was the icing on the cake, along with a delicious BBQ with great friends and neighbours. This event was held each of the four years I lived on Heritage Park. We also did an annual golf tournament in which each neighbour took turns hosting. All of this activity made our little enclave the best neighbourhood I have ever lived in.

My epic bike trips weren't done yet. The following July, Paul Dow and I headed south through a meandering connection of states to arrive at Deal's Gap in Tennessee. This is one of the premier bike roads in all of America—with 318 curves in an eleven-mile stretch. It was harrowing and exhilarating to ride, so much so that we tackled it four times!

On the return route, we took the Blue-Ridge Parkway north to Floyd, VA. Friday nights would never be the same. This small town's main street was transformed into a gathering of the local music talent from the surrounding hillsides. Yes, think gut buckets, washboards, harps, fiddles, old, beat-up guitars, and a crowd of stained, denim-wearing hillbillies playing some of the greatest country-rockin' blues I had ever witnessed. The racks of inventory at Floyd's General Store were cleared to the sides so everyone could get up and dance a jig on the weathered hardwood floors. Beers, whiskey, and moonshine flowed like tap water. It was a sight to see. It would be years later, listening to an Audible of Foo Fighters frontman Dave Grohl's autobiography, *The Storyteller,* that I would be transported back in time to the little town of Floyd. He spoke of experiencing the same Friday night jamboree fun that I had with Paul. I just thought that was cool.

That fall saw an event that makes any dad proud. My only daughter, my little peanut, Stephanie, was getting married. The beautiful ceremony took place in the historic St. Joseph's Catholic Church in Sarnia—the same church her mother and I had gotten married in, some twenty-nine years earlier. My heart burst with pride that day.

In the early spring, I got the news every parent wants to hear. Stephanie was with child. Mary and I were going to be first-time grandparents. There is so much emotion that courses through you when you realize that the fruits of your matrimonial union are now procreating the next generation of your lineage. It was almost too good to comprehend. The big surprise was the announcement, and then the anticipation of twins! This was especially significant because her mother was a twin, and we just loved that the tradition was continuing. There was so much to look forward to. These next several months could not go by fast enough.

39. The Pursuit Of Happiness

I was preparing supper in early November when I got a phone call. It was Julie and her friend Lynda inviting me over for a glass of wine. Seeing no harm in that, I readily agreed and off I went. The conversation that ensued, encouraged by Lynda, led to an awakening of feelings that Julie and I knew we had for each other but were too afraid to parley into a future. Something changed that night. We both talked with brutal honesty. The end result was that our intense feelings for each other could not be ignored any longer. Our friendship was moving beyond our self-imposed barriers, and we officially started dating. I had been waiting for this moment a long time.

Come January, my bags were packed and waiting by the door in anticipation of the word that Stephanie had gone into labour. I was not the only one hanging close to the phone. Mary, the rest of my family, and all of Pete's relatives were ready also.

It was time. I wasted not a minute getting to Welland. Upon seeing my little girl lying on the hospital bed, tummy stretched against the sheets, I knew it would only be a short time before being introduced to our first grandchildren. Mary and I spent some quiet moments together, away from the growing crowd. It was an acknowledgement of the importance of this special occasion, and the significance of our family growing.

After several hours, and an abundance of caution during delivery, Peter appeared at the end of the corridor. As he walked towards us with that happy daddy grin on his face, I felt a deep sense of relief, just knowing that everything was going to be alright and that our worlds had just changed—forever.

Leena Catherine-Anne and Noelle Mary-Anne were born January 7th, 2011, both healthy and weighing in at about 5.5 pounds apiece. What joy!

Each of us took turns holding them for a few short minutes. I marvelled at their little features and fell in love with them instantly. I called Julie to tell her the great news. It truly was hard to describe to her the emotions running through me at that very moment. She understood.

Several times over the next few months, Julie and I travelled to Welland. There was a large family gathering to witness the twins' baptism. We even had a well-attended open house back in Sarnia, to introduce my granddaughters to the world. The universe was aligned.

That July, Julie and I decided to get engaged—again. We had announced our engagement once before, only to have it end after a brief tenure. This time would be different. I was head over heels in love with her. It was a joyous occasion celebrated at a fine restaurant overlooking the St. Clair River. We immediately started making plans for the future, and the first order of business was the sale of Heritage Park. We wanted to start fresh. The house sold within a week. Now we needed to find a place of our own. We talked about wanting to hold our wedding in our new house. Once that was established, plans developed quickly—settling on a two-storey, ranch-style home on Twin Lakes Dr. This was a beautifully established subdivision in the north end of Sarnia—a great place for new beginnings. We got the keys October 31st, just in time to hand out Halloween candies to our new neighbourhoods' children.

As my realtor buddy Cordell said at the time, "She's sure got good bones, b'y." We also had much work to do—to bring it up to date. The wedding was set for December 1st, which meant we had much to accomplish in four weeks. We knew we couldn't do it all so set some priorities. We had to get the upstairs bathroom gutted and remodelled, and the reams of '70s-style floral wallpaper off the walls—this all to make way for a fresh coat of paint throughout the main living area. We enlisted the help of friends and family to deal with the grunt work. There was a parade of people with wash buckets and scrapers scratching at the walls, for days. The hundreds of yards of that hideous wallpaper was the first to go, elbow grease being the repetitive action each day. Meanwhile, I destroyed the bathroom, gutted everything, installed a new tub-surround, ceramic flooring, toilet, custom vanity, and fixtures. A fresh coat of paint finished it off—what a stressful time.

The main floor walls, after being stripped and prepped, were painted in colours of Julie's choosing. She was so good at interior design, matching colour palettes in each room. I never once questioned her design prowess.

We were married in our new home the evening of December 1st. What I thought was going to be a purely magical day turned out even better than I had dreamed. Several minutes before Julie and I were to be married, the front door opened and in walked my mother and father! I was speechless. My parents, in their eighties, had driven the two thousand kilometres from Nova Scotia to Sarnia to attend our wedding. They had actually been in the city for a few days, staying at Valerie's—all the time praying I wouldn't show up there prior to the big day. It was the best wedding gift I could have received. The whole affair was a fabulous celebration of family and friends. I had met Julie just over ten years earlier and was smitten from the start—not ever dreaming that one day she would be my wife. Dreams do come true.

Next up—Christmas. We again had a house full of friends and relatives, awesome music, great food, and lots of love. Julie had started looking into places we thought we'd like to go for our honeymoon. She's a meticulous planner, and after much online research, we settled on the Riu Palace in Puerto Vallarta, Mexico.

We spent a week in the sun, strolling the beach, doing tequila tours, roaming the town, and enjoying the all-inclusive nature of our palatial resort. It was great to get away after the whirlwind efforts of the last couple of months.

The bigger project we had discussed, and now agreed upon, was the complete "down to the studs" renovation of our kitchen and dining room. At the time of purchase, these two rooms were separated by a wall with a pocket door between. We figured the space would serve us better if opened up. Julie was again tasked to do the design. I had budgeted dollars from the sale of Heritage Park to complete this renovation in style. After many months, and true to her talents, Julie came up with a beautifully arranged room design that was truly impressive. Now it was just a matter of finding, and eventually purchasing, all the features she had included in the plans.

We had always discussed this project in terms of me doing the majority of the work after I retired. There was, at the time, no retirement date written in stone much beyond the fact I wanted to complete my required thirty-five years of service in October. This magic number of years was the maximum I would have to contribute to my OMERS pension plan. Any number of months beyond that date was a bonus. At 7 percent of my gross wages, it was going to be a significant easing of the financial burdens of living.

40. The Path Forward: My Way

The next few months were rough—shit I didn't see coming. Julie was having health issues, and she wasn't getting any relief from the many doctors she consulted. I tried to understand all that was happening, but I now realize I was incapable of comprehending the severity of her condition. I make no excuses. I was blind to her debilitating pain. She hid it well—most of the time. I only wish I knew then, the things I have learned since.

Meanwhile, back in my world, the bottom was falling out of the great set-up we had at Sarnia Fire—more to the point, it was spinning out of control. Chief Cayen, retired DC Bondy, DC Kingyens, and I had cultivated a team of crackerjack firefighters and support staff. We had turned our department around in the last several years—it now being a cohesive unit with a strong management team, and it seemed the world was ours for the taking.

In late November, I received devastating news. My friend, my mentor, my chief, had been arrested that morning on criminal charges stemming from alleged incidents in his past. I was in disbelief. Not a fucking chance in hell were these allegations true. I just knew it. He had been arrested, jailed, and bailed, all in a matter of a day. This shocking event spread across the airwaves and over social media like wildfire, and subsequently, he was told by City Hall not to report for duty for the foreseeable future. Being the senior DC in the department, I was now in charge.

There are moments in life when you make a stand. Your belief system, which you have cultivated and lived by your whole life, is thrown into question. I took a stand. I would not let any self-doubt come between my belief that he was innocent, and the eventual scorching of his character in the media—and at the firehall. I called for a full-on, department-wide, in-person meeting—attendance mandatory. I needed to get a grip on the situation and try to quell the rampant rumour mill. I was shocked and extremely disappointed by the tone of many of the members. Without hearing the facts, without a trial, without the "innocent until proven guilty" mantra of the Canadian legal system of justice, they laid him out and sliced up his character with no hesitation whatsoever. With a final plea for restraint in commenting on the issue publicly, I left the meeting. That plea fell mostly on deaf ears.

At times like this, you find out who your friends are. There were a handful of members who understood the logistics of my position and held back from getting into a discussion on the issues at hand. All we could do was weather the storm and let the legal system do its work. It didn't make for a very pleasant Christmas season, the whole affair driving a wedge between members of the brotherhood, friendships, and eventually, even relationships—such were the polarizing opinions of the armchair detectives. To add insult to injury, Chief Cayen was outright fired from the service, unceremoniously, in early January. He hadn't even had a court date yet.

I will not drag this out any longer. After several court dates over the next couple of years, one erroneously culminating in a short stint of incarceration, my friend, my mentor, my chief, was finally, and fully exonerated of all charges. He was a free man—I just fucking knew it. To this day, we speak on a regular basis. This unfortunate episode in his life took a huge toll on him and his family and, as much as he outwardly plays the jolly fella he always was, I know. I have seen the hurt, the pain, the loss of a career, the health issues that it has caused. I also know that I stood by him at his lowest point, and was there for him and his family when they needed my support. The whole thing still bothers me—probably always will. I love you, my friend.

As the initial throes of the drama played out, I was absorbing the blows as best I could. I was stressed for a myriad of reasons over the Christmas season and was hoping for some clarity, going into the new year. That was not meant to be. What happened next shocked the entire community, and beyond. My good friend's sister, Noelle, went missing New Year's Eve, and by the early morning of January 1st, 2013, it was not looking good.

Her lifeless body was eventually recovered from a wooded area outside of town. She had been abducted and brutally murdered—in the wee hours of the morning. Fuck—could it get any worse? I know how it affected me. I just couldn't fathom how the family and relatives were coping—a tragedy beyond words.

Noelle was a giver. She was known for her spunk, generosity, and love of her students at school. After a time for grieving, and the long process of healing had begun, "Noelle's Gift" was born, a charity carrying her namesake and tasked with making sure all the young students in Lambton County grew up to be *smash hits*, one of her favourite sayings. The charity raised money in many ways—through golf tournaments, health and fitness forums—and the big one, the annual gala. In the second year of the gala's existence, I was asked to be the official photographer for the event. I was thrilled and accepted readily. I would go on to do that official function the following year also—and will always cherish the honour to have been tasked with such a privilege.

Back at work, there were decisions to be made. My first priority was the continuity of operations at SFRS. This meant making sure the powers that be at city hall fulfilled their duties as laid out in the Municipal Act and install a permanent fire chief to replace the former. We had several intense meetings over the next month in which I laid it out in plain English. They needed to hire a chief, and the process needed to start now. They stalled. I put it in writing. I pointed to the exact wording in the Act in which I predicated my argument. I even suggested that I would step up, and assume the role as interim chief, but they needed to act upon this issue as soon as possible. At the last meeting with the CAO, the mayor, human resources, and DC Kingyens, I again addressed the urgency of the matter. Before the meeting broke up, I made it clear that I expected a solution to this impasse within a week. They came back with their solution. They suggested that myself, the senior DC, and DC Kingyens, junior to me in departmental seniority, should split the chief's duties, two weeks on and two weeks off. The fucking absurdity of their suggestion floored me. It wasn't that John and I were not capable of doing that, but that nowhere in the Municipal Act did it allow for such an outlandish arrangement.

I broke—enough bullshit already. I drafted my retirement notice in the form of a letter to the mayor, all members of council, and the head of human resources. I didn't hold back. In it, I expressed my gratitude for over thirty-five years of employment with the City. I was honoured to have served the citizens of our community for so long. I also chastised those who needed to hear it, for the asinine way they were handling the current situation. Once that decision was made, there was no turning back. I was fifty-six years old, about to walk out of the same department I had started my career in all those years ago, and ready to begin a new life with Julie. What could go wrong?

Finally, the big day came—March 15th, 2013. I woke up feeling a strange sense of calm. I had been a very active career firefighter for thirty-five years and six months exactly. It was time for a rest, or at the very least, it was time for a change of venue. The day started off as normal as this milestone would allow. I went to the office, as I did every day. DC Kingyens met me in the back lot with a big smile, and a reminder that the guys were gathering upstairs at 3 p.m. for cake, ice cream, and a final send-off. I had been part of this same tradition many times before—ushering a brother into retirement in this manner—but now, it was really happening to me.

Most of the morning was taken up with phone calls from my brothers and sisters in the fire service expressing congratulations and extending thanks for my years of service. Many kind words passed through the receiver that day. I took my time with each one. I wanted to remember this day for the rest of my life. My distributors, the men and women I bought our equipment from, also called with farewell messages. I would be remiss if I didn't say I relished in every conversation. These people were my extended family, and I was going to miss them. But the biggest surprise of all was the call I received from the CAO of the City of Sarnia, Ann Tuplin, asking me if I was free for lunch. I was honoured that she thought enough of me to include me in her very busy schedule. We went to Lola's Lounge and had a wonderful lunch and great conversation. Ann was getting ready to do some major renovations to her own house on the lake and she and I exchanged many tips and tricks for a successful project. We have since become good friends and I will cherish her charm and wisdom always.

I walked into the kitchen/lounge area at the appointed time. It was packed with my family, friends, co-workers, many retirees, and special guests from the Fire Marshal's Office. I was overcome with emotion. Several speeches ensued—with each one a gift commemorating my time in the service. The gathering lasted about an hour with only two more planned events scheduled before the honorary ride home in the fire truck. The first was my photograph taken in front of the digital sign on the front lawn which announced my retirement in big red letters, and the second was an interview with the *Sarnia Observer*. Not surprisingly, that interview, and story can also be recalled with a google search.

For the final time in my storied career, I climbed into the lead pump, parked and idled on the apron out front of the hall. I wish I could count how many times I had done that over the last 426 months—but it didn't matter now. It was over. We proceeded, "lights and sirens," homeward. When I exited the vehicle in front of my house, I'm sure the neighbours were wondering what was going on. I doffed my uniform cap and threw it high into the air. I was greeted by close friends and family waiting for me on the driveway. The first order of business was a shot of whisky to begin the celebrations—which I knew would go into the wee hours of the morning.

Tradition in the fire service is to have a gathering at some point after you leave the job so that friends, acquaintances, and extended family can have a venue to express their congratulations also. I chose to have mine that same night. I wanted to have a shindig and relieve some of the stress that had been lingering the last several months. This night was as good as any to let it all out.

We gathered at Side Pockets on Lambton Mall Rd. for about 6 p.m. The place filled up fast and revelry ensued—I didn't have to buy a drink all night. I was so appreciative of the outpouring of love and the kind words spoken—everyone there to celebrate the lengthy and successful career I was putting to bed. The big question posed to me most that evening was, "What are your plans for retirement?" My pat answer: "Travel, write, and take pictures."

The party continued until well past midnight. I was honoured to have been given such a warm send-off—by some of the best people and co-workers ever.

PART 4

41. Toil And Loss: Goodbye, Mom

Now retired, I had earlier laid out some goals and now needed to get to them. Firstly, there was the matter of that major renovation to the main floor of our home. With Julie's plans drawn up for an open concept kitchen/dining area with new cupboards, flooring, and appliances, it was going to take the better part of the spring and summer. I was hoping to be finished by Labour Day. The other to-do things were to renew my interest in photography, write my memoirs, and travel. If you are reading this paragraph, I must have succeeded in at least one of those items on the list.

The next day, feeling a bit worse for wear, and with Julie's encouragement, I swung the first hammer blow through the drywall in the kitchen. The renovations had begun. No different than actually building a whole house, I toiled in sweat, lost several pounds, and really enjoyed that summer of change. As planned, I was doing most of it on my own and had mapped out a timeline with September 1st targeted as our completion date. The demolition phase was labour-intensive. There were seven layers of old flooring needing to come up, and it truly was the nightmare it sounds like. Every wall was taken to the studs, shored up, and re-insulated. New plumbing and wiring were installed. The new ceiling and drywall were finished and prepped for painting. I wasn't a fool. Where I needed help with a segment of the completion, I asked. My former neighbour, Ed Teft, a master electrician and a fabulous friend, helped me with all the electrical. He performed his magic, and I was so grateful for his expertise. Sarnia Cabinets did a marvelous job of implementing Julie's design, and installation went swimmingly. We bought our appliances from Northend Appliance, and as is their standard, had everything delivered on time, and in perfect order. The only other thing I didn't do was the installation of the ceramic floor tiles in the area of the renovations. After the recent experience doing the bathroom on the second floor, I felt it appropriate to farm that job out to an expert.

After months of preparation, and several more in the actual work phase of the renovations, the project was complete, on time, and on budget. I was very proud of my accomplishments and give my dear father all the credit for teaching me the skills required to handle such a task. Julie had designed and created a functional workspace with lots of cupboards, drawers, and beautiful appliances. It was showcase-worthy, right out of *Better Homes and Gardens*. She and I were ecstatic with the results. We immediately started creating some great meals together—her fabulous design providing ample space to do just that.

For the last several months, the family was receiving regular updates on Mom's health. Her dementia was slowly edging towards full-blown Alzheimer's and was getting more acute each day. She had been diagnosed with cancer earlier in the year, so there was concern on several fronts.

The phone call came the first week of December. Mom had fallen in the bathroom, and it was determined the fall was caused by the onset of a stroke. She was now bedridden. I knew I needed to make my way east at the earliest possible moment, not knowing if, or how long she had to live. Karen and Joan were with her constantly—making sure she was taken care of, but there was Dad to look after also. They needed help. I was on a plane within hours.

I arrived the evening of December 11th and was immediately given an update on Mom's condition. We agreed to split the caregiver duties between the three of us—as many tasks needed attention. We would eventually get some more help, but the first few days were exhausting. Not only did I assist in nursing but took it upon myself to become resident chef for the duration—how long, we were not sure. I created nutritious meals for a crowd most nights. My sisters, now including Lorraine and Valerie, just in from Ontario, helped to spell me off a few nights because of sheer exhaustion on my part. Julie, sensing time was short, arrived on Christmas Eve.

By late Christmas Eve, most everyone who was coming east was home. Mom had stopped eating. Lorraine and I had been given medical permission to administer doses of morphine at regular intervals to keep her pain-free, and for the last couple of days, she was comfortable. I had hand-fed her a couple of small bites of French toast the morning before, and that was the last of her appetite. She was now only hours away from passing. We all knew it and handled it in our own ways.

So, it came to pass—on her most treasured holiday of the year, at 11:58 a.m., on December 25th, 2013, as witnessed by all who gathered around her bedside—a bright ray of sunlight broke through the clouded skies and shone through the bedroom window—directly onto her face. She opened her eyes, turned toward that ray of sunshine, sighed, took her last breath—and she was gone. She had kept her word. My beautiful mother, Helen Marie, the matriarch of our family, surrounded by those who loved her, left us to have supper with the Lord. As much as you would think this timing would be devastating to all, it wasn't. We viewed that display of rapture as a glorious miracle, just as her life had been.

Father Craig Cameron, Karen's oldest child, and now a Roman Catholic priest, said mass in the living room that afternoon. We went ahead with a big turkey dinner prepared by the nieces, nephews, and cousins in attendance, made time to pay our final respects to Mom during the remainder of the day, and finally witnessed the removal of her body from the place she had lovingly called home for so many years. We laid her to rest the following week and then got about the business of making sure Dad was going to be ok. Most of the gang who had come home for the funeral had now departed, as life's needs had to be met. I knew I was staying for some time yet, to assist in those endeavours.

42. I Fall To Pieces

Even though they had moved from Ontario to this beautiful property back in 1985, Dad was more than willing to finally sell it, now that Mom was gone. After talking to him about that possibility, he assured us he had been thinking about just that for several months, and now wanted to go spend the rest of his days close to his extended family in Truro. Joan, being the power of attorney, was going to make that happen.

After helping my sisters get Mom's affairs in order, I flew home to Sarnia. It was nice to be back. At first, everything seemed fine. I had been thinking that Julie and I had never been as close as we were those ten days in Nova Scotia. I was wrong. I also can't explain why sometimes shit happens, and there's not a damn thing anyone can do about it. I adored that girl so much, and it seemed no matter what we said or did, we couldn't right the ship. What to do? I had to leave.

Finally, just shy of a month after arriving home from Mom's funeral, I packed the truck, and left for the east—again. I knew I needed some time to clear my head and figured I could be of help getting my father's things in order—this to facilitate the ease of his eventual move to Truro. Dad was surprised to see me back and we talked well into that first night. While there, I threw myself into the daunting task of cleaning out his garage and woodworking shop. Years of accumulation, both in materials and tools, lay before me. It was not going to be a one-day job. It took me two full weeks to create a semblance of order to that space—but it was exactly what I needed to take my mind off of my emotional state.

In the meantime, after several phone conversations, I knew our marriage was rapidly falling apart. We made the decision to split the second week of March. I was totally devastated, but there was nothing I could do to stop it. I can honestly say I don't recall much from those three months at Dad's. I hadn't even begun to grieve my mother's death—and now had to deal with the loss of my wife too. Some retirement this was turning out to be.

After more sporadic conversation, it was agreed that I would return to Sarnia the first week of May, and Julie would be out of the matrimonial home by then. Making my way to Ontario, I chose to stay at Stephanie's for a few days to come to grips with the inevitable. While driving on a crowded stretch of Hwy 401 outside of Toronto, and only two hours from Welland, I suffered an instantaneous, full-blown panic attack. I seriously thought I was going to die. Miraculously, I managed to get my vehicle pulled off to the shoulder without crashing—I have no idea how. After resting and self-medicating—thankfully I had medicinals with me, I managed the nightmare ride to Stephanie's. The next several days were spent mostly in bed, my body's way of trying to cope with the mental trauma. After a needed rest, I arrived in Sarnia days later. Knowing exactly what I would be walking into—only for the fact that this exact situation had happened with Pam and I years earlier—Paul agreed to enter the house with me. As expected, it was void of anything . . . Julie. She was gone. I broke down and cried.

The next three months were a blur. All I remember for sure was the constant niggling of flight. I was not happy, and really needed to figure out what the future held. I knew almost certainly it would not be in Sarnia.

Paul had always liked the house on Twin Lakes Dr., and after some lengthy discussion about my future, he suggested that he buy the property. If I was to make a move to get the hell out of town, this was going to facilitate it greatly. But where to go?

It didn't take long to formulate a plan. I had been to Shaun's apartment in Kingston, Ont. a couple of times in the recent past and was fond of the city he now called home, so I travelled to the old town at the headwaters of the St. Lawrence River to look at rental properties. Again, the laws of attraction were set in motion. I found myself a great one-bedroom condo in the historic Prince George Hotel, right next door to Kingston's famous city hall. Located across from Confederation Park on the waterfront, the original hotel was built in 1806 and had been recently renovated into thirteen lofts. Mine was on the second floor—with an open-space design and had large living room windows overlooking Market Square, the premier gathering spot in the downtown corridor. The square was also the site of the swearing-in ceremony of our first prime minister, Sir John A. MacDonald. Still nurturing my love of history, I just knew this move was going to be good for me. What I didn't know at the time was how much of an impact Kingston would have on my future. I was to find out in short order.

Packing and purging became my everyday routine. When all was done, I had pared my worldly possessions down to the contents of one twenty-four-foot U-Haul truck. The house was sold, and all my loose ends cleared up. Julie and I met at the house the night before I left, and we talked for a couple of hours about many things. I think that was the toughest part of the move. I still loved her and knew I was going to miss her dearly.

The next day, Paul and I headed on down the highway, his car strapped to a flatbed trailer being towed behind the U-Haul. He wanted to help me move, and I really appreciated the offer. As much as I was looking forward to my new adventure, it was great to have my buddy along for emotional support.

43. Kingston

The move went smoothly and it didn't take long to get the place in order. Other than Shaun, I knew nobody in Kingston, and the feeling of being incognito was at times refreshing and other times overwhelming. That situation wouldn't last long either.

Relocating to another part of the province after spending almost my whole life in Sarnia was something I hadn't given much thought to over the years. I think I assumed I was a Southern Ontario lifer. The original draw to relocate was twofold. My sense of the adventurous spirit I'd had from my youth was starting to take hold of my thoughts again, and Shaun was now making a life for himself—post-university, in a city he hadn't grown up in. My first time to Kingston was back in the mid-'80s. During my executive board days for the SPFFA, I had attended the annual OPFFA Convention in that city, and I remember liking the old-world charm and atmosphere. I ended up renting my loft about a three-minute walk from where the convention had been held—at the Holiday Inn at the end of Princess St. In all my years being on my own, with buddies, or when married, I had never lived in an apartment-style complex. I always enjoyed having a lawn and a yard to care for, whether I rented or owned. This new set-up was going to be a first.

Lucky for me, (but not so much for my liver) the first floor of the Prince George Hotel housed three pubs. They were all owned by the same company but functioned quite independent of one another. The Tir na NÓg, or the 'Nog, as the three were collectively known, enjoyed an almost cult-like following from the Queen's University, St. Lawrence College, and Royal Military College crowds. Montes was the Friday night jazz spot, complete with a great house band playing all the standards, and more. The Old Speckled Hen was a small, narrow room that was alive with laughter and fellowship, a great meeting place for tourists and townsfolk alike. Main was the big pub with an Irish flair. Live bands were scheduled every weekend for as long as I lived there. Ironically, my loft on the second floor was directly above the stage in Main. When awake, I truly could hear every beat of the bass being played all weekend long. It's a good thing I love music. When I told of my proximity to the stage from upstairs, I was asked if the music bothered me at all. My standard answer was something to the effect that I am deaf in my left ear, so I sleep on my right. I couldn't hear but a muffled thump of the drums and bass combination when in that position.

Full disclosure: I have lost most of the hearing in my left ear and about 50 percent of the hearing in my right ear, I believe caused by the accumulated effect of various insidious noises created by sirens, loud machinery, continuous radio chatter, and a myriad of other fire-ground sounds—not to mention a rock concert or two. I have had a hearing aid for years but only wear it if I am socializing. There is certainly not much reason to wear it out in my present circumstances, as you will come to know.

The entrances to all three pubs were accessible from the lobby inside the building. I literally didn't have to go outside to socialize or experience any adverse climate conditions to get an adult beverage or some of the best in-house-made pub grub in town. I just knew I was going to enjoy my new arrangements, and it didn't take long to meet some of the finest humans I know, who I still to this day, call friends.

Still fresh off my career at Sarnia Fire—the last several as Deputy Chief—I had also been a member of the Ontario Fire Chief's Association and still owned several tees and golf shirts with various fire-related logos embroidered on the front. Wearing one such *OFC* golf shirt shortly after I settled in, I ventured down to Main to quench my thirst, and maybe grab a bite. Being still unfamiliar with the layout and routine, I sat at the first table inside the door, quickly noting a bearded gentleman walk past me a couple of times. Each time he passed, he looked me over in an inquisitive manner. By his movements—and his kilted attire, I assumed he worked there, and it wasn't long before he stopped and greeted me with a kind smile. Calvin McGregor was the manager on duty that night and what caught his eye was the very familiar lettering on my shirt. He quickly explained that his dad was a life-long member of the Ontario fire service and had retired as chief of his department. The OFC lettering he saw on my chest brought back wonderful memories of his dad, who he had lost to cancer not many years before. It was the beginning of a great friendship, forged from a mutual respect of the dedication it takes to spend a lifetime as a first responder. He and I would spend countless hours discussing the fire service, the restaurant industry, our mutual love for photography, and the nuances of a fine dram of Scotch. Cheers, my friend. I miss you.

The other T-shirt I wore often had *Sarnia Fire* stenciled across the back. Again, sitting at a window seat in The Hen one evening, I couldn't help but notice a gentleman I had seen on several occasions enjoying a meal by himself. He was the classic regular, or so it seemed. He introduced himself as John Manoll. I would come to find out that John was a former police officer, now retired from his position as police chief of the City of Brockville. We certainly had lots in common, and again, through the commitment and dedication to our public service careers, became fast friends. Even after eventually leaving Kingston, and upon my subsequent visits, I would stay with John at his condo just a block from where I lived.

Every spring, the pubs, and restaurants in the area would install their summer patios in the outdoor spaces around their buildings. This was a great tourist draw to the city, but us locals, and many of the university and college crowds, used them frequently. The 'Nog was no different. Located on Ontario St. across from the lake, it was the ideal place to kick back on a beautiful summer's eve and enjoy a burger and beer. It became my happy place real fast, and if I needed a change of venue, I only had to look across the street corner to several other outdoor patios calling my name.

The 'Nog had the best bartenders, chefs, and wait staff ever. I had never been one to claim a neighbourhood pub as my own, but my current living arrangements, and the proximity to the hustle and bustle of pub life right below me certainly changed all that. It wasn't long before I too, was a regular—treated like royalty whenever I came in for some social interaction. Calvin, Jay, Eric, Mike C, Zeek, Tyler, Mike M, Gary, Utley, Eldoo, Patrick, Dan, and Josh, plus too many more to mention, all made me feel like I belonged, and we became good friends. I specifically named only the guys in that first list of wait staff because the girls totally deserve a whole section of their own. I can't even begin to do justice in the way I was accepted by the staff of the 'Nog, and I mean that from my heart.

A day or two after meeting Calvin, I was hungry and didn't feel like creating something in the kitchen, so I wandered downstairs to eat. Looking down at my phone, I hadn't noticed her approach—until she spoke. I did a double take. Standing before me was a bronze-skinned goddess holding a menu. Her smile radiant, her long, shimmering, jet-black hair pulled back in a ponytail, her voice like silk, her gracious greeting—all combined to instantly put me at ease. If this was how I was to be greeted upon entering my neighbourhood pub, I thought, I could be sure to eat here every night. We hit it off instantly. She introduced herself as Nadra and after some pleasantries left to fill my drink order. The next action was to write her name in my notes app so I wouldn't forget it—not that there was any chance of that! There would be many conversations, and late-night therapy sessions with this one. We still keep in touch often and I will forever cherish her friendship.

Then there was Shannon. She was young enough to be my daughter, but for whatever reason we just hit it off. Her inviting smile, big hugs, and natural beauty were what I loved to see and experience just about every day. She made me feel warm. It's hard to describe. She really was my best friend in Kingston. After I eventually left for good, she too moved away, finding her way to Toronto to enter the real estate game. I told her I was venturing back to Kingston to spend the July 1st weekend there, and she came from Toronto to hang out. Now, that was fun! Miss ya, dear girl!

Charlotte, Elya, Daniela, Rachel, Amanda, Agnes, Kally, Logan, MacKenzie, Becca, Ashley K, Ashley M, Danielle, Samantha, Theresa, Carley, Emily, Jessica, Chaze Ann, and several more "salt of the earth" women all became more than wait staff at a bar. I could spend a lifetime telling stories of each of them, unique in their own right. I keep in touch with most of them today, and I know we all cared for one another deeply. I still do.

My Armed Forces buddy Simon is a national treasure. When I first met him, he was quiet and unassuming—sitting at the bar with his pint of Harp or a Guinness in hand. A veteran of several nasty war-time conflicts, he never really talked about it openly. It was only after getting to know him on a deeper level that we had a great chinwag one night about our life choices and how what we had seen, and done, had affected us in a personal way. He and his chocolate lab Charlie Bear still live in Kingston, and when I go back to the city, we make sure to get together to quaff a few grogs. Miss you, brother.

I finally got a family doctor about a year after relocating to Kingston. Dr. Marion Luka was small in stature but large and in charge—smart and sophisticated. Upon initial examination, and after talking to her about my previous health, she immediately decided, among other things, that I needed a sleep study. Once arranged, I was to go to Kingston General Hospital to their overnight sleep clinic to determine whether I had sleep apnea. All the classic symptoms were present, but a clinical diagnosis was appropriate. It didn't take long to hear those life altering words: "You need a CPAP machine."

Truth be known, Dr. Luka most assuredly saved my life. My breathing was stopped or obstructed over thirty times an hour and it was having a hugely detrimental effect on my sleep patterns and amount of quality sleep attained. Because of all those factors, my blood pressure was affected, and heart function too.

The testing and subsequent diagnosis had taken place in July of 2016, and within a few days I had been given a loaner machine to assist me in getting used to it prior to obtaining my own. I had heard horror stories of wearing such an archaic device while trying to maintain some sort of normalcy during sleep. To my surprise, I found immediate relief from my headaches, dry sore throat, cessation of my cough, and general exhaustion during the following days. It didn't take me long to get used to wearing the head gear to bed. Today, I am past my seventh anniversary of use and on my second machine.

Along with bloodwork to determine the path forward in my health journey, she adjusted my blood pressure and cholesterol meds that I had been taking on a regular basis. I was in relatively good shape. And lucky for me, Dr. Luka was determined to keep me that way.

I was enjoying my new surroundings and especially the wonderful friendships I was making, but what I really enjoyed was when folks from Sarnia would come through town and we would visit. Some would stay overnight—either at my place or at one of the local hotels in the area. This happened several times, and I so appreciated the company. Stephanie and family, Lorraine, Shannon, and Rebecca, Kat and Aaran, and several others made their way east for a visit. One such couple, Jill Carroll and Graham Emslie, whom I worked with at SFRS, happened to be on their way to Nova Scotia in July of 2016 to see friends when they stopped for the night. It was great seeing them again and we sat on the patio at the 'Nog for hours reminiscing through laughter and tears, at the antics we had been through together over the years. Graham and I both attended that convention at the Holiday Inn down the street, as previously mentioned, and his memory was much better than mine in recalling some of the highlights of our first time in the Limestone City.

What makes the world go around is the fact that we cannot do one damn thing about the past except preserve the memories, good and bad—again, my true reason for penning this book. The future is a giant unknown, only to be influenced by the things we can control, which in reality is not much at all. All we have are our todays in which we can make a conscious effort to affect a positive outcome on life in general.

That evening spent with Graham and Jill will forever be a fabulous memory for me. You see, less than three months later, Graham would be diagnosed with a terminal illness, and succumb to that dreadful death sentence a short six weeks after finding out the news. He and I had some great times together. His loss devastated me. Fuck cancer.

Living above an Irish Pub really came in handy on March 17th of each year. St. Patrick's Day was quite the celebrated event in Kingston, and especially at the 'Nog. I'm sure fire-code occupation limits were exceeded several times during the course of these particular events. A group of us, including Chris, Keith, John, Simon, and of course Shaun, were guaranteed a free pass to the festivities—no waiting in line for hours like most pub crawlers did. I truly felt at home any time I walked down that flight of stairs to enter any one of the three bars. It wasn't uncommon to venture to all three, several times a night. After all, each had their own vibe, and there was no way I wanted to miss out on any of the fun. It did help that I knew every one of the staff on duty on any given night and really just wanted to hang with all of them. I thought of them as family, and they did me also.

44. Soup Anyone? The Restaurant Years

You might be wondering why I really chose Kingston of all places. Besides the fact that Shaun had moved into a vacant, upper loft of a building on Princess St., the main corridor through the town a year earlier, there was so much more to it. His girlfriend, Yasmin, had been born and raised there, and as they were planning their future together, it was only logical the Limestone City was the place they would put down roots and raise a family. I hadn't spent much time with Shaun over the last several years during his university days, so it was also a great opportunity to get closer to my son. The other reason was huge. He and his in-laws had been brainstorming, scheming, and now putting plans together to open a cafe on the ground level of the same vacant building that housed his loft, owned by Yasmin's parents. Although I wasn't going to be a part of that future operation, I thought I could help with logistics, and even do a celebrity chef gig once in a while after the place got up and running. Shaun and I had always loved to create great meals together, ever since he had started working in the restaurant industry during his four years at Guelph. Through several years of apprenticeship in some of the best dining establishments around, he had become quite the talented chef in his own right, and I just knew I wanted to be closer to that action.

Much preliminary work had been done to move the project along, and I could see the sparkle in Shaun's eyes when we talked about it. Being only four city blocks apart, he and I would meet at my local pub several nights a week to discuss the progress. It truly felt great to be starting a new life in a new city with nothing but the future I would design ahead of me.

It was about the 15th of November. I had only been in the city for six weeks. I walked over to the yet-to-be-opened cafe, only to find Shaun and his mother-in-law standing in the space they were hoping would be occupied by the future kitchen facilities. The looks on their faces reminded me of a grieving family. Something was definitely wrong.

As fate would have it, the plans for the construction, outfitting, and opening of The Small Batch Cafe, their dream, had suddenly come to a screeching halt. The financing they had thought was assured was not. The hard facts of reality were being discussed among them when I walked in. Upon hearing the first snippets of the bad news, my heart ached. I felt so bad for Shaun. He had moved to this city, built up his hopes of owning his own business—of being a successful young entrepreneur—only to have them dashed by unfulfilled promises.

Later that day, sitting in my loft, stewing about my son's predicament, I did what most dads would do. I started to entertain the idea of lending a helping hand. I had just closed the deal on the house in Sarnia and had some liquid cash coming to me by the end of the month. As had happened almost ten years earlier when deciding to take the deputy chief's position at SFRS, I mouthed the same words that would change the course of my life—yet again.

Shaun met me at the pub, and after plying him with a couple of drafts to calm his nerves, I presented my proposal. I had been thinking about the intricacies of taking on this financial burden for most of the day and came to only one conclusion. As a father, I could not bear to see my son's dream go down the drain if I could at all help in any way. So, I uttered those words again: "What about me?"

His first reaction was one of misunderstanding, I'm sure. After he had grasped the comment and applied it to his immediate dilemma, his face lit up again. As was expected, he declined the offer on the grounds that he didn't want me to take on such a financial commitment. We discussed the pros and cons of such a partnership and in the end decided to go ahead with our discussed arrangement. I promised the partners I would give them three years of my time, and finances. I was going to look after the books and give Shaun a hand in the kitchen when needed, which for the first year turned out to be every day. I would reassess my role when that time period passed.

After a week or so of getting the papers signed, and making sure the others involved were good with all of it, the planning continued full throttle. There was much to do. We hired an architect to design our ideas, and once that was done and signed off, we hired a contractor to oversee the renovations and construction of the new facilities.

The building was gutted to the studs, and everything from new wiring to a complete drywall job, new flooring, washrooms, and fully functioning kitchen, rose from the shell of the old futon store. It was an exciting time for sure. Recipes were perfected, specialty coffee was agreed upon, staff were being interviewed, and new equipment was arriving daily.

All the while this was going on, I tried to maintain a semblance of privacy, and enjoy my retirement. To that end, I researched and finally bought my first semi-professional-grade digital camera, a Nikon D5300 DX. I had no idea how to use it but was determined to learn. This time around, I was not going to keep it in automatic mode as I had with my Canon AE-1 many years earlier. I didn't have a clue at the time how this seemingly normal purchase would again change my life in immeasurable ways. Looking back, it was the single most important thing I did for me, and my plans for my future.

After some hiccups with Hector, the initial contractor we had hired, bailing on the job three quarters of the way through, we hired a new contractor to finish the interior. In record time, after applying the final spit and polish to the space, The Small Batch Cafe was ready to open. We had done the impossible.

One of the best things to happen that first day was the surprise visit from my great friend Carole from Sarnia. She had driven all through the night to make the cafe opening at 7 a.m. It was so good to have a familiar face to help out and calm my opening-day nerves. And yes, we even put her to work making one of our first batches of veggie stock. Carole was a trooper, and I am so grateful for her friendship. By the end of that first day, we were all exhausted. Oh ya, we grossed a whopping $175.

Getting any new business off the ground, especially in a very competitive market such as Kingston, was no easy feat. We had done lots of advertising, met with the right people, and developed a top-notch operation from the get-go. Still, it was a slow start, at least in our opinion, but by the end of the first month, we were seeing a larger clientele, and even had our regulars coming in every day to enjoy the fruits of our collective labour.

Everything we made was from scratch. We blended our mayonnaise and aiolis fresh every day. Our salad dressings were crafted by Shaun and I and were so good, we should have bottled them. We used our two industrial-strength panini presses on our sandwiches, which made them quite out of the ordinary. Brie and pear, pastrami on rye, porchetta made in house, exotic egg salad, Cuban, rare roast beef, just to name a few, were all hits with the university crowd. We had a breakfast sandwich made fresh every single morning, and it sold out every day. I can still taste it.

Our crowning achievement, and the go-to for almost anyone entering our cafe, was our homemade soups. One reason for this success was our base stocks, made fresh every day. Vegetable stock went into most of our creations and formed a delicious base to work from. This also allowed us to make vegetarian options, another huge hit. When called for, we would roast pounds of chicken bones and scraps purchased from the butcher for our chicken stock. This gave several of our soups the wow factor. Roasted broccoli and aged cheddar, chicken noodle, North African lentil, carrot and thyme, carrot and ginger, roasted squash and pumpkin—just a few of the winners.

Shaun and I both had our specialties when it came to making these bowls of flavour—his being the Hungarian mushroom, and mine being the East Coast clam chowder. We eventually got into a routine of having certain soups ready to go on certain days. The regulars knew this schedule off by heart. I was quite pleased to see the lineups every Friday morning— our loyal customers anticipating a steaming pot of chowder coming fresh from the kitchen at any moment.

The baked goods started off slow. We didn't have the capacity or the cash to hire a baker, so we were importing a selection of sweets from a baker off site. This lasted a couple of months, but in the end it proved to be very costly. We decided to get into the desserts end of things, with Shaun's mother-in-law taking on the baking duties. This move proved an instant hit, so much so that Marlene was coming in every day after we had cleaned up our mess from the day shift. I was impressed by the number of different items she made—every one so delicious. The other hit in the sweet and savoury department was

Shaun's scones, truly the best thing I ever put in my mouth. It didn't take long for him to invent about twenty different flavours of these buttery flakes of goodness, and again, they sold out every day.

Still, we were finding it hard to make ends meet. We had a great location, awesome staff, some of the best food around, and a great clientele—but were barely scratching the surface of sustainability. After several months of attempting to stay one step ahead of the bills, I cashed some of my personal RRSPs to buoy up the flailing ship. This was above and beyond the initial investment I had put out. Part of the reason for our struggles was the cyclical nature of the university crowd. They flocked to us in droves when in school but once May rolled around and until the end of August, many students went home. This created a "must rely on the tourist crowd" mentality for the summer months, and it just wasn't enough. We did manage to keep the doors open for that first summer, and when September 1st came, it was like an adrenaline shot in the arm. The place filled up, and we were again off to the races.

Christmas time saw most of the students go home. We wanted to thank the staff for sticking by us that first year, so we organized our own Christmas party at the 'Nog and had a wonderful night of fun and companionship. We felt like a family and it outwardly showed. That's not to say we didn't have our issues. Working in such close quarters with extended family does tend to be tedious at times. There were many moments when I had to bite my tongue, lest I get into trouble saying the wrong thing, and I'm sure the others felt the same.

Our second year in business started off well. I was getting some of the construction bills paid off, and most of the kinks were ironed out as far as the daily operations went—but that was all about to change drastically. We had heard rumours for some time about a major construction project most likely being ramped up in the early spring. The *Big Dig* was definitely going to put a damper on our bottom line—this we were sure of. Major road, sewer, and infrastructure projects, a continuation of the upgrading of services to the downtown core, had been going on for the last couple of years. The construction schedule slated our section of Princess St. for total reconstruction, and there wasn't a damn thing we could do about it. Actually, the mild winter allowed crews to start the dig early and by spring it was outside our doorstep. Could we weather this storm too?

Perpetual Motion

To their credit, the City of Kingston did everything in their power to maintain access to the businesses along the main thoroughfare. That still didn't help with the 60 percent drop in customers and revenue. The Big Dig, combined with the student exodus in May, spelled disaster. Things were not adding up. We marched on.

The summer was brutal. We tried everything from changing operating hours, closing on Mondays, opening on Sundays, catering, and a myriad of other options designed to keep the doors open. Finally, September rolled around, and again, the students came back in droves, this time to a newly refurbished street and a hint of better times to come. We had, by this time, hired a baker to take the load off Marlene. She still came to help when she could, but the onus was taken off her to keep up with the goods. Through all the adversity, we still maintained our standards of producing the best local fare at a very affordable price. Our loyal regulars continued to come, and we were so grateful for them. In hindsight, it still wasn't enough.

Shaun, our other partner Sarah, (Yasmin's sister) and their mom were the backbone of the cafe and would continue to operate The Small Batch for the foreseeable future. I needed to make some hard decisions about my own future, eventually informing my partners and the rest of the staff that I would be leaving Kingston for good in August of the following year. That would give us the time needed to figure out a way forward. I had retired from the fire service four years earlier and had never wanted to work full time in my post retirement years. 2017 was going to be the year I finally got to do the things I wanted to do when I left the employ of the City of Sarnia. By now, my passion for photography was taking off again, I was writing, and had the bug to travel. The stress levels had become too much—affecting my health—so I was really looking forward to the next chapter in my life.

Winding down my stay in the Limestone City was both exciting and sad, for the fact that even though I was starting a new gig, I was sure to miss my newly minted friends in this great city. I would miss the loft, my home for the last three years, my local watering hole where I seriously had some of the best times of my life, and the ease of getting around the downtown core—with all its great amenities so close at hand. I most certainly would miss my weekend wanderings, getting out on a regular basis into my natural environment to hone my ever-improving photography skills. I had covered hundreds of kilometres of roads in and around my adopted city. All of them led to such creative opportunities to shoot the Ontario landscape.

It had been decided by others that there was going to be a farewell party for me the last weekend I was in town. I was never so humbled to see the turnout of just about everyone I had ever met from Kingston show up. Such kind words were spoken of what my friendship meant to many, and I had to confess, the feelings were mutual for sure. Much drink and many hugs were doled out in between the laughter and tears as the evening wore on. Nadra presented me with my own special tulip-style glass that, for the past three years, she had kept clean, cold, and at the ready for me, any time I would show up for my bottle of Bud. I could not have asked for more. I knew I would miss everyone like crazy, and I was right. To this day, I totally count my time in Kingston as some of the best times ever, and often keep in touch with many of the kind souls mentioned above. Friendship and love with this crew, still makes my world go round and round.

There was one more thing to do before I really felt comfortable leaving. I had mapped out my next year of travels for exploring new parts of the world I had not seen before. I just needed a place to live. To that end, Paul had suggested me taking possession of the thirty-foot trailer he had bought about fifteen months earlier. It was a toy-hauler, and perfect for my travel ambitions going forward. We agreed on terms, discussed the transfer, and I was ready to begin life in a camper for as long as I deemed fit to enjoy that style of living. My 4Runner was not up to the task of hauling that bad boy so, in anticipation of such a journey, I traded it for a new Toyota Tundra Platinum, my dream truck.

Finally, after three long years in Kingston, years that saw me endure some of the greatest stress I had ever known, coupled with incredibly happy memories of being with family, meeting so many lifelong friends, and rediscovering my passion for photography and writing, it was time to leave. In the past month, I had purged most of my worldly belongings, and what I didn't want to part with went to storage. I knew I would retrieve those mementos at a later date.

45. Southbound Travels: Shaun Gets Married

Time to embark on a new journey. The trailer had been secured and my Tundra was ever so capable of hauling it anywhere I desired. I arrived at Paul's place on September 1st, late afternoon. We immediately drove over to where my future living quarters was being stored, to go over the details of ownership. I had been busy prepping for this next adventure in many ways, not only outfitting the trailer with all the necessary equipment for smooth operations, but finalizing my itinerary also—where I was going to stay, and for how long.

My first site-lease was Branton-Cundick Park on a beautiful stretch of the River Rd. leading south from Sarnia to Sombra. Once settled, I just knew this lifestyle was for me, certainly for the foreseeable future.

It was good to see Julie again. After several years, and many miles between us, she came to the campground for a visit. Yup, the spark was still there. Even though it had been a bit of a rough go prior to moving to Kingston, I knew—no matter what—we would be able to repair our friendship, and who knew, maybe even start fresh. There was no rush. We knew this time around we had to take it easy going forward.

Having now freed up much more time to finally do the things I had dreamed of for years, I prepared to make the journey to Cape Breton Island for my very first Offbeat Community Workshop, an endeavour that would see me up my photography skills greatly. Even though I had been taking pictures on a regular basis for a couple of years, I just knew there had to be more to it than what I was currently doing. I really didn't have a clue how to handle my digital camera properly. I knew advanced instruction by some of the greats in the business was just the ticket. I had taken the leap by registering for this adventure almost a year previous and was eagerly awaiting the coming fall season. My cousin Erin's husband, Dave Brosha—whom you may recall I met in 2008 at our family reunion—was now a world-renowned photographer in his own right, and he was leading this outdoor workshop to the Highlands on the island. Of course, any excuse to get back to my home province was ok by me. Was I in for a treat.

After safely securing the trailer, I made my way to the Keltic Lodge in Ingonish, NS—on the northeast shore of the island. I had only been around the Cabot Trail once, many years ago with Gayle, so I was anticipating a fabulous week. It was the height of autumn foliage, an attraction in this area known worldwide for the vibrancy and splashes of colour from the maples and birches, all interspersed with the coniferous greens as far as the eye could see.

There were to be about twenty-five to thirty participants and I didn't know anyone. I did, however, have an online social media connection to several who would be in attendance, so I wasn't going in totally blind.

This workshop was where I first met Ian Proctor—in person. We had graciously commented on each other's work through different Facebook photography pages we posted to—but that was the extent of me knowing him before that week. Ian lived in Calgary; he was an oil patch worker, originally from Montreal. He and I were about the same age, balding, white facial hair in whatever style we felt appropriate for the day, and a passion for taking pictures. It was also the beginning of a great friendship—which continues to this day.

As mentioned previously, I was quite green with the technical side of photography. So, when it came time to introduce ourselves, and say a few words as to why we were there, I explained in no uncertain terms that I needed to learn shutter speed, aperture, and ISO—the three main building blocks to a well-crafted image. Much to my surprise, there were no moans, groans, hisses, or boos from the crowd. It turns out, this group of *OffBeatles*—a term I can proudly say I coined shortly after this first workshop—would become the most supportive gang of creatives I have ever had the privilege of collaborating with. We spent a grand time the whole week staying at this iconic lodge, touring the highlands and the Cabot Trail—all in the name of creating fabulous images. I was hooked!

The other two mentors alongside Dave were Curtis Jones and Jon Brown. Jon lived in the area for quite some time and knew it well. What this meant for the group was that we were taken off the beaten path to some really special places not known to the tourists. Curtis, a free and adventurous spirit if I ever met one, was the perfect accompaniment to Dave and Jon. His knowledge of the art of photography was a priceless commodity to this newbie—and he was just as generous with his one-on-one time in the great outdoors as he was in the classroom.

After spending long days taking hundreds upon hundreds of shots with my little Nikon digital, we were to submit two edited images for a gentle critique on the last day. I was so nervous. Did I even get a shot worthy enough to actually put out to the world? With very limited editing skills developed thus far, I had an uphill battle all the way. I settled on a landscape image taken at one of the iconic stops along the trail. It was just before dusk, the sun was setting—casting a brilliant gold and orange hue on the fall foliage across the bay. There was a small coniferous tree, which initially gave me grief, as I felt it was in my way and could ruin the majestic scene in front of me. I chose in that instant to leave it in the shot. I am happy I did. My critique was stellar—done by none other than Dave Brosha! His comments made me so proud. Not that my image was the best one out there—no, my image was the best I'd ever taken. I had actually done it. My focus in coming to the workshop was to improve my image quality and performance. I felt I'd accomplished those goals. Dave's words, even though he probably has said the same to many of his mentees—rang deep and true, straight to my heart. More than that, the acknowledgement of my work as being good, even if it was only one image, instilled in me a passion, a fire burning so fierce and hard that I just knew at that moment I was meant to be on this creative journey. I absolutely believed in that moment—I had found my calling, my retirement gig. I was right.

In a sentence, I was totally blown away by what I had experienced in Cape Breton. The education gained by creating art together in a large group of like-minded individuals was so foreign to me and I loved it. Each of us vowed to keep in touch through social media and, at any time we found ourselves in another's neck of the woods, we were to stop by to say hello. Ian and I took it much further. We had already made tentative plans for me to fly to Calgary at a date in the future, and spend some time with him in the Rockies, that breathtaking part of Canada that I hadn't been to for over forty years.

On the way back to Joan's house, where I was visiting when not in Cape Breton, I was overcome with emotion. I called Julie and tried to explain to her just what it was that I had experienced in the last seven days. I'm sure she was pretty confused by much of what I tried to convey. Hell, I was confused by it all too. All I really wanted her to know was how my life had changed that week. I knew I was not the same guy that recently lived in Kingston, and I was on a path forward that even I couldn't stop. At that moment in time, ironically—as I was driving past my hometown of Antigonish, in my beautiful home province of Nova Scotia—I just knew, no matter what life threw at me ever again, I was going to weather the storm—I would beat the odds and come out the other side a winner. Now that, my friends, was a "full circle" moment!

Now that my workshop was behind me, there was a little matter of getting ready to head south to Florida for the winter. In all the years I lived in Canada, I had never really entertained the notion of actually spending the winters in the sunny south. That is, until I started thinking about my future, after Kingston. I had sold my house to Paul three years earlier, moved to a new city, rented a loft for the first time ever, and now, that period of the grand adventure was over. I needed to get on to the next big thing. Living full-time in the trailer was definitely going to be different from anything I'd done in the past. I had worked on my itinerary for the past several months to the point where I believed I was ready. Even though I had never pulled a thirty-foot trailer more than a few miles at a time, it was all part of the journey, and I wasn't worried. My first three-month stay was scheduled for a trailer park in North Fort Myers, via the long drive south and east over to the Atlantic Ocean. I chose that route because it created a chance for me to visit some of the old cities of southern charm where I had never been before. Lexington, Knoxville, Charleston, and Savannah were picturesque towns with great history. I knew I could get some great photographs of some of the historical areas in these beautiful enclaves.

Perpetual Motion

I spent the first few days of November getting the trailer ready for the journey. I said my teary goodbyes to my family and Julie, then departed on the 5th. Despite some intense rain through the mountains of Kentucky, and Tennessee, and a fair amount of traffic to maneuver through, I took my time on the road, not rushing the experience. Some memorable times were spent near the ocean in South Carolina. Savannah, Georgia was just spectacular. I arrived at North Fort Myers on November 12th. It had been a great trip south with no major issues—now to get set up, unleash Big Blue from her cage, get me settled in, and do some exploring.

I had a week to get settled. Shaun and Yasmin got engaged while I was still in Kingston—and now had booked a destination wedding to the Dominican Republic the third week of November. I was to fly from Miami to Punta Cana for the festivities. I was really looking forward to congregating with the whole family at the Riu Palace on the ocean.

This irony was not lost on me. I usually flew south from cold weather in the north to enjoy the warmth of the south sun. This trip, flying from sunny Miami to sunny Punta Cana, was different to say the least. The more interesting fact was me flying back to the south of Florida and staying put all winter. It took some getting used to when I tried to process those facts initially.

The week prior to my flight to the DR was filled with exploration. I put many miles on my bike and truck—with my camera always around my neck. After getting supplies, loading the fridge, and making sure I had all the staples for an extended stay, I went to Home Depot and bought a Masterbuilt Bullet Smoker on sale for twenty-nine dollars US. What a steal! It performed flawlessly all that winter and would continue to serve me well for years after I came back to Canada.

The wedding week was so much fun! Everything about the resort was first class, and our family posse was taking advantage of all the Palace had to offer. Free drinks, food, and entertainment filled our unlimited time. The wedding on the beach took place at the end of the week—which had given us plenty of time to acclimate to our surroundings. The twins were flower girls and looked so cute in their matching outfits. They really stole the show. Yasmin was a beautiful bride and Shaun very handsome in his tux. What a fabulous couple they made. The weather was clear, dry, and hot. I managed to get through the ceremony, soaking wet from sweat after running around trying to get a few good wedding images to keep. I had come prepared, having several clean, dry shirts to trade as the day went on.

Leaving the island after that glorious week was somewhat hard, knowing I wouldn't be seeing any family members until at least the following spring. I thought I had prepared myself for that eventuality, but when the time came to say our goodbyes, there were a few tears shed.

Back at the park, it was time to get to know my surroundings. I needed to find the ocean. Fort Myers Beach and Sanibel Island became my go to destinations for most of the following three months I spent in that part of Florida. Naples and the Everglades were other destinations I spent time exploring. I drove the back roads through the swamps of the Everglades National Park. I saw and photographed over two hundred alligators of all sizes—most lying beside the road or swimming in the shallow ponds nearby. My camera was my constant companion—almost never out of my hands. But was it equipped to take the kind of images I was starting to dream of?

After contemplating it for some time, and not long after returning from the wedding in the DR, I made the most significant purchase to date—in my quest to move my photography forward. I ordered a Nikon D750 full-frame digital camera, and several accessories, from the online web portal Adorama, out of New York. My excitement was palpable. This equipment arrived a couple of days before Christmas and I was thrilled. Not only did it improve the quality of my images through the improved technology, but it had a bigger sensor that could record more information on the SD Cards. It drove my passion for getting out and exploring the area even more than before—becoming another huge milestone on my creative journey.

Christmas of 2017 would be the first holiday I would spend without loved ones near. Although it was taxing on me emotionally, I could sense a change in the way I processed these thoughts. I was feeling ok with it all. What helped me through it was having this amazing piece of equipment to experiment with. Christmas Day saw me exploring Pine Island and many stops between my campground and Naples to the southwest. The camera responded flawlessly to my every need. I was happy with some of the first images to come out of it. It continues to serve me well to this day.

Perpetual Motion

Shortly before Christmas, a couple moved their trailer on to the lot behind me. They introduced themselves as Frank and Franki, and they were characters for sure. Frank was a handyman who worked for the sole purpose of drinking Budweiser beer. It was an everyday, all day occurrence. Franki, his girlfriend, was a sweetheart. I'm not sure what she did except wait hand and foot on Frank. But they made it work. We got along well and enjoyed many bottles of Bud together. Super Bowl Sunday in early 2018 was spent with them in the gazebo between our trailers. I had the big screen pointed at us, so we got to see the game in style. When I finally did pull up stakes to move north, they were sad to see me leave. We promised to keep in touch, and we still do, sporadically.

It hadn't occurred to me at that time, but I can now see what the attraction is for many Canadian snowbirds flying south for the full winter, especially seniors. I don't mind the inclement weather in the north, but it sure was a pleasure not having to worry about shovelling snow, ice-caked windshields, and heavy winter wear. Yes, sandals, shorts, and, on occasion, flip flops, were the dress of the day.

I rode Big Blue a lot. Two-hundred-mile days were not uncommon. A ride from my park up to Sarasota for lunch, across the state to the orange groves, and back home did my mind a world of good. Little by little, I sensed that I was actually learning to love myself again—be comfortable in my own skin, and not have to rely on anyone else for my happiness, a pattern I was finally starting to rid myself of. A sort of forced isolation was not something I thought I needed until it happened, but once set upon, the benefits were almost immediate. I found my mind much clearer. There were no dark, foreboding shadows lurking behind my eyelids. My memory improved. My sleep patterns improved, and with that came a healthier me. I know my CPAP had played a significant role in the improvements I was seeing—but taking stock of my overall outlook on my life at the time, I knew it was because I was finally giving myself the attention I deserved. I wasn't squandering it trying to please everyone else. I was truly happy. I sure wish it hadn't taken sixty-one years.

All that winter, I kept in touch with the people I cared about back home. It made for a more bearable time away. I know that may sound strange, as I was in the sunny south, perfect Florida weather and all, but I am still a social guy, and I found myself missing family and the few close friendships I maintained. Besides immediate family, Paul, Carole, and Julie were the three closest to me, and it was nice to keep in touch.

Florida was ripe with photographic opportunities. I put lots of miles on both modes of transportation while chasing the elusive shot. One such opportunity was a favourite. My adventure over to the Kennedy Space Center to witness the inaugural flight of the Space-X Falcon Heavy Rocket, designed by Elon Musk of Tesla fame, was incredible—a sight to behold. At launch, I was witnessing two firsts. The triple rocket design was making its historical flight, being the heaviest object ever to leave earth's orbit, and its payload was Elon Musk's personal, cherry-red Tesla Roadster being sent into perpetual space with a mannequin at the wheel, for all future aliens to see. He even had David Bowie's "Space Odyssey" playing on a loop through the radio. How strange was that? Well, it is something my grandkids should know, right?

My departure date from North Fort Myers, March 15th, had come around and it was time to head a bit further north. My next stop was a spot between Dunedin and Tampa, where I had a two-week stint booked. The best part of this location was that my good friends Rick and Barb, Lynn and Leslee, and Shawn and Judy, from Ontario, were living on the coast just outside Dunedin. I had never been to this area and really looked forward to exploring the Gulf Coast.

I hadn't even finished setting up camp yet when my neighbour came over, introduced himself, and asked if I liked fishing. Well, yes, I did, so he invited me on a charter for the following Wednesday—with five other locals. I was quite hesitant at first, not knowing him or any of the others, and maybe a little fearful thinking about being out on the Gulf of Mexico in a boat full of strangers, no one knowing where I was. It was risky, but what the hell. You only live once, right? I accepted, and he said he would keep in touch with further details.

In the meantime, I did get together with my Ontario friends and had a wonderful day with them, hanging out on the patio, going for a boat ride, and later that evening, supper at a seafood hut down the street. I told them about my invite on the charter, so at least someone was aware of my activities.

Perpetual Motion

The fishing charter turned out to be one of the major highlights of my whole winter south. My neighbour was a great guy—the other fine gentlemen just as nice. We all got on real well and netted about one hundred and fifty strippers total. We had them cleaned and fileted by the shore crew and later that week had a huge fish fry next door. Between that, my friends from Ontario, and a great visit with retired firefighter Kevin McHarg and his wife Sue, those two weeks were packed full of fun. Now it was time again to continue my northward movements. I was headed to the Florida Panhandle.

During my journey south, I had stayed in many campgrounds. All were relatively clean, and I really had no complaints about my accommodations at all. I next arrived at Emerald Park Resort in Panama City Beach, Florida and was truly blown away by how perfectly manicured everything was. Even the many streets the trailer sites were lined up on were paved with interlocking brick. It was by far the nicest place I had stayed—or probably will ever stay that was labelled a trailer park. The word "resort" in its name was so apropos. I had originally booked for three weeks, but after seeing the ridiculously great amenities available, I went straight back to the counter and added two more weeks to the stay.

Camping and living in a trailer for such a long period of time can be taxing, not for the lifestyle, but as mentioned previously, for the fleeting friendships that are forged through a common bond of camaraderie and the love of the outdoors. Again, while at the Emerald, I met several great couples, and we also became fast friends. To this day, I still keep in touch with some of them. They still talk about my culinary skills on the smoker during our potluck dinners. I was blessed to be able to freely give myself to the fellowship of others during a time when we were all strangers. For the first time in my life, I felt like I was truly alive and living my best life. I sometimes wish I could bottle that feeling.

Shortly after I arrived in Panama City Beach, I remembered that Lisa, a co-worker from my Securitex days, was living in Panama City, the town next door. It took me a few days, but I summoned the courage to call her at work and see if she wanted to get together for a drink. Well, that was an understatement. She was thrilled I called, and we made arrangements to meet a few days later at a restaurant in town. What a wonderful reunion, as if we had seen each other last week. Of course, we had so much to catch up on, having not spoken since about 2003.

Lisa and I hung out three times while I was at the park, the most memorable of which was on St. Patrick's Day, and our visit to Tyndall Air Force Base. She explained that she had been married (tentatively still was) to an airman, so she had a pass to the base and all its facilities. I was in luck. The base actually has one of the most beautiful beaches in all of Florida. The crazy thing is—that long stretch of sand is not open to the public, being on the private lands of the base itself, so just air force personnel could use it. I was amazed to see miles of emerald-green waters and smooth sandy beaches as far as the eye could see, with not another soul to occupy it for almost the whole time we were there. I think we ran into maybe two or three people in the many miles we walked that day. It reminded me of the opening scene to a very old movie, *Planet of the Apes*, barren and desolate with ocean for miles. We hit an out-of-the-way seafood shack, a couple of bars for some Irish social time, and enjoyed a beautiful day in the sun. It was one of my best day tripping adventures that winter.

The other activity I spent much time doing that winter was exploring the Florida State Park system. From the Everglades in the south to the Caverns in the north, I think I entered about twenty state parks while I was wintering in the warm climate. Each had its own uniqueness—which made for more fabulous photo opportunities.

The Canadian spring was approaching and given the fact that I had a six-month limit on my stay in the US, it was time to start making my way slowly back to the more northerly climes. I had several stops to make before re-entering Canada—which I hoped would be as memorable as the last four months had been. Julie and I had made arrangements to meet in Nashville, TN the third week of April. Neither of us had ever been there before, so we thought it would be a great way to explore the history and the country feel of this famous city. But before that time arrived, there were other cities to explore en route.

My first stop north was Montgomery, AL, famous for many things including the home of the Confederacy movement which, along with other factors, sparked the Civil War of 1861-1865, during Lincoln's presidency. I toured many of the historical landmarks. Jefferson Davis was named president of the newly formed, Confederate States of America, and resided in the short-lived Southern White House near the state capital. It was beautiful in its ornate decor but nothing like the present-day White House for sure—all this being part of a controversial historical record—but history nonetheless.

The fifty-four-mile Freedom March from Selma to the state capital in Montgomery in 1965 in support of African American citizens' right to vote, and which Martin Luther King Jr. participated in, was well represented with plaques and markers telling the story in great detail. I wandered this hallowed ground for hours, just feeling the energy and determination of the marchers of so long ago. You can read all of this in the published records, but to actually stand where history was made is food for my soul.

What would Alabama be without a big ol' feed of Southern BBQ? I did a little research and ended up at Dreamland BBQ on Jefferson Avenue, a large pub-style brick building with their smokers outside and visible to the public. The whole area was intoxicating with the aromas of smoke and sauce. Smoked ribs, chicken, sausage, mac and cheese, slaw, and beer all got in my belly that day. I rate it as one of the top five meals I ate while on my southern trailer adventures. I sure hope to get back there someday.

Moving north again, my next bucket list adventure was to Muscle Shoals Recording Studio in Muscle Shoals, AL. If you are into classic rock at all, you will most likely be familiar with this shrine. Many of the greats from the late '50s and well into the '60s, recorded there. Wilson Pickett (of "Mustang Sally" fame), The Rolling Stones, Cher, Lynyrd Skynyrd, Bob Seger, and a host of others graced those sound-proof rooms. My claim to fame that day was sitting in the actual seat, at the actual piano, on which Bob Seger recorded the song "Old Time Rock 'n Roll." It really felt like I was walking in the footsteps of music royalty, and for those of you who know me well, you know music is a huge part of my life—still. No different than attending a rock concert, I bought the T-shirt.

I had booked a site at a fishing camp in Decatur, about twenty minutes from the studio, situated right on the border of Alabama and Tennessee. I was greeted at the gate by a loud, heavily Southern-drawl-accented, cowboy-hat-wearing redneck, and it was one of the best welcomes I've had to this day. He introduced me to his sidekick, Joey Harrington, to help me find my way down to my spot by the river. After some tight maneuvering to get my trailer situated—with Joey's help—he left me with the invitation to come over to his camper later that afternoon for some fishing and beer. I knew I had made the right decision to pick this spot to stay. With a six-pack in hand, I ventured over. Joey set me up with a rig made especially for the channel cat and largemouth bass we anticipated putting in the bucket. He also plied me with tales of the giants that got away and more folklore from the deep woods—can you hear the banjo playin' yet?

We were about fifteen minutes into it and we hadn't had much luck landing any lunkers—a few bites, but nothing. I looked over at Joey and saw a puzzled look on his face. Upon inquiry, he told me that one of the reasons for non-activity in this stream was predators. Before I could get any further explanation, he pointed across the river. Headed our way was what I could only assume was a snake of some sort—by the way its slithering body made ripples in the otherwise still waters. Joey calmly explained that the creature heading towards us was a snake called a Cottonmouth or Water Moccasin, a highly venomous viper capable of killing a human with its poisonous bite; its presence in the water was the probable reason for the scarcity of fish biting our bate. I had no idea whether to believe him or not. He wasted no time in retrieving his rifle from the trailer. Now, having heard his previous explanation, I would have assumed that in a situation like this, the weapon of choice would be, at minimum, a .22 cal rifle, surely enough fire-power to do the job Joey had in mind. My next thought was, *Why the hell does he not have a .12 gauge shotgun?* What he did have in his hand . . . was a fucking pellet gun! *What??*

Joey poured some pellets into the chamber and, with a pump, took aim at the slithering mass of reptile—which by this time was about thirty feet away from the dock we were standing on and heading directly for us. He aimed and fired. Every time he pulled the trigger, he had to manually pump another pellet into the chamber. It was comical—in a terror-filled, possibly-gonna-shit-my-pants sort of way. The third shot was a charm—*thank God*—though not a kill shot by any means. The fanged beast kept coming—*shit, are you kidding me?* Two or three shots later, I thought Mr. Cottonmouth had slowed somewhat—*ok, now we're getting somewhere, folks.* The stubborn, never-say-die piece of reptilian shit reached the sand-strewn shore moments later—but kept up its relentless forward motion. A small squeal may have emanated from my throat. Fucking Godzilla was now only five feet away. Joey was about eight shots in at this point, when finally, a direct hit to the head—*praise Jesus!* Again, movement, but somewhat laboured—*was this cursed creature from the deep ever going to die?* It took another close-up round to the head to finally stop the snake from moving—*ok, finally I can breathe.*

Joey then picked up his next killing implement, a flat-head spade. He explained the need to remove the viper's head from its body in order to stop it from doing any damage to any land critters. Dogs, cats, rats, and mice—all were prey if Mr. Cottonmouth decided not to die right away. With a carefully placed strike, the viper's head was severed from its four-foot torso. Joey picked up the head with the shovel to allow me to get a better look at it. With that, he dug a hole in the dirt—about fifteen inches deep, tossed the head into the pit, and buried it with the loose soil. After throwing the torso into the river, he was now satisfied this killing machine would cause no harm to the world's vulnerable population ever again. All in an evening's entertainment in the deep South.

The next two days were awash in torrential rains and high winds. Tornado warnings—very frequent in this area of the Midwest, had been issued for the surrounding three hundred miles, and I was in an ultra-lite trailer by a viper-infested river. What could go wrong? Thankfully nothing—except a little bit of boredom, and when the threat of severe weather abated, it was time for the two-hour ride to Nashville.

Julie and her friends, Karen and Mark were on their way to Nashville by car. I was really looking forward to finally seeing people I knew. The last time had been in the DR with my family back in November. The Two Rivers Campground, my new patch of real estate, was located only a mile or so from the new Grand Ole Opry building in east Nashville. I settled in, bought some groceries, and waited for company to arrive. It was then I got the phone call.

My ninety-one-year-old father had been having medical issues off and on for a few months, and we knew with his failing health the end could come at any time. We had already gone through a few scares in the recent past, and so with that, I had thought my plans through for if and when the time came while I was still on the road.

Dad was not responding to his present treatment. My sisters feared the worst. I looked over my exit plans, and started making inquiries as to flights, and storage for the trailer if I needed to get to Halifax in a hurry. My biggest decision was whether I pack up and go home now or ride out the medical information I was being provided, and get to Halifax in time for the funeral. I was torn. Just as I was getting all that info together, we got breaking news. Dad wasn't ready to go just yet. With a sigh of relief, I made the decision to stay in Nashville at least for the three days my guests were going to be there. I hoped it was the right one.

It was so good to see Julie, Karen, and Mark again. After months of just talking over the phone, a hug was exactly what I really needed. For the next three days, we toured the downtown hub of activity in the music capital of the USA. We hung out in the honky-tonks, did some sightseeing, drank beer, and ate some fabulous foods. I enjoyed it as much as my mind let me, knowing of my father's ill health. But despite that, from thereon out, when someone asks me which city I loved the most from my years of travelling, the answer is always Nashville.

It was decision time. I had booked the Two Rivers Campground for two weeks. Now that my company and I had had a wonderful time partying in those crowded bars for a few days, it was getting on time for them to leave, and after some thought, I decided to cut my Nashville stay short and head back to Canada also. Julie and I discussed it, and she decided that she would like to travel home with me. I was thrilled. It would be a three-day drive with two nights at camping facilities along the way—so that is what we did. Karen and Mark left to venture back home on their own and the next day we packed up the trailer and set out for Ontario. I enjoyed the road trip home with Julie. We took our time—but I was tired. It had been almost six months to the day since I'd left Sarnia, and I needed to just—stop.

46. No Moss Under My Feet: Goodbye, Dad

It was good to be back in Canada. I hadn't been out of the country for an extended period of time ever, let alone six months. The time away was worth it. It gave me the clarity to be me again. The past six months had also given me ample opportunity to reflect on my upcoming retirement years without concern about the cafe. Those reflections always led me back to my love of photography, writing, and travel, the three main elements of my original retirement plan. I had put them on hold to go into the restaurant business, but now, even though I was still financially involved with that venture, I had the freedom to create new memories around my passions.

I had also paid in full for a year's lease on my site at Branton-Cundick Park, downriver. The park opening was not until the first weekend in May, but I received permission to set the trailer on the site early—given the fact that I was homeless otherwise. It was good to just stop—for a month at least. June would bring plans to once again hook up the trailer, head east for some new adventures, and enjoy some Canadiana.

May gave me time to regroup. I needed to refresh a few items that warranted attention after having lived in the trailer for the last eight months. I visited family and made a few dates with friends to hang out, knowing I was leaving again soon. Overall, it was a very relaxing month. Julie and I spent several occasions together and our friendship was again blossoming into something special. We both knew what we were getting into, having been through it before. This time it felt more natural, more at ease. I liked that.

Since last July when I had met Ian on Cape Breton Island, and we had hit it off as instant friends, we talked about getting together for some photography and fellowship. The original plan was for him to fly south to wherever I was at the time and hang out with me, exploring new locations we both had never seen before. For whatever reason, that didn't happen. We kept in touch, and eventually decided on me flying to Calgary for a visit and some photography in the Rockies come September. Ian's wife Jenn was excited to finally meet me and had already started on the itinerary for the week. It was going to be quite a nostalgic trip. I hadn't been west since the summer of 1974, when Jim and I thumbed our way across the country.

I hadn't seen family for about seven months. Before even thinking about Calgary, I wanted to start my summer off right by visiting both of my children and their families—prior to enjoying my itinerary for PEI and Nova Scotia. With the trailer maintenance taken care of and loaded, I left Sarnia for Welland, having registered for a two-week stay at a campground only a few kilometres from Stephanie. It was a wonderful time having the twins for visits and sleepovers—lots of snuggles and hugs for Papa. I also enjoyed several winery tours and some great meals—the Niagara area ripe for those activities. The time went by way too fast.

Next stop—Kingston. This time at the KOA, not far off the Gardiners Rd. This would be my first time back to the city since departing last September. It actually felt a little strange not having my loft to comfort me. I knew family and the many friends I had made would certainly make me feel welcome. Shaun, Yasmin, and I spent quality time creating some great meals together, as was the norm for us. I always felt so lucky to have such great bonding time with them over our shared passion. It also felt somewhat strange going into the Small Batch. I only went twice in the ten days I was there—it just wasn't the same. The highlight of my visit was a great get-together at the 'Nog for Canada Day celebrations. As mentioned earlier, my bestie, Shannon, drove in from Toronto to hang out for the weekend. We had a blast.

It was time, again, to hit the open road—I know, seems like a recurring theme, right? I had four days to get to the KOA on PEI. Travel time to my final destination was about sixteen hours, so I broke it up, only motoring about four hours a day. I took my time to see this part of Canada a little deeper, having been through on many occasions but never stopping to explore.

Perpetual Motion

The day before heading over the Confederation Bridge linking New Brunswick to PEI, I stayed in Shediac, NB, just northeast of Moncton. A former co-worker of mine, Fire Chief Bruce Morrison, had retired to the area not long after I left the service. We made arrangements to meet for dinner and drinks. It was great to reminisce about our time in the fire service, even though he was in the industrial sector and me municipal. We had a great laugh during an impromptu phone call to my former chief, and our good friend, Pat Cayen.

The drive over the infamous, thirteen-kilometre-long Confederation Bridge was especially memorable for two reasons. I had never been to PEI before, and, ever since the bridge was completed in May of 1997, I had wanted to navigate that expanse. I had been warned of the possibility of high winds during the crossing and attempting it with a thirty-foot trailer could pose a challenge. Fortunately, all was good.

My first impressions of this beautiful island were off the charts. The canola fields awash with bright yellows against the blue backdrop of the Northumberland Strait took my breath away. I knew I was in for a treat. My planning had me staying the full two weeks at the picturesque Charlottetown KOA, nestled on the shores of Bass Cove. The first week was all workshops, and the second week was all mine to explore in depth the only province I hadn't been to, until now.

Land & See—described as a fun-loving photography camp for adults—was a week-long landscape and portrait workshop, held each year in Dave and Erin's century-weathered barn on their farm property in Long Creek. This was the third annual gathering, and having heard so many great stories about the itinerary, speakers, entertainment, and photography opportunities, I just knew it would be special. What made it extra-special is that Erin is my first cousin. Her dad—Uncle Joe—and my mom were brother and sister. I remember her as a toddler, clinging to her mother's dress when we would visit the Boyle family farm—just another reason to acknowledge it being such a small world after all. It was great to see many old friends, and even better, meet and make new ones. If ever I felt like I had a family outside my blood relatives, this gathering proved it. Come to think of it, every workshop I have attended has felt like hanging out with my closest family. I give the Brosha's and the Zizka's total credit for creating OffBeat, the best photography community ever. The instruction, the atmosphere, the models, the breathtaking beauty of the landscape—all combined to make my first L&S so magical. I was instantly enamoured by it all, and it wasn't fifteen minutes into the first day that I approached Erin and said to her something to the effect of, "I don't know what you have to do to make it happen, but I definitely want to come back next year." She just gave me a wink, smiled, and said, "Done."

Being among such creative talent can only lead to more creativity. One of the new ideas presented to us prior to arriving was the call for participants to the first annual Land & See Lip Sync Battle. I immediately thought back to my fifteen minutes of fame doing "Mustang Sally" on stage for a talent show years before. Knowing the words by heart, I could definitely put on a show for the crowd. With Ian and our friend Candy as my backup singers, we rehearsed a couple of times the afternoon of the show and declared ourselves ready—and ready we were! We took first place in the inaugural competition, and I even have a video recording of the performance. What a fun night.

Dave, among all his other talents, is a Sigma Lens representative. Sigma is a Japanese company that manufactures lenses for several different brands of cameras. This would not be significant to my story except for one fun fact: Because of his affiliation with the company, he received permission to borrow a dozen or more new lenses of every configuration, all done in the three most prominent mounts, Canon, Nikon, and Sony. We, as participants, were able to sign out any lens we wanted to try. What a perfect way to experiment with new technology before committing hard-earned dollars. It just so happened I was in the market for some upgraded glass, and I was happy with the samples I got to try. Even more fun was that he didn't have to return those lenses back to Sigma Canada for several days after the workshop ended—so he loaned me the full complement of Nikon mount lenses to use on my journey of discovery around the province, all that next week. I was in heaven. Having a range of lenses from 14mm all the way to 500mm in my arsenal for even a few days made me try that much harder to put all the lessons I had learned to good use. I think back to those early days and can't help but be thankful for all the wonderful opportunities I was given to advance my creativity in photography.

Perpetual Motion

Artificial lighting or OCF (off camera flash) was something I was not familiar with at all. Until this workshop, I wasn't even remotely thinking I wanted to do creative portraits. That all changed upon receiving some of the best instruction, and guidance from the gifted mentors Dave and Erin had assembled. I had so much to learn and began to absorb all I could. New skills flourished. Before leaving the workshop, I had already ordered the Dave Brosha Lighting Kit from StrobePro, a lighting and accessories store in Calgary. This was billed as a beginner's lighting set, something I just knew I would put to good use. Scheduled delivery was set for Karen's cottage in Bayfield, NS, my destination after I left PEI. At the time, I didn't realize the significance of that purchase—but soon my new equipment would play a huge part in the most important images I have ever taken in my fledgling photography career. I also made inquiries as to where I could buy two of my favourite lenses I had tried at the workshop. I was quite fond of the Sigma 14-24mm Art, and the Sigma 24-70mm Art lenses. The best deal was at The Camera Shop in Kingston—ironically, only two blocks from the cafe. I placed the order and was assured they would be ready for pick-up when I came back through Kingston in late August.

The week spent on the island after the workshop was so grounding—adding more healing time to my body and mind. I had all the time in the world, my little home on a beautiful campsite, more photo hardware than I could ever afford, beautiful weather, and one of the most amazing places on earth for creating strong images. Ian wasn't leaving for a day or two, so we did a day trip to the north part of the island to hang out and get some shooting in. After he left, I went right to work, putting my newly acquired knowledge to the test. Lighthouses, ocean vistas, little fishing villages, quaint and homey restaurants serving the best clam or seafood chowder anywhere—all competed for my time. When it was over and time to leave, I knew in my heart I'd be back.

I love hanging out at my sister's cottage on beautiful Bayfield Beach. Overlooking the Northumberland Strait, the Camerons had found their little piece of heaven many years before, and over time fixed up the place that now served as a gathering centre for their growing family. How lucky was I to be able to park my trailer just beyond the cottage doors, hook up to power, and relax in this gorgeous setting. Not only that, but Stephanie and family arrived from Ontario for a few days also. We made room in the trailer for all of us to sleep—which was real cozy, to say the least. My lighting was delivered, so I immediately recruited Peter to be my first test subject. Yes, I had a lot to learn, but it felt good being able to up my game in such a creative way. What fun we had over the extended long weekend. It wasn't my first time at the cottage, and certainly wouldn't be my last.

The logistics of hauling a long trailer everywhere you go sure presents unique challenges. You can't just pull up to someone's house and go in for a visit. No doubt you would be blocking a driveway or creating some type of inconvenience for others—so, it's always good when you have relatives in the area. My cousin Bill, and family, owns several seniors' homes in the Truro area, and as luck would have it, that was where my father now permanently resided. Bill offered me a secluded spot behind one of the villas, complete with power. I had no need for the trailer for the next several days, as I was staying at Joan's house on the outskirts of Truro—so I graciously accepted his offer.

I had one goal to accomplish while in Truro. I wanted to take quality portraits of my father. Even though he was in failing health, Joan had asked him if he was up to sitting for me, and he said yes. We all knew this was most likely the last chance we would have to create lasting images of the patriarch of our family. No pressure, right?

On August 22nd, the seniors home staff made sure Dad was looking his best—haircut and clean shirt, the order of the day. Dad had been confined to a wheelchair for months, so it was an easy task getting him out to the manicured grounds of the estate while I set up my equipment. I was nervous, hoping all would go off without a hitch. We all congregated around the chosen bench I had scouted out. Dad, sitting in his usual slouch in his wheelchair, seemed quite nonchalant about the whole affair. We moved him to the bench and I explained to him what I hoped to accomplish. When I was set, I gently asked him in a jovial manner to sit up straight and look into the camera, not expecting much of a reaction. The surprised look on our collective faces will not soon be forgotten. Dad, as proud as he had ever been in his whole life, sat up ram-rod straight, held his chin high, looked right into the camera—eyes bright, and sporting a cheeky grin. Taken aback momentarily, I knew this was the time. For about twenty minutes, everything I asked him to do he did with grace. I snapped about one hundred raw images, and after a moment to check a couple to see if I had nailed at least one, we called it a wrap. When we were done, tears ran down my cheeks—knowing what I had accomplished for the ages. Back in his chair, and in his familiar slouch, I showed Dad just a quick sample of the images. He smiled and said, "Thanks." He always was a man of few words.

As I said earlier, I didn't know the significance of my lighting purchase at the time. It soon became quite obvious to all of us—the importance of some of the decisions we make in our lives, whether impromptu or deliberately planned.

A few days after my father's portrait session, I went to visit him one last time before I headed back west. This moment was not lost on me. There had been many times in the recent past when I had said goodbye—not knowing if I would ever see him again. This time I was sure. My last memory of my father, my lifelong mentor, was of him sitting in his chair by the window in his room. As I was leaving, I turned and blew him a kiss. He returned the gesture. I left.

Not knowing is hard. I had to continue my journey of discovery to other places and pray that when the time came for my father to leave this world, I would be somewhere where I could drop everything and return to the East Coast for his funeral. But it wasn't the time now to dwell on that. I still had to get the trailer back to Ontario and prepare to fly west for a week.

The adventure home was just as rewarding as it was heading east. I stopped at a different area each day—having taken a never-before-travelled route through northern New Brunswick into eastern Quebec and along the St. Lawrence River. I had nothing but time; I wasn't flying to Calgary until the second week of September. Gorgeous sunrises and sunsets were captured along the way, and I was increasingly happy with the quality and output of my images. As with any other skill learned during one's lifetime, being mentored by some of the best photographers in the world surely elevated my craft and would continue to do so; I had many workshops and photography journeys yet to take. After stops in Kingston and then Peterborough to see Greg and family, it was back to the park on the river.

Now safely back home, it was time to see the people I continued to miss while on the road. Julie and I spent the brief time I had well. Even though I hadn't seen her much, she understood my desire for exploration. Her job and lifestyle precluded her from dropping everything and joining me on my adventures, but she was always supportive of my need to go. Contemplating those thoughts now, I was probably viewing this through rose-coloured glasses.

I got a call just after I got home. The Small Batch Cafe was closed permanently. I felt so bad for Shaun, and our other partner, Sarah. They had really put their all into keeping our little cafe open for as long as possible. It just wasn't feasible any longer. As much as I wanted them to be successful, there had to be a time to stop the bleed. It was not an easy decision. The issue, however, was that I was still the sole investor, and now there was no more income to pay the remaining bills—or any way to recoup my initial investment. I had to think hard to overcome the worry this was going to cause me, financially. It put in motion events I never would have dreamed would happen to me; my life was about to take another turn. What I knew to be true was that I couldn't let it control me. I had put in the hard work to see my healing progress to where I now was. This was only a test. I told myself repeatedly—I would come out the other side better than I went in. That remained to be seen.

It wasn't long until I was boarding a plane in London, bound for YYC Calgary. The Proctors had invited me west and had my suite ready—a bottle of Scotch on hand just in case I needed a drink when I got there. After all of the emotion experienced in the last couple of weeks, that was an understatement. Thankfully, the flight was uneventful. What I didn't expect was the biting cold and snow that had presented itself the evening before my arrival. I had left some stellar fall weather back in Ontario. It was a bit of a shocker, but I was assured it was a normal occurrence to get inclement weather in September, in the foothills of the Rockies. I didn't mind, I was on another adventure and so looking forward to seeing the mountains again for the first time since I was a teen. My return flight was not until late Monday evening, so I had several days to explore this part of the country again. Ian would be a great tour guide—after all, he had lived in the area for several decades and knew his way around the mountains well. I was in good hands.

Perpetual Motion

We set off the next morning, west to Banff National Park to see the majesty of the mountains—all good, except for one problem. It was such a foggy morning, we literally couldn't see twenty feet above the car roof. The foothills, and subsequently, the mountains, were just not there. Ian was not happy. As we drove further towards Banff, he just kept pointing in every direction and, with exasperation, explaining the scenery that I was missing. I was thankful I had seen all of it years ago, so I knew what he was pointing out. Still, I was somewhat disappointed. All was not lost. As photographers, we try to see the good in any scenario, and with Ian's knowledge of the area, he soon had us at Two Jack Lake. I was really enjoying the surrounding views when Ian, pointing afar, informed me that Mt. Rundle—the famous mountain on the outskirts of Banff was right over there—yes it was, unfortunately covered in a thick blanket of fog. We did end up getting some great shots as the day wore on. The fog bank lifted intermittently which let us do some magic with the camera. I actually have an image of a beautiful scene from the Banff National Parkway printed on canvas and hanging in my home—a reminder of the great trip west, and also the need for perseverance in anything we set out to accomplish.

A day doing portrait work and two more days in the mountains made for an awesome stay at the Proctor residence. Even though Ian and I hadn't known each other long, and this was the first time meeting his beautiful wife Jennifer, we all got along like we were old school chums.

It was time to check in for my return flight home, so Jenn, being quite computer savvy in the ways of navigating the Air Canada website, started the process online. We were soon to discover a grave error on my ticket.

When originally booking my flight, I had received a written itinerary with the specific dates, arriving Thursday morning and flying out Monday night. However, that is not what the actual ticket said. It had me flying out Sunday night, late, and I hadn't picked up on the error. After a couple of attempts to book my flight, we realized the issue and now, here I was, late Sunday afternoon, thinking I was not flying out until the following night at midnight, and it was now too late to do anything about the flight I was going to miss.

Thank God I always use a travel agent and didn't just book online. Rose Davidson, my girl Friday, has for many years been my go-to travel assistant. I started using her to book my flights way back in the mid-'80s and have never looked back. Not only is she a top-drawer travel agent, but now she is one of my great friends. It was time to give her a call. After some intense conversation as to the who's and why's of the matter, it was determined there had been a printing error. Within an hour, a new ticket was issued for the following night. I will always be grateful to Rosie; she never leaves me floundering. She would prove herself again a year later, dealing with another booking error when I ventured overseas—customer service, baby, customer service.

It all turned out well. Back at the campground again, and now having completed my travel itinerary for the year, it was time to consider my living accommodations for the winter. I knew I was not returning south and could not stay in the trailer in the off season, so I started making inquiries about house-sitting. This idea was presented to me in conversation with some friends over beers one night. I thought about it and decided it fit my current lifestyle perfectly. I was game to get my name out there and see where this adventurous avenue led. After my initial post on Facebook, I was inundated with suggestions, recommendations, and inquiries. I really didn't expect it to be that easy, but having the background and credentials I did sure helped. It wasn't long before I had a three-month booking, right in Sarnia. Rick and Barb, friends for many years, saw my post, and immediately contacted me to discuss a possible match. They had been travelling to Florida every year and staying all winter. Their two children had graciously agreed to look after their house and property each year and were thrilled to hear they didn't have to take on that responsibility again that winter. We reached an agreement—I was to take over their residence the first week of January 2019. I was thrilled that most of the winter was booked.

I still needed to find accommodations for October to December, given the fact that the trailer park closed Thanksgiving weekend. Julie and I were talking one night when she mentioned that our friend Lynda's boarder had recently moved out. Even though she was not actively seeking another, I thought I'd give her a call. I really only needed a quiet room with a bed to get me through the three months until Prentice St. was available. I don't think I could have asked for a warmer greeting. She was thrilled to have me stay with her and I just knew we would get along perfectly. Now having the matter of my accommodations taken care of until April, it was time to relax. I still had at least three weeks before I had to be out of the park.

"The best-laid plans of mice and men," a loosely quoted line from Scottish poet Robert Burns, refers to the fact that no matter how careful we are in planning a project or an event of any kind, there is always the chance that something can go wrong.

It was only days later, on September 24th, at about 12 p.m., that the patriarch of our family, my father, Maurice Bernard Pitts, ninety-two years young, veteran, father, mentor, and friend to all, passed away in his sleep, of natural causes. All the time I was in the west, I had kept in touch with my sisters back home and received the daily updates as to Dad's condition. Still, nothing prepares you for that eventual phone call.

All the mental preparedness I had exercised in the recent past, all the "what if" scenarios, came in handy now that the reality of life and death was at my doorstep once more. My first call was to my brother Martin, asking if he was up for a road trip, or was he flying to Halifax. He was all for accompanying me in the Tundra, at least for the outbound leg. I had put about twelve thousand kilometres on my truck already that summer, and now it looked like, unexpectedly, there would be a few thousand more. I obviously would not be back in time to winterize the trailer, so I called Sarnia RV to make arrangements for them to do everything needed. It was fortunate that I could do that, knowing of the issues I would have faced if I was still on the road somewhere. Once all was taken care of, Martin and I headed east.

The next week was another test. We stayed at Joan's new house in the town of Valley, outside of Truro. The family dynamics had each of us doing whatever we could to contribute to the ease of each moment. We prepared the visuals for the funeral home. We prepared meals, sometimes for twenty or more. We attended the funeral and burial services. We consoled each other, and mostly, we felt the presence of our now dearly departed parents surrounding us with their years of wisdom and love. As it was with Mom's time of passing, we came together as one, a strong bond between us, nurtured and nursed by the memories of two of the most loved humans to ever exist.

It was a lot to take in, a moment most children don't relish happening. Now that Mom and Dad were gone, what was to become of us as a family? They most certainly had been the principal draw to us as siblings making the annual trek back to the motherland. I had made more than one hundred sojourns east over my adult life. Ironically, amidst the chaos and intensity of the moment, I suddenly felt the need to run—and I did.

The next three days were spent on the South Shore. A great little motel on the shores of the Peggy's Cove area, and a motel on a hilltop—overlooking the colourful, waterfront structures of the historic town of Lunenburg—served as my refuge, massaging my need to get away to clear my mind. I met Peter Zwicker, a fellow OffBeat photographer, for a day of image making. It was exactly what I needed to ease the trials of the past week. Thanks, Peter.

Soon after, I was alone again and heading down the highway—Martin having flown home the day before. Like the many hours spent previously doing the same thing, I found this time somewhat liberating, and at other times stifling. As in the past, music blasting through the Bose speakers helped calm a troubled soul. There was more to life, there just had to be. I had accomplished so much and was proud of how far I'd come—through many trials and tribulations, but now what? I had much to discover, I just didn't know it yet.

47. My Future—Reinvented

I moved into the upper loft in Lynda Buckland's home on Elgin St. in Sarnia on October 20th. She had converted the upper floor, at one time an attic, into a spacious bachelor den, nicely appointed and perfect for my immediate needs. Lynda had been kind, gentle, and loving to me from the moment I had met her several years earlier. This being the first time I was to share a home with another human in some time, I am grateful to this day it was her. She is a born healer, a Reiki Master, and a deep thinker. As a bonus, she loved to cook. We hit it off right away, talked for hours on end, and for the next ten weeks, enjoyed each other's company almost daily.

When Lynda would go away for the occasional weekend, Julie would come over and we would create some culinary delights together in the kitchen, enjoy some wine and each other's company. But, truth be known, I had sensed a widening void in our communications over the last several weeks. In that time we did spend together, there was a palpable distance between us. Something was up. Everything changed December 18th, 2018.

Sometimes, just sometimes—even if you love someone with all your heart, knowing you've tried the best you know how—it still doesn't work out in the end. Julie and I had been together in some capacity, for almost fifteen years. The highs and the lows, the ebb and flow, all made for beautiful music at times, and cat-scratch-fever at others. Our lifestyles had become polar opposites. Me travelling, wandering the world with my camera, trying to capture that elusive, perfect shot, and her, grounded in her work, teacher of meditation practices, Reiki Master, and a genuine empath to the world. Deep inside, we both knew. After a satiating meal, fueled with some red wine, we had the talk. Julie had met someone in the recent past, and needed to feel free enough to pursue the possibility of a new romance. I certainly could not blame her one bit. Truthfully, I was feeling a bit selfish, hanging on to what we once had, knowing it was probably wrong to do so. After a time, and through many tears, we both agreed that no matter what, we would keep in touch. To my surprise, I was ok with it. Judging by the way I had conducted myself in the past, and the severe depressive episodes brought on by such a situation as this, my head was surprisingly clear, and I could see a brighter path forward.

Since then, and through it all, no matter the circumstances, Julie and I still remain very close. It hasn't always been easy, and sometimes we don't talk for weeks—but we always find a way of coming back to centre. Maybe, just maybe, all that self-reflection and time spent alone has done some good after all. I love you, my dear Julie, and that's forever.

Lynda and I had decorated a real tree for Christmas, something she hadn't done in many years. She was thrilled with my gift to her and loved how it added the perfect touch to the festive decorations already adorning the living room. Despite all that had happened in the recent past, I felt at peace while staying at Elgin St.

I spent Christmas with my family in Welland and had a wonderful time just enjoying the calm I felt inside. It was obvious that the universe had new plans for me. I had no idea what they were but was anxious to find out.

I had always wanted to write my memoirs. My first inclination came several years earlier when researching our family tree. I found a lack of written information about previous generations of Boyles, Murphys, Pitts', and Pettipas', so I aimed to change that. My original idea was a story written to my grandchildren, at the time my twin granddaughters Leena and Noelle. I figured a brief written history of what their Papa did in his life would become a keepsake for them and also a historical record of the life and times of Dana A. Pitts. The more I thought about it, the more it started to percolate. I had already started taking notes and writing down dates. I had talked to my siblings about my childhood to see if there was enough information to compile a chronology. After a while, and after reviewing the notes, I felt it was time to get at it. What better time than now. When I got to Prentice St. and settled in for the winter, I pulled out the laptop and started pecking away. I was actually surprised at how easy the words, ideas, and information—stored away in my cranial matter—came flowing out. For the next three months, I wrote. It was a great routine. Coffee and a couple of hours of writing in the morning, a walk, and some photography in the afternoon, and if needed, more writing in the evening. I was definitely on a roll.

I'm not sure if it was all the sitting, a lack of actual exercise, or something I just manifested, but I woke up one morning with a pinched nerve running down my butt cheek. I knew right away it was an inflamed sciatic nerve. The chiropractor confirmed my diagnosis. I had experienced this pain twice before, and just knew it was going to be a long journey. But come hell or high water, I was not going to let it get in the way of me living my best life.

The three months looking after Prentice St. flew by. To be clear, writing wasn't the only thing on my mind. I was loving my advancing skills with my camera and took every opportunity to make images. While there, I had the privilege of meeting and photographing the incomparable Rae Stoetzel, a truck driver, and fellow OffBeat photographer, during one of his layovers in the region. Again, a reminder that the images we make hold so much power. I cherish the portraits I made that evening. Rae passed away in July of 2023. Miss you, my friend.

I knew the more I practiced my photography, the better I would become. I also knew I wanted more hands-on education in that discipline. The workshops I had taken in the past had served me well in feeding my creative addiction. To that end, I had done lots of research into just how and where I wanted to invest my hard-earned funds. The obvious answer was the OffBeat Photography workshops sponsored and organized by my cousin Dave Brosha and his co-creators.

After careful consideration for timing, budget, and travel itineraries, I settled on four different workshops for 2019, namely: my second Land & See at the barn on PEI in July; my first Character Portraits workshop in Elora, Ont. in September; a new offering, The Art of Storytelling, hosted by Dave and Paul Zizka, in the Rockies in early October; and from there, over to Skye High in Scotland for late October. It was an aggressive schedule but was sure to be fun. Even though my sciatica was still raging, I vowed to work on it so I could continue my education. What I didn't know was the eventual importance of the timing of these now paid-in-full workshops.

Critical life events don't seem to happen at convenient times, as witnessed previously, and that would soon be evident in the events and the final outcome of my extensive year of travel.

The trailer park officially opened the first weekend in May, so I needed to occupy my time for a month. That's why we have kids! I spent time in Welland and Kingston, enjoying my time with each of them. It always makes me extremely happy to do that.

Stephanie and Peter had bought a digital camera—the same make and model as my original from my early days in Kingston. The twins, now nine years old, had expressed an interest in taking some pictures with Papa so, each happily outfitted with cameras, we headed outside the city to the surrounding bush and farmlands. I wanted some unique space where they could take their own photos with their own camera. They were very keen to learn and took instruction well. I only wish someone would have given me that opportunity when I was their age. When back at the house, I taught them how to edit their photos in a simple editing program. To this day, they have those photos hanging in their bedrooms. Yes, one proud Papa moment.

At Shaun's, I taught him how to use the Masterbuilt smoker I bought him for Christmas. He and I still had a passion for creating great meals together, and we had now upped our game. Ribs, chicken, and salmon all got the treatment. They had gotten a puppy some months prior, and she was a handful at first, but with patience and training, Winnie became one of the best dogs going. We spent time walking her—me with my wonky gait—tasting new craft beers and creating delicious meals for the family. Yasmin and Shaun had made the grand announcement that they were pregnant—she was in her first trimester. Gramma and I were thrilled for them, and we were getting our third grandchild. A new, exciting world was opening up for them, and seeing the smiles on their faces just made me cry tears of joy. It was eventually revealed they were having a boy! That just made my whole year. I was going to have a grandson. Another proud Papa moment.

Back at the campsite, I was getting everything up and running for another great summer by the St. Clair River. This area had become like home to me because of the neighbours, the beautiful scenery, the quaint village of Sombra just down the road, and the best neighborhood pub for miles. Rum Runners Speakeasy was currently run by a dear friend of mine, whom I had originally met in the early '80s. I hadn't seen her in quite some time, until one day, I walked into Rum Runners, and there she was behind the bar. I love chance meetings such as that. We have kept in touch ever since. I was truly looking forward to another summer in the park.

To an outsider, all appeared well in my world, but to me—knowing there were some financial issues continuing to brew—things were not sitting well. The demise of the cafe and my assumption of that debt, was the first issue. The other, and related to the first, was the arrangement as to how Paul and I dealt with the financing of the trailer.

Ever since that chance meeting with Paul on the marina dock back in 2004, we had become best friends. We had seen, done, and accomplished so much together in the past sixteen years—most of the time we were virtually inseparable. But if there is one thing I've learned—the hard way, of course—it is that it's never wise to get involved with friends or family financially. Because of the cafe debt, I tried to borrow, but was refused funds to pay for the trailer outright. So, in writing, we agreed to defer the title exchange and ownership for a year until the previous hit to my credit score could be resolved. This arrangement worked for a time. Because Paul was restructuring his debts and assets at the same time, wanting to raise the capital to build his dream home on the water, he asked periodically how my situation was playing out. It was never good news, and I told him so. Without going into the details of what eventually happened, we will just call it the perfect storm. His needs and the desire to finalize the outstanding trailer issue, coupled with my lack of progress on getting my finances straightened out, finally came to a head.

At that time, Paul was working in Qatar, a country in the Middle East, having landed a teaching position a year earlier through Texas A&M University. Something had to give. Although his name was still on the title to the trailer, I was making the payments, including the insurance, e-transferred to him faithfully, each month. He now deemed this an unsatisfactory solution, wanting our arrangement finalized so he could get on with his financial needs. I hated it being this way. If I could have robbed a bank or won a lottery, he would have been paid in full immediately. It was not meant to be. Our friendship had sustained us to this point but was becoming strained due to the lack of a resolution.

Come the last week in June, I received an email from Paul stating that he was coming home by the Canada Day weekend. I was surprised to see he had penned an ultimatum to me. It basically stated that if I could not honour my commitment to him, and pay for the trailer in full, he would be left with no choice but to re-possess the unit, return it to the original seller and have them re-sell it for him. I completely understood his frustration and need for such actions. It still didn't change my ability to rectify the issue. It was time to make some very stressful decisions on my part. I knew there was no way to "borrow" the money from any source, including, as he had suggested, some of my rich family members. Say what? That would simply be throwing gasoline on the fire. I know he didn't look at it that way—thinking it was a viable solution to resolve our outstanding issues.

Until that point, no one knew of our arrangement, so after discussing my dilemma with a trusted friend, I knew what had to be done. Finding no other alternative, and completely understanding that he would not be ok with the decision, I still needed to take Paul at his word. I would give the rig back to him as suggested—for disposal, any way he saw fit. After all, he still owned the trailer, legally. This also meant I was about forty-eight hours away from being truly homeless—a humbling thought, for sure.

If I have learned anything in my sixty-plus years on this planet, it is that I can be resilient in the face of adversity. Lord knows, I've seen my share. It was not always easy, but as I got older—maybe a little wiser, I started to feel the need to survive at all costs. When presented with a choice in the past, I might have thrown denial at it—not this time. I had the distinct feeling this was my time to change—the time to take total control of every aspect of my life was in the here and now. But what did that look like?

I called my friend Lynda. After explaining my dilemma, she was more than happy to help out. The accommodations I had used the last three months of 2018 were still available to rent. I let her know I was not sure of the timeline. I needed a secure place to keep my stuff for at least six months while on my preplanned workshop schedule. She understood completely and welcomed me home.

Now that I had a secure roof over my head, the next several days were occupied by the task of removing all my possessions from the unit, making sure it was secure, power off, water shut down, and locked. At times like these, it isn't hard to feel like a failure, but I knew all I had done was for the best. I wasn't happy having to change my life plans on the fly, but after it was all said and done, walking away from the trailer felt somewhat liberating. I could feel the stress leaving my body. I had an afternoon of saying my goodbyes to friends in the park, and after leaving a note for Paul, I was gone. It wouldn't be the last of our conversations.

I have always prided myself on being self-sufficient. I had held a job on an almost continuous basis since the age of fourteen, not once collecting unemployment benefits to support me when temporarily out of work. I don't think I actually thought about it much, but failure to meet my financial needs had never been an issue in the past. I always had the ways and means to pay my bills. This new feeling of utter helplessness in not being able to meet my commitments to Paul, the cafe, and other such entities, was unfamiliar territory. I hated it. The stress I was under was also affecting my health. My sciatica was raging to the point where I couldn't walk twenty steps without intense pain. All the stretching and chiropractic appointments had not helped. To finally admit that yes, I had made some bad decisions and now was in over my head financially—well, that was truly humbling. If ever there was a time for outside help, it was now. Again, this was not how I had envisioned retirement.

48. Just Can't Wait To Get On The Road Again

I happened to be visiting a close personal friend for coffee and was spilling my heart out to him about the oppressive weight on my shoulders. Having been in a very similar situation in the past, he pointed me in the direction of credit counselling. Just the thought of that scared me, but I knew he was coming from a place of knowledge. Although he had claimed bankruptcy, I knew that was too drastic a step to take in review of my issues. What I needed was a solution that wouldn't steal my soul.

I contacted the advisor he had dealt with and set the process in motion. The first thing she did was put me at ease. She then explained what could potentially happen. Following through with this would eventually save my credit rating and restore my ability to enjoy life again. She gave me a list of statements I needed to compile, several goals to meet, and finally set up a meeting for August to sign any documents needed. I left her office feeling like the world had been lifted off me. It wasn't cast in stone yet, but her assurances meant everything. The month or so until the next meeting gave me all the time I needed to think this through.

With all that behind me for now, it was just about time to head to PEI for round two of the Land & See photography workshop. Ian and I had made plans to meet in Ontario and drive east together—a road trip for the ages. Or was that the aged? The way I was still hurting from my sciatica didn't help with moving forward. Ian flew to London in the early afternoon, and we headed to Kingston before stopping for the night. We were quite tired from the drive in the heavy traffic so there was no visiting any of my friends. I just wasn't up to it.

Ian had booked us into Brennan's, a Victorian-style B&B in Fredericton, NB, for two nights. It was fabulous. Our Offbeat friends Joni and Candy met us during our stay for some fun times and great conversation. Candy even helped Ian with some portrait work, with me being the main subject. I had grown quite the beard over the past several months, and it was a unique look for me. As per Ian's usual work, he nailed it. Breaking up the road trip into manageable drives because of my leg pain made for a more pleasant ride to our PEI destination.

Each year, the Land & See experience is totally different from previous efforts. A new cast of characters intermingled with some of the stalwart regulars makes attending the week-long workshop unique. This year was no different. I limped around the grounds, getting to know Elena, Rae, Erin, Marcel, Jeanene, Dave Mc, Mark, Jesse, Susan, and so many more fabulously talented humans. Ian and I rented a cottage overlooking the south shore of the Northumberland Strait, which only added to the ambiance of the week. Without sounding too repetitive, this workshop proved yet again, my love for photography.

When the week was over, we headed for Halifax. Jenn, Ian's wife, was flying in for a few days of rest and relaxation. They were also in the process of considering a huge move from their current hometown of Calgary and relocating to the Halifax area within the next year. There were, no doubt, exciting times ahead for my friends from the west.

In the past, I too had verbalized how cool it would be to relocate to the East Coast—not thinking it would ever happen. My friends were in Sarnia, and my siblings, kids, and grandkids were in Ontario, so a move east didn't make sense in my world. Feeling Ian and Jenn's excitement as they described the salt air blowing across their faces while standing at the Atlantic shore, or the natural comfort level they felt while touring the area, sure made me long for those experiences on a more permanent basis also. They still had about a year to wrap things up out west, so no rush. I put those thoughts on the back burner, but as the saying goes: Be careful what you wish for.

The growing sense of freedom in my life was having a profound effect on me. My next workshop was not until mid-September, so there was no rush in returning to Ontario. Other than the pressure I was getting from

Paul, and the meeting date set for my financial issues, the rest of my emotional parts were keeping me grounded. I still had my sciatic issues but was learning to live with that disability.

The one place I had always felt grounded was Karen's cottage. Every year, her extended family continued to have their own mini family reunion around the third weekend in July, and this would be the second year of me attending. Having family around me at that time really helped with the lingering anxiety I was feeling about my issues back home. After a few days of relaxation, it was time yet again to head west—alone. I had really enjoyed Ian's company on the road trip out, but he and Jenn had flown back to Calgary a few days earlier. This now familiar trek home would give me time to secure my judgements and beliefs in the decisions I was about to finalize. I had so much going on at that time and just wished for a distraction of some sort to get me through the next few weeks. It happened shortly after I got home—again, the laws of attraction, at work.

I got a text from my good friend Wayne Simpson, a world-renowned portrait and landscape artist in his own right. Wayne was putting together a photojournalistic hardcover book of his portraits and had entitled it *Resilient*. It would have images of a cross section of society, all with a story for the ages. Each of his subjects had been through some real tough times and now found themselves on the mend; there were tales of resilience behind each photo. In his text, he asked me if I was available to assist him on a shoot he was doing in town. Hell ya! Of course I was—anything to assist the master!

The shoot was being done at a private residence just outside of Sarnia, in the bordering indigenous community of Aamjiwnaang First Nation. The subject—none other than Wayne's mother herself. He explained this was going to be a tough one because of such a close connection to the subject, and that her story was so hard to fathom; there were things about her life he was just finding out. We met Wanda at her home, and after introductions, set up the lighting and camera positions to capture her as he wanted to present her in the book. The shoot took about an hour. Just before we wrapped for the day, Wayne asked if I would take a couple of images of him and his mother—together. I was floored, and instantly nervous as hell. The mini-shoot in her living room, of mother and son, turned out absolutely perfect. So good in fact, that he included my photograph as the last one in his book! Now folks, that shit is cool. Before departing, Wanda gifted me with a Spirit Catcher she had hand-crafted. To this day it hangs on the rear-view mirror in my vehicle, placed there that day, and never removed—a reminder of a truly resilient woman. R.I.P. dear Wanda. I am a better human for knowing you, so briefly.

One decision that had to take precedence upon returning to Ontario was the issue of trading my beloved Tundra. I had purchased it specifically to pull the trailer all over the country. It had performed well, but was not needed anymore. The recommendation from my counsellor was to trade the truck for a more practical vehicle, at a reduced payment rate, prior to my proposal going through the system. This would help me cope with the loss of the income going towards my debt. Prior to acquiring the trailer and the Tundra, I'd had a Toyota 4Runner LTD in a beautiful, pearl-white colour. It was the perfect vehicle for my needs, dealing with the activities of the restaurant while in Kingston. I'd really enjoyed that vehicle and thought an updated one was in order. Bailey Toyota in Sarnia was always my go-to dealership, with Brian and Carole as owners, so I traded my white Tundra for a black 4Runner. It turned out to be the right decision.

Unfortunately, my relationship with my now former best friend, Paul, had deteriorated to the point where, after several texts, I was feeling somewhat harassed. I knew he was pissed, and rightly so. This was not the way he had envisioned our dealings playing out, but neither had I. I wished for nothing more than to be able to pay him off and rescue a once very strong friendship, but that was not meant to be. I made the painful decision to unfriend him from my social media accounts to stop the texts. I truly wish it hadn't happened that way. I can't tell you how much it hurt to remove his presence from my life. I still miss him.

With the financial papers signed, the new vehicle delivered, and my personal issues somewhat at bay, it was time to pick up the pieces of my creative journey in photography and head to Elora, Ont. for my first full-on portrait workshop. As a bonus, I was booked to stay at Martin's condo in Kitchener for the week. He had been working at Home Hardware's head office in St. Jacobs for several years, and this would be the first time staying with him at his home away from home.

The week in the Elora region was very educational. I learned so much more about off-camera lighting techniques from some of the masters in the business. Dave Brosha and Wayne Simpson, as mentioned earlier, are two of the best portrait artists in the world, and to have them at our beck and call, teaching us their tricks of the trade, only served to elevate my images greatly. It gave me so much more confidence in using my own light setups. The models were extraordinary, definite characters all. I had chosen this journey of discovering my renewed passion for photography, and even though I could hardly walk by this time, I continued to push through the sciatic nerve pain. The aggressive itinerary I had mapped out was my main focus.

Each evening I would come back to Martin's and spend some quality brother time together, something we often tried to do but only when he was home in Sarnia. It was great to have him all to myself each night.

The workshop wrapped up on the Friday morning, but because it was perfect fall weather and the leaves were changing into beautiful autumn colours, I made arrangements to meet Mark Heine, another workshop attendee, the next morning at one of his favourite spots in the area, for a sunrise shoot. That decision proved costly.

The morning was foggy. I found my way to the Flats, as the area was known. The grass was very damp. Mark and I had set our tripods and cameras in a great spot to capture the anticipated sunrise. I still had my camera bag on my back. I took a step backwards and the next thing I knew, I was lying on my back, camera bag under me. It happened that fast. I don't actually remember the fall. Mark hadn't seen it either. I immediately got up but noticed the extreme pain in my right shoulder. I couldn't tell if it was broken, dislocated, or torn. I suspected it involved the rotator cuff. Great, sciatica, and now this. I still had the cross-Canada and overseas workshops to eventually attend—this was not good.

That night, my last at the condo, was a non-starter in the sleep department. I could not find a comfortable position and gave up trying. All I knew was that I had three weeks before I was to embark on the most intense part of my travel schedule.

Those three weeks sucked. It was a confirmed rotator cuff tear, and my leg pain was bad. I had received some chiropractic help from Dr. Jeff at the Sarnia Sports Injury Clinic, and some take-away exercises to help with the injuries. I worked as best I could preparing for my travels, buying the cold weather gear I knew I would need for the mountains of Alberta and Scotland, packing the right amount of camera gear for the different environmental challenges I would be facing in both countries, and making sure all my travel documents were in order—a lesson carried over from my last trip to Calgary. By the time I was ready to fly west, I was as ready as I could be, pain be damned.

I have mentioned the laws of attraction in previous chapters. Even though it seems bad things happen to us, we all still have the energy and the power to will those issues away. I was really dreading the cramped plane ride to Calgary, knowing that the plane would be full, and there would be very little opportunity to move around and stretch. I gave my injuries up to the Universe. It was a long flight. Upon landing, I stood up slowly, expecting the shooting leg pain to knock me back in my seat. To my utter amazement, there was no pain. I had to stop for a moment before reaching for my bag in the overhead compartment, to take stock of this revelation. I moved to my left, my right, stretched a bit, and even bent over as best I could in the crowded aisle. There was still no pain. Yes, I still had the sore shoulder, but whatever had been pinching my sciatic nerve all the last several months had suddenly released its grip, and I truly was pain-free. I almost started to cry.

Ian was waiting for me when I made it to the baggage carousel. I knew he was expecting a limping traveller, and he had probably thought of securing a wheelchair. He looked quizzical when he saw me skipping along the concourse with a big grin on my face.

What a relief. Barring re-injuring it, I was going to be alright. The pain in my shoulder was definitely not as severe as it originally had been, and now I had no leg pain. Praise the Lord!

The workshop we attended was held at a beautiful lodge in the mountains of Kananaskis Country, not far from Canmore, Alta. It was the ideal location for the subject matter of *The Art of Storytelling*. I had known when I first saw this course offered that I was going to attend, no matter the cost or location. It fit exactly where I saw my craft going. Each time I attended another workshop with OffBeat, I came away with a powerful drive to create in a new and completely different way. I had always thought there was more to photography than just taking good images. I found myself seeing a story evolve while looking for a composition, using that inspiration to frame my subject in a way that married it with the story in my head. These four days of intense education directly related to my vision fit perfectly into the timing of my creative journey.

The mentors of OffBeat are so proficient in their style of teaching, and they go deep in their desire to instill that same passion in their students. One of the ways they accomplish this is by presenting a creative challenge to the group at any random time during the workshop, sending us out to interpret the challenge in our own way. During my first workshop on Cape Breton Island exactly two years earlier, I hadn't even known the technical workings of a camera, let alone know how to go out and intentionally create an image good enough to present to the instructors. I must have been paying attention the last couple of years, because the image I presented at this workshop was chosen to take the prize during one such exercise. I was beyond thrilled to be recognized by my peers for a photograph that I had conceptualized and saw to fruition.

What many people don't realize is how a kind word, an acknowledgement of effort, a pat on the back, or even a small, insignificant token of their appreciation in any form, goes a long way in spreading personal joy for both the giver and receiver. Inspiration fuels the drive to succeed. Where many creatives tend to keep their styles and processes to themselves, through the passion and drive of the OffBeat mentors, the community they have nurtured has embraced the philosophy of encouragement and non-judgement. The group of participants for this workshop was so cohesive, and I came away with several new friends for life. It goes without saying, when one succeeds, we all succeed. It is a powerful lesson I continue to live by. (I see you, Shyanne!)

The second to last day, I received a phone call. Shaun and Yasmin were the proud parents of a beautiful and healthy baby boy, Lochlan Shaun Pitts, born October 17th, 2019—exactly forty-two years to the day after I started my career as a firefighter. I was filled with joy for them. The feeling of knowing that your bloodline will live on is one of the best moments in a father's life. The group acknowledged the great news at supper, and Dave bought me a shot of Scotch to toast my good fortunes. I still had many days of travel yet before I would eventually hold my third grandchild—my first grandson—but it is future events of that magnitude that sustain us and keep us moving forward.

I came away from the storytelling workshop with a whole new look at my craft, and more importantly, I was going to be able to put my recent education to practice at Skye High in Scotland in just a few days. My shoulder was healing slowly, and my leg pain had healed completely. I was ready for the biggest travel adventure of my life.

It's hard to believe, given my enjoyment of travelling, but I had never been overseas. That was all about to change. After a great evening with the Proctors, I was off to the airport. My itinerary consisted of twenty-two hours of flight and airport time. Calgary to Halifax with a four-hour layover, off to Glasgow, Scotland, arriving at about 7 a.m. local time. From there, a train ride through the breathtaking Scottish countryside to my final destination—a great boutique hotel on the banks of the River Ness, in Inverness. By the time I arrived at my hotel, I was tired from the long hours of travel and really needed a siesta to recharge. Check-in at the front desk immediately became an issue. It was soon discovered that my reservation had not been secured, or at least it appeared that way. I knew it had all been taken care of by Rose when I booked my itinerary, but the hotel staff was questioning that fact. Again, the memory of Calgary and my incorrect flight date from a year earlier came to mind. Knowing I had again booked through a proper travel agency, I didn't panic. I called Rose, and within fifteen minutes, she had it all taken care of. Thanks again, my friend. I truly value you!

I was looking forward to exploring the ancient city and finding a great restaurant to nourish the body. Dave's smiling face greeted me the next morning for the short drive to our home for the next week. It was great to see him again, even though it had only been a few days since Canmore. Any time spent with such a passionate photographer and mentor—and for me personally, family—was good for the soul. By the time we had filled the van with some of the other participants, the air of anticipation was thick. We had been briefed on our accommodations and itinerary, and all of us were acting like a bunch of little kids seeing Disneyland for the first time.

The fourteen-kilometre drive on the left side of the road was thrilling enough, but pulling into the long driveway, and approaching the perfectly manicured grounds of a fourteenth-century castle, was mind blowing. Yes, we were staying at Erchless Castle in the Highlands of Scotland. I felt like I was dreaming. Better still, travelling alone, I would come to find out I had my own room and a private bath—in my own wing on the second floor of this majestic structure. Somebody pinch me. I felt no stress, and nothing was going to stand in my way.

A Scottish regimental officer in full dress uniform bagpiping us into the castle was almost too much to comprehend. It was a fairy-tale beginning to what would eventually become one of the most memorable weeks of my entire existence.

Dave, Wayne, and Kahli were the consummate tour guides, and they were available for any help, suggestions, and mentorship. We explored castles, lochs, ruins, rugged landscapes, ancient bridges, and ate at some of the best roadside pubs ever. We were even graced with a rainbow or two every single day. I could spend a month writing of the extraordinary sights seen. Loch Ness and Urquhart Castle, Eileen Donan Castle and the infamous Hairy Coo's were but a few, but the most memorable day was our ascent to the top of Storr.

On the Isle of Skye, there is a peninsula called Trotternish—some very rugged landscape overlooking the Sound of Raasay. The Storr—the Scottish refer to it as a hill—is a rocky outcropping rising 720 metres above the sea. The main attraction, The Old Man of Storr—a pinnacle of rock rising above the surrounding landscape—can be seen for miles when approaching the area by vehicle. We were to spend the day hiking this ridge. It was more of a climb.

Having just come off months of almost total immobility due to my sciatica, I knew I was not in the best shape physically to be attempting this strenuous climb. Even though the pain had gone away, I still felt the exertion of any walking or climbing on an incline. This, coupled with some anxiety about the physical aspects of the day had me in a bit of a state by the time we parked the van. Just the view from the parking lot of the majestic structures high above me was intimidating. I knew I needed a reset. With a moment of quiet reflection, and feeding off the excitement of the group, I steeled myself for what lay ahead. I was not going to let this moment pass me by. It was a matter of pride that I make every effort to complete the climb and enjoy every step forward. I was secure in the knowledge that we as a group had all day to make the almost four-kilometre hike up and down the forty-five-degree incline. Our guides knew of my recent inactivity and were keeping an eye on my progress with much encouragement—and a little teasing too. Slowly, but ever so determinedly, I made it to the grouping of rocky pinnacles with the rest of the group. The view from that height, looking out over the waters and valleys below, is forever etched in my memory.

It was then that I lost it. Standing upon a truly otherworldly piece of God's creation, overwhelming emotion poured from me. It was a culmination of what I would later determine to be years of pent-up feelings. In that moment, I purged the ridiculous notion of my inadequacy. I tore the scab off of the "I'm not good enough" syndrome, and then, just for good measure, I threw in some of the "I fucking did it" wails, loud enough for all to hear. I stood there and wept. Kahli, bless her heart, knew exactly what I was experiencing and just hung out beside me for a few moments, allowing me to freely take it all in. With a big hug, she told me how proud she was of me for rising above my fears and pushing through the doubt to reach the apex of the moment. She grabbed my iPhone and took several shots of me hamming it up, capturing the release of so much of what I had been keeping inside for years. It was my "aha!" moment, a clean break from my past aggressions and finally, my path forward.

I wandered off on my own for a bit, taking pictures of the beautiful vistas—Kahli in her flowing red dress from afar, and the group wandering around below me. At one point, I knew I had to put a final exclamation point on the day, so I climbed an eighty-degree, rock-strewn incline, high above anyone else there, and touched the face of the huge granite wall rising straight out of the earth on top of Storr. For the next several minutes, I steeled myself—just breathing. My grandchildren danced in my head. My children were with me at that moment, in spirit. My family, my friends, my life passed before me in an instant. After sixty-three years, I finally understood what true peace felt like.

The last night in the castle was magical. The cast of characters I hung out with that week will live in my heart forever. How could it get any better? Well, I did win another photo challenge for a silhouette shot taken up on Storr! Two workshops, two wins! I was ecstatic!

The ride back to Glasgow was also magical. I held a return ticket for the train back, but Dave had rented a car and was taking the scenic route back to the airport the same day. When he asked me to join him for the drive, I was elated. We had a fabulous three hours together, just the two of us, one on one. I'm not sure there was a silent moment the whole ride back. Sorry if I bent your ear right off you, Dave!

A last night in Glasgow with a meal at one of the world's best Indian restaurants, ended my dream vacation to Scotland. It was off to the airport, and after a few minor glitches with connecting flights, I was home.

49. Some Grandson Lovin' Before The World Goes To Shit

Finally, I got to meet baby Lochlan. Only days after arriving back to Canada, I was on the road to Kingston—one more time. I had arranged a week at an Airbnb, the Horse Ranch and Resort in Battersea, about twenty kilometres northeast of the city. I wanted to give the new parents unfettered room to deal with a newborn, sleep when they could, and not have to worry about Papa being in the way. It worked out perfectly. I spent time with them at home. They came to the ranch for a photo shoot and a visit, all the time trying to adjust to their new life. Proud is not a strong enough word to describe my feelings towards their growing family.

Christmas was again held at the Mazza's in Welland. Shaun, Yasmin, and the baby arrived late Christmas Eve to everyone's delight. Lochlan was introduced to his extended family for the first time. I would love to say it was a great time, and all was well, but the truth is, my flu symptoms (but were they really?) started shortly after I got there. I spent almost the whole time in bed, sequestered away in the basement—only seeing the girls open their gifts and saying a quick hello to the other guests. I finally felt somewhat well enough to travel home on December 27th. There was no way I could have known it would be the last time seeing Shaun and family for over a year. Even harder to imagine was the fact it would be almost two and a half years before seeing Stephanie and family again.

And then it was 2020. Nobody the world over, was prepared for what was to take hold of our lives for the next many, many months.

I had just arrived at my latest house-sitting gig on Sandy Lane in Sarnia two days earlier. The eleventh floor of the third high-rise closest to the lake—overlooking the Sarnia Yacht Club—was just what I needed to get back to a healthy state. I was determined to make this next year the greatest ever.

The world then quietly whispered, "Hold my beer."

At the time, my only nagging concern was how my future plans looked after this three-month stint in the condo. Where would I go? What would I do? Normally I would have my direction mapped, many months of plans already in place. There was one idea however, kind of a far off thought out in left field, that was starting to take shape, and it was so different from anything else I'd done in the past that it was beginning to consume my everyday thoughts.

I was excited and somewhat apprehensive moving into the condo. Not because it wasn't nice—no, quite the opposite. It was beautiful—and that view! I was pretty stoked to be getting some great sunsets and changing scenes of the twin Bluewater Bridges during these winter months. The apprehension came because of my lack of enthusiasm for living in apartment-style housing. I had done that for three years while residing in Kingston, and although the location of that building enhanced the experience fully, I was still not sold on being in such a densely populated structure. I was more of an outdoors-space type of guy. However, the arrangements that my good friends, Bill and Arlene had offered were quite sweet. After some careful consideration, we agreed to terms. I was set up on Sandy Lane for at least three months.

My camera remained my closest ally. I would go for ten-kilometre walks—returning with hundreds of images just ripe for editing. My good friend, Cathy lived one building over and loved walking too. It was going to be a good winter. All the while, still that thought in the back of my mind—what's next?

I had been in Ontario since 1959. Wasn't it about time I changed things up? My parents had dreamed of moving back to their home province of Nova Scotia and talked about it on a regular basis. Words became reality when they finally made that move in 1985. What was this little niggle in my brain—testing the waters of this same notion?

The thought of moving to another locale—as I had done for my three years in Kingston—had entered my mind on past occasions, but because of my life and career path at the time, I had not been ready, willing, or even able to entertain a vision of moving across the country to my home province. My career was definitely the big stopper. My family, my relationships—or lack thereof, and my friendships, people I did not want to part company with, were also deciding factors in staying put in southwestern Ontario. I had probably resigned myself to the fact that I would live out my life in the city where I grew up.

But, as has been told in many a tale, things do change. My family was grown and married with children of their own. Any romantic relationship in my life at this moment was non-existent, some of my close friendships that I valued greatly had, in the recent past, ended, and my career had been over for years. I kept thinking back to my conversations with the Proctors in July, and again in October of the last year, about how awesome it would be if both of us relocated to the East Coast. Now I found myself thinking: *What reasons—if any—were stopping me?* In a word, nothing!

Being winter in Sarnia, I knew I had time to do the research and, if I was serious about it, get some real plans in place to finally "blow this pop stand." The more I thought about it, the more I knew it was going to become a reality, and definitely in the near future too. I had exhausted my stay in this city and could not stop thinking about the excitement of all the new adventures that would come my way because of this move. I could feel an awakening.

When this possibility began to feel real, it became all I could think of, and the hard planning started in earnest. I had definitely made up my mind. I was moving back to Nova Scotia!

In the past many years, ever since the 9/11 tragedy in the United States, I had not been a TV watcher. I chose back then to purge the negativity from my life and concentrate on the positive. It had not always been easy, but it had helped me through some rough times over the years. It did help that over the last few years of my self-imposed nomadic lifestyle, I hadn't had much access to the sensory bombardment of cable news. Yes, I remained aware of world news to the extent I needed to, but certainly was not a news junkie. But here I was, staying in this condo for the next three months, with total access to TV—if I cared to turn it on.

What did matter to me, only because I am a history buff, and especially American political history, was the fact that the forty-fifth President of the United States, Donald J. Trump, had recently been charged with two articles of impeachment, just a month earlier—this being only the third time in history that the act of impeachment was put before Congress and the Senate. Full disclosure: I have conspicuously—but consciously—not included much, if any, of the political controversy surrounding the role of his presidency during his one term of office. Let history be the judge of such actions. If you, dear reader, are finding these words at a much later date, you will, if interested, have a much better understanding of exactly what I refer to. I do include some reference for clarity because of its lead-up to later events.

The subsequent trial, held before the congressional body and covered extensively by the media, was now just getting underway. It was a historical event like we hadn't seen in many years. I considered it newsworthy. I sat in front of the TV for hours on end, absorbing all the talking points laid out in dramatic fashion. Adam Shiff, a member of Congress for California was also the senior member of the House Intelligence Committee. He had been selected as the chairman of the impeachment proceedings and was brilliant in his opening address to the American public. This was counteracted by the rallying cries of the Senate Republicans who, led by a dowdy old Kentucky member, Mitch McConnell, decreed from the get-go that the trial was a complete sham. In their opinion, there was no way they were going to vote to impeach this president, no matter what he had said or done. I know, riveting stuff, eh?

CNN, the Cable News Network, was at that time my choice of stations to view the proceedings. Whether it was because the talking heads that reported this spectacular event held the same beliefs as I did on the matter being juried or not is irrelevant now. It seemed at the time to be what I needed to hear. History will certainly be the judge of whether I was on the right side of the truth—or not. In true CNN fashion, the coverage was all consuming because of its political and historical nature—and not much else was reported to any significant degree during the ongoing hearings.

So, it was for this reason in particular that I was slow to hear—along with most of the North American population—of a small problem with an apparent outbreak of an unknown virus, all the way over in China. Oh, how the world would soon change.

Without going into great detail of how this virus started, media reports did come out in the early part of the year that it had something to do with a live-foods market in Wuhan, China. More importantly, it was spreading quite rapidly throughout the region. The reports went on to say that China had known about the spread of the virus for a couple of months. Did they choose to keep that detail from the World Health Organization (WHO), so as not to bring unwanted attention to yet another lethal pathogen emanating from their country? I'm not so sure we will ever know the truth.

During the last week of the impeachment trial in late January, as much as the news was all about the wrap-up of the House and Senate hearings and the inevitable outcome, the news of this virus (SARS-CoV-2) or Severe Acute Respiratory Syndrome Coronavirus 2, now with a given name of Covid-19 (Coronavirus disease 2019), was being talked about in much more prevalent terms. We were learning in rapid fashion that there had been, and continued to be many deaths related to the spread of the disease throughout Asia. With no known cure or vaccine, things started to spiral out of control. Each day the news was more grim. The numbers of newly infected people and subsequently the deaths attributed to Covid, were now being counted in the several hundreds, inching their way to the thousands. It was anyone's guess where those numbers would stop.

The coronavirus was now dominating the headlines. President Trump, as expected, had been acquitted of all charges against him by the Senate, and just in time—because the world had a new problem on its hands, much more severe than the economic impact of an impeachment trial.

As it was with SARS, H1N1, Ebola, and other pandemics in the past, this new medical issue was not outwardly affecting my life in the first week of February. It was discussed at length by all the talking heads, but the word "pandemic" was still not being spoken out loud. If anything, even given the news of the rapid spread of the virus throughout Europe, we in North America seemed ambivalent to the threat.

Super Bowl Sunday, February 2nd, dawned cold but dry. It had snowed the day before, so I decided to take a walk around the grounds of the building complex before watching the game later. Of course, I had my camera with me and I am sure glad I did. I took an image of the four trees sitting on a small spit of land, separating the nearby Cove from Lake Huron. It turned out so well that it has now become my most sold print as of this writing. Cathy, Cindy and John, Ann and several others have a version of it hanging in their homes. I am so grateful for these moments. They sustain me. And how was I to know that the shit that was happening the world over would soon crush my dreams for another good year.

Bill and Arlene's plan was to be back home by April 4th. I had my own plans to make, and there were about six weeks left to make them. No problem, lots of time—or so I assumed. The terms *social distancing* and *stay home, stay safe* were not in our normal vocabulary yet—but soon would be.

Sometimes, the universe just looks out for you, and for reasons unexplained at the time, things started falling into place at an accelerated pace. Writing this after the fact certainly proves that—again, more proof that the laws of attraction are real.

My research into the East Coast housing market had started in earnest. I spent some time looking through the different rental sites to see some properties that—quite frankly, seemed too good to be true. Given the cost of lakefront rentals in Ontario, the much more favourable initial offerings I found for Nova Scotia were proving to be the norm for that province. Location was not a major factor as far as where I was going to set down roots. My siblings, Karen, Joan, and families, my many cousins, aunts and uncles, all lived quite spread out—so, no matter where I landed, I was going to be relatively close to people I knew. Being true to my past nomadic lifestyle, I also hoped to do lots of travelling out of the country in pursuit of my greatest passion.

As Mom had years ago, I too had criteria for the ideal living arrangements, or at least dreams of such. They included: a single family, two-bedroom dwelling, not very big, in a rural area outside of the big cities. The dream part of this would be all of it resting on the shores of one of the many thousands of lakes throughout the province. The bonus scene in that dream would be if I could get all of this for rent that was affordable. No harm in willing something into being. I have always believed in the laws of attraction, and this was as good a time as any to put it all into practice—once again.

My plan, as initially formulated, was simple. I figured I needed to be in Nova Scotia sometime before the 10th of May, which would give me plenty of time to see my family and make the trek east. I had already spoken to Joan and determined that I could initially stay with them for the time it took me to find a place to rent for June 1st.

I was going to pack up my worldly belongings and leave Sarnia for Kingston on or about the 4th of April to spend some quality time with Shaun, Yasmin, and Lochlan. During the month, I would head to Welland for a week or so and visit with Stephanie and family before heading back to Kingston. There, I would get the U-Haul loaded with the stuff from my storage unit—finally—and make my way to Joan's. It was a simple plan, and quite doable. Or not.

By about the middle of February, the world—and more importantly, Canada and the USA—were taking note of the inevitable spread of this deadly virus to our shores. This was when I had another "aha!" moment. It came during a report on CNN by one of the nightly news anchors. Don Lemon matter-of-factly stated that at the time of his broadcast, there were 721 reported cases of the coronavirus in the USA and over 30 reported deaths. He then went on to solemnly state that in a week's time, these numbers would triple and would continue to triple or quadruple every week thereafter. Man, this guy was as serious as a heart attack. It was a heady statement, but the gravity in his presentation made me sit up and take note. Something needed to be done, and fast, to control the spread of Covid-19. But what?

Travel was slowly being restricted more and more. Countries were being outed as the ones we as citizens could not travel to or receive visitors from—mostly from Asia and Europe. The infection rate and death toll were mounting exponentially, with no end in sight. Talks of finding a vaccine, or even eventually a cure, were many months away at best.

The next two weeks were crucial. The world did see a huge spike in the infection rate as the virus spread to all corners of the earth. No country was safe, and almost no country was spared its wrath. China, Italy, and Spain were especially hard hit. The US was seeing their numbers growing at an alarming rate. Canada, meanwhile, was also starting to feel the rapidly growing effects.

As I and many millions of others sat around our TVs, trying to absorb the information that was coming at us daily, the governments of our nations started taking measures that, frankly, no one thought they would ever witness in a lifetime. In order to stop the spread of the disease, drastic measures had to be enforced.

It started with the call to self-isolate. That in and of itself was so foreign to a world that thrives on human connections. This led to social distancing, another thing I couldn't wrap my head around in the beginning. I am a huge hugger, and for me to not shake hands or hug someone upon greeting was insane. This led to a government-imposed shutdown of all non-essential businesses for a period of two weeks initially, and there was talk of shutting down all essential travel out of the country. Living on a border town, this included what we had taken for granted our whole lives: day trips to the USA. All of this uncertainty was beginning to tweak the fragility of my mental state—mind games I thought were not possible. More importantly, my already laid-out travel plans were not looking so solid anymore.

Reality set in. I still didn't have a place to rent in Nova Scotia, and it was all but certain I was not going to be able to stay at Joan's because of the social distancing factor. For that matter, I was definitely not going to be able to stay at my children's places for an extended visit before I made the journey back to my home province. Having to make those calls was excruciating. To not be able to say proper goodbyes to your children and grandchildren—well, there are no words. My children, having listened to the news everyday as we all did, understood the reasons for the change of plans, and agreed with them fully. I assured them I was only a short flight or a day's drive away. After the pandemic had subsided, we would see each other again. It still didn't make it any easier. After all, how long could this last?

I came across an ad for 163 Eagle Rock Dr. in early March. It was addressed somewhere in Springfield, NS. I had no idea where that was but would soon find out. What caught my eye were interior shots of the kitchen and bedroom loft area. It seemed some accent walls were painted orange, my favourite colour. I delved a little deeper. The more I read, the more I couldn't believe what I was reading. It was perfect! An eleven-hundred-square-foot, single family dwelling on 2.6 acres of property, in a rural location, on a lake in Lunenburg County. The stated rent was well within my doable range, and for the second bedroom, the owner had built a sixteen-by-eighteen-foot bunk house just down the lane. Could I have painted a better picture? If someone had been around, I would have asked them to pinch me.

The universe was definitely looking out for me. I emailed the owner and started down the path to securing my next residence. It took less than two weeks to get all my ducks in a row. Now, Butler Lake was mine. What I didn't anticipate, and should have, was the continued rapid spread of the virus throughout Canada and around the world. By the time I signed the deal on the rental, the Canadian government had essentially eliminated travel. We were encouraged to curtail all movement out of the country for the foreseeable future. To make matters even more grave, all non-essential travel between provinces was being halted for the most part, and all travellers were questioned at makeshift checkpoints at each of the provincial borders.

Shit was getting serious. Time to revamp the plans—again. Bill called from Florida. He let me know they were coming home a week early because of the border issue. This meant that now I had to be out of the condo by March 26th. What to do?

I text my future landlord who, by the way, resided in New Brunswick. I asked him if I could arrive much earlier than originally anticipated because of the impending travel restrictions—giving him a projected date of April 4th—the original date I was to leave Sarnia. He was kind enough to reply immediately in the affirmative. Good, one issue solved.

Now to figure out timing for the U-Haul rental, hotels, and Airbnbs all the way to my new home. These plans were not without their challenges. Fortunately, U-Haul was deemed an essential service so did not have to shut down. I made my rental reservation from Sarnia to Bridgewater, NS, instead of the original plan of picking the unit up in Kingston. I also confirmed hotel reservations in Kingston—having to go there to load my belongings from my storage unit. I certainly was not going to take any chances staying at Shaun's, given that baby Lochlan was only five months old.

I then confirmed my Airbnb in Grand Falls, NB at the Maple Lodge Resort, a place I had stayed a year earlier. What I didn't have covered was the recently opened window of time that I now had—because of Bill's early arrival. I booked a week at the Sincerely Airbnb Retreat in Corunna, a little village fifteen minutes downriver from Sarnia. Plans were finally coming together—again. When I finally got to Corunna, I was as organized.

That final week in Corunna was relaxing. It helped me de-stress somewhat from the turbulent weeks prior. The proprietor, Ida Swartz, was very charismatic—a charming lady with a storied past. The pandemic was raging, but Ida made me feel welcome at Sincerely. Social distancing was in full swing, and as much as it was very foreign to most everyone, we all began to accept this as the new normal. Ida and I would sit in two large, wing-back chairs six feet apart and enjoy a few moments of conversation each day. We regaled each other with tales of our lives, enjoying the human connection—something that had been sorely lacking. She cooked me some delicious meals—comfort food for the soul—making me feel safe in a world that was out of control. My time spent at Sincerely was exactly what I needed to set my mind to what lay ahead. Thank you, Ida, you are a treasure.

The hardest part of my imminent departure was not being able to physically say goodbye to anyone. Here I was, leaving the province permanently, and I couldn't even hug my friends, family—anyone. That hurt bad. The only thing to buffer the sting was knowing my future adventures were going to be epic. I just knew it.

50. Last Man Standing As A Troubled World Sighs

April 1st, April Fool's Day. There was nothing foolish about this day. I was about to begin my journey eastward, to a new life in my home province. I picked up the U-Haul and loaded it with the minuscule belongings I still had with me. Prior to leaving, I stopped at Lynda's to say goodbye. She had allowed me to store some of my belongings at the house for the winter. It was all packed up in no time. We spoke for a few minutes, finally embracing each other—social distancing be damned. The last stop before hitting the road was Val and Rob's. That was a tough one. It all became quite real when, saying goodbye to them, we didn't hug.

Sarnia now in my rear-view mirror, I settled in for the ride—Kingston on the horizon. This was really happening—the hardest part of the journey soon to come. Driving past the Hwy 403 exit to Stephanie's was difficult. I didn't know when the next time I would see them again and I fought back the tears. I arrived at my accommodations for the night on the outskirts of Kingston—the new Motel 6 near Hwy 401.

Shaun and I had agreed he would help me load the trailer the following morning. We were going to keep our distance as best we could. I didn't require his help and was done by noon. After a shower to freshen up, I went to their place about 4 p.m.—needing to grab the few remaining items I had stored in their garage. The trailer was now fully packed. We hung out in the driveway—just visiting. Yasmin and baby Lochlan stayed for a short time—at a distance. This was tough on them too; with a tearful goodbye, they went back inside. Shaun and I had a couple glasses of wine to toast the impending journey, and then it was time to leave. I teared up as I drove away and cried for a good while afterwards.

Sleep that evening was sporadic. My plan was for a good night's rest, and on the road no later than 6 a.m. My body thought otherwise. I was wide awake, showered, and gone by 2 a.m. The next twenty-four hours would be the strangest time ever spent on a road trip—anywhere.

I was starting my trek to Nova Scotia, the trailer filled with my worldly possessions, and the Covid-19 pandemic reaching Biblical proportions. All non-essential retail was now closed—including restaurants and most other public places. Although gas stations remained open for fuel, the public washrooms were off limits to anyone but essential workers. Truckers, police, fire, EMS, and those who travel for work—doctors etc.—could use them, but not the motoring public. Fast food restaurants such as McDonald's and Tim Hortons were only open for drive-through. It was a challenge to stay fed and hydrated. I had stocked up on non-perishable foods and a supply of bottled water in anticipation of this issue.

I now know what it's like running through an apocalypse. On the normally very busy Trans-Canada Highway from Kingston to Grand Falls, NB, I drove through a vacuum, a virtual ghost town on the other side of my windshield. The first three hours to the south of Montreal, I saw five semis and no other cars. The absence of the many large trucks—used to move the essential products to keep the country running—was a scene ripped from *The Twilight Zone*. I will readily admit, it was at times somewhat intimidating to feel like you are the last person on earth. This social being struggled with that feeling.

The weather cooperated. Maple Tourist Home Bed and Breakfast in Grand Falls was a welcome sight. The proprietor and I had spoken a few days earlier—having assured ourselves we had been taking all the right precautions to fulfill the reservation without concern. It did help that I had stayed at this same place the previous fall. Victoria remembered me. I fully understood her line of questioning in these troubled times—her children were concerned for her well-being, and rightly so. Even with that, she still offered to make me a full breakfast the following morning. I politely refused, putting her at ease. In the morning, she had laid out fruits, muffins, and some bottled juice. Victoria had provided a welcome oasis—when all around me, uncertainty reigned.

The original plan for the rest of my journey consisted of a stop outside of Salisbury, NB. I was to meet my new landlord, Bryce Reede, at the Big Stop just off the highway, to exchange greetings and the keys to the property. This, unfortunately, did not happen. Because of the newly imposed restrictions on province-to-province travel, which included a mandatory fourteen day quarantine after entering Nova Scotia, Bryce could no longer do his usual deep clean prior to my arrival. He did, however, get an agreement from the departing tenants to make sure the place was presentable and to leave the keys in the decorative birdhouse on the front porch. Bryce also contracted a team of painters to come in and spruce the place up—a thoughtful gesture on his part.

Speaking of the newly implemented fourteen-day quarantine imposed by the government of Nova Scotia—that included me too. This created a whole new set of issues. I would need groceries to sustain me for two weeks, and at least something to sleep on until I could get some furnishings ordered. Enter dear Joan. I had forwarded her a list of essentials I would need to get me by while self-isolating. She was kind enough to do my grocery shopping for me and supply an air mattress with sheets for temporary usage—or so we thought at the time. The plan was to enter the province and, contrary to the official rules, go to her house to pick up these items before heading south to Eagle Rock Dr. I arrived in Valley, just east of Truro, at about 12:15 p.m. to a wonderful greeting party. Joan and Graham, along with my nieces, Cara, Natasha, and their puppy, Finn, all came out to welcome me to the province. They also had my bags of delicious edibles and supplies waiting for me at the end of the driveway. Again, it was a difficult moment in not being able to hug my family—damn pandemic.

The final leg of the journey from Truro to Franey Corner/East Dalhousie—the little hamlet just northwest of the rental property—was filled with anticipation. I had finally arrived in the province of my birth for about the hundredth time—but for the first time in my adult life as a resident of. Over my sixty-three years on this earth, many stories, adventures, trials, and tribulations had seen me to this day. I could not help but think of my parents. Moving across the country so many years ago in search of a better life; they sought out meaningful work and a lifestyle that would sustain their growing family. The significance was not lost on me in that moment; it was sixty-one years to the day since the Pitts family arrived in Sarnia—and now, that many years later, I was arriving back in Nova Scotia. I truly wish with all my heart that they were still with us to help me celebrate this momentous occasion.

51. My Nova Scotia Home! Beautiful Lunenburg County

Of the many times I had been back to this province, little time had been spent this far southwest of the Halifax/Sackville area, so each kilometre towards my new home was filled with new sights. What I was not prepared for, even though I had located the property on Google Maps, was just how rural the area really was.

The community of Maple Hills is located on Butler Lake, in Lunenburg County, off the Forties Rd. My new residence was located almost a kilometre down Eagle Rock Dr., a winding dirt road, maintained through funding by the fifty-three property owners in the area. My GPS was surprisingly accurate—leading right to the proper address. As I drove the two-hundred-foot driveway towards the house, I proceeded at a crawl. I wanted to take it all in—for the first time.

Bryce had assured me the keys for the place would be accessible and located in the colourful birdhouse I now saw in front of me. The moment of truth had arrived. What if I didn't like the place? What if it was a pigsty inside? I was about to find out.

I grabbed the keys, sorted out which one opened the front door, and entered the cavernous space. To my pleasure, and amazement, the place was perfect—for real!! Even though I had no furniture—actually nothing but the borrowed air mattress, two lawn chairs, and a few of my personal belongings from my storage unit—I was home. It was going to be a long two weeks of quarantine. But then again, cousins come to the rescue! Covid be damned, Christine Beck showed up with a couple of bottles of wine and some eating utensils—things I sorely needed. Thanks, cuz!

Priorities came into focus quite fast. I needed heat. To that end, I had asked the previous tenants to leave me a smattering of firewood to tide me over until I could get some delivered. They were kind enough to supply me with about a week's worth of good clean, and dry wood. The airtight wood stove was immediately put to use and was a godsend—considering the still chilly temperatures that are a constant in April in Nova Scotia. Next up was cell service, internet, and power hookup. All of that went quite smoothly—but looking back, my cell service was shitty to non-existent, and my internet cost me an arm and a leg. Power was rather affordable, so I had no issues there.

Once settled, I needed to furnish the place. A bed and mattress were my top priorities for initial creature comforts, but unfortunately they took four and a half months to be delivered from the Brick Warehouse. Pandemic issues were causing havoc with every aspect of life at that time.

What happened next was downright frightening. On the morning of April 19th, just over two weeks after coming home, I got a text from my sister asking me if I was ok. A little perplexed, I inquired as to why she was asking me this. I would come to find out that central Nova Scotia was under attack by a deranged serial killer. At the time of the text, this monster was still on the loose. Damn, as if I didn't have enough to think about, just trying to stay safe from the pandemic. I gathered as much information as possible, and felt somewhat safe as the incidents of death and destruction were occurring about two hours from me. That gave me little solace, considering my in-province family members were right in the thick of it. The killer was finally neutralized later that morning at a Big Stop rest area in Enfield, culminating in the worst mass murder spree in Canadian history. And, if you're keeping score, this was another traumatic event to scar my senses just a little more. Truth be told, I'm still not over that one. Meanwhile, life had to move on.

I continued to source the things I needed to make my place a home. I discovered the company Wayfair, and even though I had never ordered much online before, I ended up outfitting my complete home with this company. They did live up to their name and were way fair to me with any issues I had with deliveries, damaged goods, and such. The whole process took five months to complete—given the supply and demand issues caused by the world doing a reset. In the end, after all those months, it all came together. I was very satisfied with my fledgling interior design skills. Those same skills, just newly exercised, would later be justified when life threw me another curve ball.

For someone who had shunned the online-buying lifestyle for so long, I finally stepped up my photography game that August and purchased from Amazon, a Nikkor 200mm to 500mm f:5.6 super-telephoto lens to "reach for the stars," so to speak. It is a decision I have never regretted. I pride myself on my restraint when it comes to gear purchases—having never bought anything camera-related that didn't enhance my progress towards better images. The new reach was fabulous, and I levelled up big time.

Amidst all the negativity surrounding the health issues of the entire world, there was some good news. Ian and Jenn, (accompanied by their trusty feline, Nyx) had finalized plans to move to Nova Scotia. After a very long drive from Calgary, and having experienced most of the same issues I had, they made it to their new province in early June, safe and excited for the future. They settled into their condo-style unit in Halifax and began to enjoy the area in earnest. It was great to have my friends so close.

The pandemic however, continued to worsen. In November of 2020, the USA had surpassed 230,000 deaths, and the infection rate climbed to well over a thousand humans a day—with no vaccines to counteract the spread. Canada was not much better off. The only bright side to this issue was our own "Atlantic Bubble." In time, the governments of the four Atlantic provinces had shut their borders to any and all outsiders. If you wanted to enter the province, you had to prove your residency, quarantine for a mandatory, fourteen-day period, and get tested for Covid at least twice in that time period. This strategy worked for a time, keeping our infection rates near zero, and almost Covid-free. Wearing a mask in any public place was also mandatory—this rule had been in place for months. Hand sanitizer was located everywhere, and again, it was mandatory to use it prior to entering just about any public establishment. Social distancing—at a six-foot measure—became the norm. These requirements, put in place by the government, went completely against anything we had ever come to know, and there was no end in sight.

With the vaccines still in the development phase, most of us knew a second wave of infections would be coming, and it did. In late November, with the virus raging around the world and literally on every continent, our little bubble burst. It was inevitable and unstoppable. Most indications were that a segment of the population, between eighteen and thirty-five years old, were increasingly becoming infected. The Halifax metro area, or officially the Central Region, was seeing a huge increase. It was suggested by our provincial health minister that we not travel to that specific region, and the residents of that same region were not to travel outside of it. Think about that for a second. We were actually being instructed to remain in our own communities—and God help us if we were then caught breaking that rule. It sounded so draconian. Even so, I did understand why such restrictions were needed—we had to get this virus under control.

The development of a viable vaccine was happening at breakneck speed. To everyone's amazement, the first approved vaccines came out in less than a year. To some doomsday-scenario skeptics, this was perceived as a life-threatening move. On a personal note, I sure hoped the vaccine would work—so to me, it was a no-brainer. I felt it was imperative we get this virus under control and eventually eradicated—so we could become social humans again. I was willing to receive my jab to make that happen. After much controversy and debate, the newly developed Covid-19 vaccines started going into the arms of the masses in early 2021.

In the meantime, and even prior to me being able to book my first dose, I continued my solo explorations, plying the province for photo opportunities. I was becoming quite successful at seeing much of the area in the three different seasons I'd experienced to date.

I had set a goal when I arrived in the province earlier that year. I was going to try and navigate every road in Nova Scotia, and so far, I had managed to add a few thousand kilometres to my 4Runner's odometer while attempting to do just that—my creative passion for photography driving the efforts to succeed.

I had moved from Ontario during the beginning of this worldwide pandemic and had landed, oh so softly, in a beautiful home on Butler Lake. Other than not having my family and grandchildren close by, I had everything I could possibly want. I felt secure in my surroundings. So, when I received the email from the landlord in early December, inquiring as to my intentions to rent the lake house for another year, I had to take a breath. It couldn't be that time already? I was caught a bit off guard, having not even given it much thought, and being only nine months into the original term. After looking at my lease, I quickly learned that I had to give at least three months' notice to vacate the premises—if that was my intention. Damn, I didn't even have intentions—because I hadn't even thought that far in advance. After weighing my options—staying put versus finding a new place to live, I committed to renting Eagle Rock Dr. for another year. Bryce and I agreed to terms. Now that my decision was made, I settled into a nice winter routine.

Christmas and New Years of 2020 was so out of the ordinary for me. I was invited to Joan's for a couple of days to celebrate with family, but as luck would have it, we were getting increased numbers of patients in the area infected by Covid, so I thought wisely that as much as I would have loved to do *normal*, I needed to think of the big picture—that being that I truly wanted to see my own family and grandchildren again someday. I needed to keep myself safe. I stayed home and had a quiet Christmas at the lake house. I rang in the new year in the same fashion, and now that the holidays had passed, I felt good about my decision. I was determined to get to the other side of this pandemic and experience a normal life—once again.

Not being able to be as active as I would have liked, I had gained a few Covid pounds—as they were fast becoming known. I'm sure we've all been there. On the positive side, I wasn't going out to restaurants and bars anymore, so the dollar savings were substantial, and I was routinely making every meal at home—three times a day, every day. This became challenging. Not for the fact I had to figure out what to make every day, or even that I had to cook it—I knew my culinary skills were on point. My issue was portion control. Coming from a huge family, I was always taught that if you were going to make supper, make enough for everybody—a mantra my mother often preached. So I did, for an army! The ultimate issue then became self-discipline, and the portions sizes I would serve myself. I enjoy my own cooking and try to make each and every meal as flavourful as possible. This would include pairing my meals with the perfect bottle of wine. And of course, it tasted so good that I would inevitably have seconds. I began to realize this was not a healthy way to eat or live and started devising a plan of action. I hate diets—so that route was immediately dismissed. There had to be a better, more natural way. It wasn't long before I was on my way to a healthier me.

Significant events in one's life are often a catalyst for change. The substance of an early-evening phone call from Shaun was exactly the catalyst I needed. As much as I was happy, healthy, and safe, there was such joyous news in that conversation, I knew it was time to get back to exercising. When he told me he and Yasmin were expecting a wee sibling for Lochlan, I was brought to tears of joy. This was the kick in the ass I needed. I had to maintain my health in order to one day get back to Ontario to meet this little treasure. Not only that, but my next birthday was the big one. You only get to go around the sun the sixty-fifth time in your life once if you are lucky—so no more excuses. It would be a couple of months before we knew the sex, but I told Shaun instantly that he was having a girl. I love being right!

My story wouldn't be consistent if I didn't continue to include snippets of significant world events that influenced my life. Having said that, I have purposely continued to leave out the excruciating details of the presidency of "forty-five." As much as I love American politics, I just can't for the life of me justify bringing that level of insanity to print. Way too much media has been dedicated to this era, and unfortunately, it continues.

Here, I make an exception—for one significant day. January 6th, 2021—the day of the Capitol riots. It pains me to think that one man, in today's world, garnered enough power and influence to try to overthrow the government of the United States. It pains me even more deeply to think that so many Americans actually believed his rhetoric and went along with his antics. What a bunch of fu . . . Oh, never mind. I just hope I live long enough to see how history is written—for future generations to study.

I, for one, was ecstatic with his defeat, and as January 20th approached, I made arrangements to spend the day with the Proctors so we could immerse ourselves in the revelry of President Joe Biden's Inauguration Day. Was Joe the right man for the job? I don't know, but I suspect history will reveal those answers eventually. Like it or not, politics is a divisive institution. We will never agree on everything, so for those of you so inclined, let's just agree to disagree on this subject and move on—'nuff said.

The next day, January 21st, I made the monumental decision to attempt to walk a minimum of ten thousand steps a day, every day. This was the one thing I knew I could accomplish—given my present location and circumstances. I had no end goal in mind, and no idea how long I would last—or if I would even make it past a day or two. I just knew I had to try. As will be noted later on, I did alright.

The winter dragged on through Covid waves. Catastrophe was everywhere, but Nova Scotia seemed to ride the tide of our self-induced isolation rules, and we fared well. Yes, there were deaths, and the hospitals were overwhelmed at times, but compared to the rest of Canada, we were going to be ok.

Vaccines, consisting of two separate doses, were finally given approval for distribution. Nova Scotians stepped up to the plate—big time. The roll-out started from the seniors on down. I got my first shot in late March. After almost fifteen months of concern for my well-being, I felt I now had a fighting chance to fulfill my wishes of seeing my two children and grandkids again. Little did I know just how long that wait would be.

The saving grace to all the isolation and down time was seeing life through the lens. Travel was obviously out of the question. I was also struggling with the motivation to add to this story—so I made it a habit to get outdoors several times a week. I wanted to continue to create a new body of work that I would be proud of. There were more ICM (in-camera-movement) techniques learned, a few Zoom seminars attended, and trips with Ian to the water's edge—visiting the many picturesque fishing villages along the Atlantic and Bay of Fundy coasts. Today, I just can't imagine my retirement life without my camera, the incredible friends I have made, and the knowledge I have gained through this medium.

I also wanted to upgrade my hardware. A shiny new iMac 27" desktop computer—heavily equipped with some badass shit for editing purposes—did the trick. Purchasing this was more of a mental crutch than an absolute necessity. I had a MacBook Pro, quite sufficient enough to do any of the editing I needed, but psychologically, I needed the boost—it totally did the trick. Not only did I really enjoy editing my images on the big screen, but my passion for writing picked up considerably. There is something to be said for having the right equipment for the job at hand.

Winter finally gasped its last breath. We had experienced some fairly severe weather in March—with high winds and about forty to fifty centimetres of snow. I had been quite lucky until then to be able to get in and out of my long driveway over the past few months. This was different. The giant road grader was plowing Eagle Rock Dr., so I asked about the possibility of him taking a swipe at my lane. After negotiating a fair price, he brought the behemoth down the drive. All was going swimmingly until the driver asked me to move my vehicle over to the side. Unfortunately, I got a little too rambunctious in complying with his wishes and ran my vehicle into the side of a tree while backing up. The crunch was sickening but there was not a damn thing I could do about it. I sheepishly parked the now-damaged vehicle where he wanted it. I'm sure he was just as shocked as I was—witnessing this bonehead move. When he was finished throwing the snow around, he hightailed it out of there, and never did come back for payment. I guess he figured it was going to cost me enough already. The 4Runner was still operational, but the front left quarter panel was in rough shape. This was the first time in thirty-five years that I had done any sort of damage to a vehicle. I eventually had it fully repaired with OEM parts at a great facility down the road—the claim going through my insurance, so it didn't cost me a dime out of pocket. Lessons learned—pay attention to your surroundings when in control of your vehicle (my father's driving lessons from fifty year past, still ringing in my ears).

The snow finally melted, and spring smells permeated the air. I had purchased three cords of dry, split firewood shortly after arriving at the property a year earlier and now, having enjoyed a cozy warm winter on the lake, needed to replenish my stock. It was prudent to get it delivered in time to allow the wood to season for the following winter's heat. I liked being prepared. I called the same supplier as before and, remembering me, he said yes to another three cords—to be delivered the following week at the same price as last year. I was happy with the deal and looked forward to the workout—stacking the split logs into my woodshed. That's the greatest thing about buying firewood in bulk. It warms you twice—once while stacking it and once while burning it.

Perpetual Motion

The distinct smell of fresh-cut firewood is intoxicating to me. It always brings me back to the many trips to Nova Scotia in the early fall—helping my father with his huge stack of long logs, which had been deposited in his driveway earlier in the summer. We would use the chainsaws to cut the logs to length, lay them on the power splitter, throw the split logs in a huge pile, and then stack that pile into the woodshed he had built, just for that purpose. That was fine country living for sure.

My delivery was set for April 24th. That morning dawned frosty and clear, perfect conditions for a good day's work in the yard. By this time, I hadn't missed my daily ritual of taking my ten thousand steps, and with the physical labour required to move the three cords, I knew this day was going to be a high-water mark. The stake truck arrived, deposited the load in a spot just beyond the shed doors, and was gone. And now before me—hours of manual labour. I was in my element.

52. Now What

I was two hours in, and close to a cord stacked, when my phone pinged. As it was a beautiful morning, I had it next to a water bottle on the shelf in the shed, and knowing that the signal was weak at best, hurriedly picked it up to retrieve my message. It was from my landlord. I read the message. I read it again. I think I actually read it a third time. Comprehension has always been one of my strong suits, but my brain was not quite grasping the gravity of the text. After all, I was elbow-deep in a very large pile of firewood—just delivered, all to make my life comfortable and warm in the ensuing winter, which, giving my head a shake as I tried to reason, was still eight months away. WTF?

So, if you recall, the real estate market was in overdrive during the Covid pandemic. For reasons unexplained in this writing, but which can be seen and read about anywhere, people lost their collective shit when it came to pricing strategies for housing. Bryce saw an opportunity. He was no fool. He had attempted to sell this piece of property several times over the last few years—to no avail. There was no doubt in his mind that now was the time to act. Bryce did have one immediate problem. He had recently agreed to another year-long lease with me on this same property. It must have pained him to send that text. There was a conciliatory air to the words on my screen. He said it was just an exploratory venture—maybe to see if there was any real interest in his holdings. He also assured me that I was safe, and if things did happen, he would make sure I was included in the dealings. What exactly did that mean?

Well, this was an unexpected turn of events. I put the phone down and proceeded to stack the rest of the wood into the shed. It took me exactly eight hours in total—working non-stop, all the while running these latest developments through my head. Bryce let me know he was sending a real estate agent out to the property—to advise on a competitive price to bring to market. He was only giving the agent a thirty-day window in which to see if there was any interest from the buying public. There would be minimal interruption to my life. I would only need to step out for the short time the buyers, if any, would be viewing the property. He also mentioned a short window of opportunity for viewing—a Friday, a Saturday, possibly a showing on the Sunday. The last thing mentioned, again in a conciliatory manner, was that many potential buyers for this type of property came from out of province. It was quite possible there could be an opportunity to stay right where I was for the upcoming year. My mind was whirling.

I have a small, framed plaque on my desk that has been in place for well over two decades. It is a five-by-seven image of a door cracked open, a sunburst shining through the small opening. The message reads: OPPORTUNITY—*When one door closes, another opens. Seize the opportunity while the path remains lit.*

This has been a mantra of mine, and I have lived by these words for years. It dawned on me, if ever this mantra rang true, it was now. I cleaned up, poured a Scotch, and began to plan my future.

Bryce's realtor, Kane Smith, was coming to the house in two days. True to my nature, I made sure the place was in showroom condition when he showed up. We hit it off instantly, and after an hour or so of observation—drone footage and still images—he couldn't help but say he had never dealt with a more cooperative tenant in all his years in sales. I knew there was no sense in being negative about my circumstances. I was taking all of this as a sign. It was my opportunity to possibly relocate to a new area of the province, thus assuring me a whole new canvas in which to create images. I also knew that the universe would provide, as it always had. The laws of attraction were still hard at work.

The promised couple of days of viewings stretched into five. There were nineteen showings—with multiple offers—and within days, a *SOLD* sign on the property. During this time, I had put out feelers to the prospective buyers—through Kane—that I was willing to sell my brand-new furniture so they would have move-in ready accommodations upon closing. I really didn't expect much of a reaction, but I was wrong. There was strong interest in my furnishings from many of the clients, and even a few willing to have me stay as a tenant—a caretaker of sorts. In the end, the property was sold locally. I was put in touch with the purchasers to negotiate their wishes for the available furniture.

You may be wondering why I wanted to sell perfectly good and almost new furniture. It all came down to where I eventually decided to move. Once I gauged the overwhelming interest in the lake property, I knew I would be relocating, so I needed to find a place to live—and soon. Legally, I had three months to vacate the premises. Kane had suggested a couple of resources I could use in order to find suitable accommodations. I wasn't choosy and could live pretty well anywhere, so I had already done some digging. What happened next really was the epitome of attracting what I needed—yup, feeling that vibe again!

When I first talked of moving east in early 2020, Joan had mentioned that she worked for a gentleman who builds duplex rentals, and that he had a unit being built in the little town of Milford, NS. Being in a huge cauldron of uncertainty from the emerging pandemic, my need to find my way across the country before everything was shut down was paramount. I had no idea where Milford was and didn't really have the time nor the inclination to put an effort into research. I had already found the lake house by then, and that was where I was to take my chances. I hadn't given Joan's suggestion another thought—until this moment.

I called her and nonchalantly asked if her friend had any places for rent. Wayne, who just happened to be her boss, did indeed have a new double unit being built right then—again in Milford. This time, I took a much closer look at location, what was being offered, and ultimately, how much closer it was to Joan and Karen. I found my way to the build the next day. Wayne noticed me prowling around and introduced himself. We hit it off straight away. He knew right away that I was the right fit for his rental. Within the hour, I had secured my new home. The unit was just a shell at this time, drywall not quite done, no flooring, no cupboards, no bathroom—I listened as he described the upscale decor. It sure sounded sweet, so I took him at his word. We agreed to a move-in date of June 1st.

With that minor detail out of the way, preparations for dealing with the sale of my furnishings and firewood was next on the to-do list. It all worked out perfectly with the new owners, Amy and Robin. They had offered me more than a fair price for the wood and several of my pieces. I wouldn't have to move any big-ticket items. The proceeds from the sale would also allow me to decorate the new place as it should be—instead of trying to shoehorn my existing furnishings into a smaller space. Again, thank you, universe.

53. Milford... For The Moment, Anyways

On June 1st, with immense thanks to my great friend Ian, I moved into a brand-new duplex—on a ridge overlooking some beautiful farmland, complete with an eastern exposure from the back deck. I just knew the sunrises were going to be spectacular.

I didn't realize how much I had missed being a part of a small community. There were actual humans walking the streets instead of bears and coyotes. This little hamlet included a Timmie's, a pizza shop, and a Foodland right down the street. I took to it like flies on shit! Being such a social person for my whole life, and then to basically isolate for what seemed like forever, this move was a huge boost to my mental attitude—as well as my soul. I needed this change. Today, I think back to the hours and days I contemplated staying at the lake house for another year. I know I would have made it work, I always do—but without a doubt, landing in Milford was the better move.

The day after the move, I drove back to the lake house to finally meet Amy and Robin in person. We had communicated several times by text and phone, and I was coming back to pick up the cash for my items. We knew from previous conversations we had many things in common—wine, food, and nature—but spending time with the two of them that afternoon sealed the deal. What a wonderful couple. Before leaving, they insisted I come back for a weekend to get better acquainted. I had found new friends just by being open to what possibilities there were out there. I knew we would do just that. In late August, I spent a fun-filled, action-packed, wine-drinking, gourmet-food-eating, friendship-making weekend with them, and even stayed overnight in the bunkie I had renovated while still residing at the property. It will always be a treasured memory.

Perpetual Motion

After being in perpetual motion for the last four years straight, uncertainty ruling much of my life, Milford felt like home. It would take me a few months to get this nest outfitted to my liking, but that was okay by me. I knew it was not going to be as much of an ordeal as the lake house had been to furnish. I could just feel my outlook improving every day.

Then came August 5th, 2021, a very special day. I turned sixty-five years old—a true milestone. I went for a drive, explored some quaint little fishing villages along the Atlantic, stopped for a celebratory drink, and ate some fabulous seafood at a family restaurant in Sheet Harbour. I met a couple who were on a grand adventure on two wheels, all the way from Winnipeg. We talked for an hour, comparing stories of the open road—they having more recent experiences than I. Before they departed, I took a few images of them standing with their ride—with a promise to send prints. Afterwards, on the drive home, I had time to reflect on my life up to this point. I concluded my day with the thought that I had lived a good life, and this might be the proper moment to put an end to the written sojourn of my time on this planet. Many stories had been written, tales told, and memories made. I closed the file. I would take a break for a few weeks—knowing there was a full edit still to do.

Three weeks later, on August 30th, I got the phone call. Yasmin and Shaun had just welcomed their second child, my fourth grandchild, Mila Yasmin, to the world. If I had finished the book on my birthday—the original goal—baby Mila would have missed out, so I continued to write. I could not have been happier or more excited for them, and of course for me—remember that reason for me staying healthy? I had to get back to Ontario to meet sweet Mila. Now, if only this damn pandemic would just fuck off. With the promise from them to send lots of pictures, I resigned myself to the coming fall and winter— again without the hugs I so needed from my family. It would, however, give me lots of time for the book editing process. I embraced it.

Fortunately for me, this wonderful community of Milford has also embraced me, and I did feel some relief from the stress of not having a shred of intimacy the last two years. Because of my continued daily walks, I met and eventually became friends with several neighbours. Out of this came several photography opportunities, including portrait work, both individual and group sessions, some fine art canvases hanging on their walls, and several other unique shoots. I was feeling good about the progress I was making in my artistic endeavours. Ian and I continued to make images together, enjoying our ever-growing friendship.

Early September brought another gift. My sister Valerie and her husband Rob, after retiring from their respective careers in Sarnia, sold everything and moved back to Nova Scotia, eventually buying a house five minutes from Joan's, and a half hour from me. This was truly a blessing. Valerie and I have always been really close, and it was very hard for both of us when we said our goodbyes as I was leaving Ontario—way back at the beginning of the pandemic. This move remedied all that.

Even though the viral crisis is still news, I have not let it affect me negatively for the most part. I have continued to make new friends, kept in touch with old friends, taken many photographs, catered suppers, walked millions of steps—and attempted to remain relatively healthy. Best of all, touch wood, I have never had Covid.

I had made plans to drive back to Ontario to see my friends and family once again, especially Miss Mila, whom I had not yet been able to hold in my arms. Unfortunately, some painful medical/mobility issues arose, and I had to postpone that trip for a few months. I chose to remain as active as possible and started playing my guitar faithfully, every day. Yes, my damn fingers hurt for a couple of weeks, but when I got past that vile stage, I enjoyed making music again. I kick myself for not following through with it years ago.

Still more adventures were around the corner. I spent another fabulous week on PEI at the annual Land & See photography conference with Ian and the gang. Travel restrictions were lifted in the latter part of 2022, just in time for my long-anticipated ten-day trip to the west in September. I spent some time with Jesse, Susan, and friends, camping and hiking into the Great Bear Rainforest in British Columbia—finishing that trip off with some quality time in Vancouver, hanging with my old travelling buddy, Jim Butler. The months of October and most of November were spent travelling back to Ontario to finally meet Mila, and getting reacquainted with Lochlan, Leena, and Noelle. I fell in love with my grandchildren all over again! Quality time was also spent with many of my family members and close friends.

My minor health issues, femoral neuropathy and plantar fasciitis, have all but disappeared. I did get orthotics to help with the wonky gait.

I finally made my way back to Ontario once more this past spring. Stephanie was celebrating her fortieth birthday and I sure didn't want to miss that affair! I spent some quality time with my brother Greg at his cottage on Sturgeon Lake, and a week in Kingston with Shaun and family. I needed the family vibes so bad. I don't know how I went so long without it in the past. Most recently, I was back on PEI for the finale of the Land & See Conference and Workshop. It was a very emotional affair to say the least. My world is a better place to exist in because of the many years I attended those "Barn" sessions.

I know the next several years will bring more adventure to these old bones—God willin' and the creeks don't rise. And you can bet the farm on this one sure thing: The three activities I promised myself I would pursue in retirement—travel, photography, and writing—will continue to sustain me, now and for many years to come.

My frame of mind is good, and so am I.

Bring on the next sixty-seven years.

Afterword

So, is this how I finish this tale? No, I don't think so. If I am blessed with more time and good health, the stories will continue. The world is vast and alluring, and I have not seen anywhere near enough of it yet. Could there be a sequel in the works? Maybe...

We as a collective human body have had a real scare. We endured a three-year Covid-induced pause on our known ways of living and interacting with one another. It wasn't easy, and not everyone came out of this intact, but humanity itself has survived and will live to fight another day.

This type of global reset does not define any person's lifetime. The moments we have experienced and the lessons we have learned over the course of our existence—and how we apply them, is what makes up our legacy. It is up to us to use those many lessons for benevolent purposes—making me hopeful for the future.

It is with humility that I have learned many of my life's lessons, and I accept those teachings with gratitude. Things such as living a good life, loving deeply, grief, turmoil, and pain—both mental and physical—resilience, lifelong friendships, not-so-friendly humans, comedy, gut-wrenching laughter, giving freely from my heart, and so much more—have all come from my experiences on this patch of dirt. Some of those moments were very minor, and some... mind-blowing and life-altering. It hasn't always been an easy road. Some of those moments caused me to question my existence at times. But some—with the preverbal exclamation "Aha!" to emphasize them so eloquently—were the best times of my life. I will always cherish those moments. I have also worked tirelessly on my mental health. I am proud of myself for overcoming the challenges I have faced. *I am a survivor.* There are so many incredible humans who have helped and guided me on my path to a fulfilling, enriched retirement. I could not begin to name all of you. Just know that I am forever grateful.

And finally, even though my intended audience has somewhat grown from the initial concept of this book, I still think that wrapping it up requires some afterthought. Now that I've committed my life to print, and after reviewing the many stories told, I can assure you, the life lessons I have penned next are applicable to all who take the time to read my musings, my grandchildren included. I only wish I had known these antidotes while I was growing up.

Life Lessons

Learn How to Make Soup: This simple act of self-preservation is key to staying alive, not much different than boiling water. If you can graduate beyond that skill and become proficient in the culinary arts—to whatever extent—your life will be exponentially richer.

Get an Education: I don't mean you have to go to college or university, although that's not a bad idea. I mean really educate yourself in the ways of life, and don't stop learning. Even at sixty-seven, I learn every day. I will readily admit, I have gained 95 percent of my knowledge and education post high school. You can too.

Read a Lot, and Then Read More: Find a genre—or several—that interest you. Absorb every word you can get your hands on. You will thank me later. Share what you have read—and as a bonus, turn off the damn TV.

Keep a Journal: This one's obvious if you have read my book, and especially if you think you may write your own story someday. Don't rely on memory alone—after all, you are a part of the historical record, and accuracy is paramount.

Embrace the Music: It is the language of the world. Listen to your favourite sounds daily. I do. Sing and dance like no one is watching. I do. And while you're at it, try your hand at an instrument. If you stick to it, the satisfaction you get out of mastering your chosen implement will sustain your life—along with the soup.

Perpetual Motion

<u>Get a Job with a Good Pension</u>: You can take this literally—or not. This advice has been around for almost one hundred years. I am not dismissing the many professions that do not support this goal—especially self-employment. There are many entrepreneurs in this world who have gone on to greatness, supported themselves and their families, and have been successful saving a fruitful nest egg for those retirement years. My path was one of public service—and a good pension, post retirement. I am quite comfortable in my choices, which created my present income and lifestyle. There is no shame in working a meaningful career and, after paying into a good pension plan, reaping the benefits of such sacrifice in your golden years.

<u>Start a Savings/Investment Account</u>: This may sound so trivial, but you would be surprised at how many young people have never been given this advice—me included. I did not invest in any type of savings plan until I was forty-two years old. Don't make the same mistake I did—and while you are at it, invest in real estate. You can't really go wrong there, at least in my experience. It's a great way to learn finances.

<u>Buy the Hockey Cards/Comic Books</u>: This is a metaphor for so many things. If you can afford it, invest in memorabilia. That shit is gold—if you can hang on to your stash long enough. Just ask my brother Greg! I recently found out that my concert ticket stubs from the '70s are worth money. Who would have thought?

<u>Talk to Your Relatives</u>: Absorb their stories and consider how they relate to yours. The history your parents, aunts, uncles, and grandparents keep inside will be lost if you don't ask. There is a connection. Reach out.

<u>Take Time to Grieve</u>: Seriously, when the bottom falls out and you lose a loved one—whether it be a person or a pet—don't let others dictate when or how long you need to grieve the unimaginable loss. The damage to yourself comes when you stifle the needed process. This step is imperative to your future health.

<u>Realize When You Need Help</u>: If you scrape your knee, you put a Band-Aid on it. If you break your leg, you get a cast—and hopefully get it signed by the doctor. If you have chest pains, you get a checkup. If your head breaks—proverbially speaking—you need to get that fixed too. No stigma. No shame. Go see your doctor and get help. You do not need to suffer alone. You do not need to feel small. You do not need to feel inadequate. You do not need to take your own life. Wait! Let me repeat that: You do not need to take your own life!!! You do, however, matter to everyone who knows you—they are all in your corner. Medication is not taboo—if used correctly. It is your lifeblood to healing. Just do it. And remember this: If you fall down, get right back up. It will take effort. Just know you have the strength to do it.

<u>Don't Smoke, and if You Do Drink, Drink Responsibly</u>: Smoking just sucks. It makes you stink—in every way possible. Drinking on the other hand, if done responsibly, can be socially acceptable, of course—in my opinion only. I smoked when I was young but quickly realized my destructive pattern. I was one of the lucky ones to get out early. I have been a social drinker for all of my adult life. I am ok with that. But it can be a potential trigger for alcoholism and many other social issues—so if you find this is an issue for you, quit. No excuses, just quit.

<u>Take Chances</u>: Even in adversity, opportunity knocks, and doors open. Fight for the right to a better tomorrow. The situation you find yourself in, or the job you are offered today, can also be a stepping stone to better tomorrows. I see this in my beautiful children every day. They have both overcome dissatisfaction in previous ventures to get to where they are at present. I am so damn proud of them, forever and always.

<u>Admit When You Are Wrong</u>: Yes, this is a tough one. It takes practice, and I only wish I had practiced it much sooner. It would have saved me much grief. No, I am not saying you must give in, succumb to someone else's will. What I am saying is you must own your part. Almost inevitably, there are three sides to an issue, yours, theirs, and the truth. By calmly talking through it—and both of you accepting responsibility for your own

actions—there will be resolution. This is no more evident than in a marriage. Damn it, that shit takes work, and I should know. I have intimate knowledge of such things—you can right the ship.

Travel: Even if it means driving a few miles down the road to the next town. I have met many people on my travels who have not been thirty miles from their home, ever. The world is worth exploring, and if you start that savings account when you are young, this life lesson will become a reality much sooner than you think. Memories are so much more valuable than material things.

Take the Photograph: The world is a photographer's dream. I know this firsthand. You don't need to own an expensive piece of equipment. With a camera phone in your hand, most likely at all times, there is no excuse. The memories captured will have a greater impact when you can refer to those moments and relive them time and time again. And to add to this lesson, get your ass in front of the camera too. Those who love you will appreciate the view.

Go Fishing: Another metaphor. This sport is most often accomplished alone. It allows us to spend quality time with and by ourselves. Learning to be alone—as opposed to being lonely—is one of the greatest skills to master in life. Trust me, I know. It only stands to reason: If you love being with you, then others will too. When that skill is mastered, fishing becomes a shared sport. Friendships blossom—and as a bonus, you get to eat fish!

If You Go In, Go All In: Just recently, during a conversation with my friend Carole, she spoke a truth about me: "When you choose to do something, you are all in." Yes, I am. When I joined the fire service, I was all in. I retired at the top. I chose to be the best I could possibly be. When I started my walking journey, I never faltered—not one day. The same can be said for my photography. I take pictures every day and continually educate myself in its creative flow. Just recently—and this is the reason for her comment—I finally re-committed myself to my guitar. Yes, I am all in. Be passionate about life. You too can be all in.

Make New Friends, Even When You Are Old: This doesn't always work out, as witnessed in previous chapters, but I do truly believe that if you put your best foot forward you will be rewarded by strong human interaction at all stages of your life. Those wanting to hang out with you will want to know you better, and yes, most likely they will become good friends. This has been no more evident than in the last five years of my life. For all you young'uns out there—this holds true for you too. Just be a good person, and good will come to you.

Be a Giver: Do this without expectation. Donating to charities, helping friends in need, paying it forward at your local coffee shop drive-through, shovelling the neighbour's driveway after a snowfall, volunteering in your community . . . I could go on and on. You get the picture. Just do it. The health benefits of these acts are immeasurable.

Laugh Till It Hurts: Need I say more?

"What You Think—So Shall Be" (D.A. Pitts, 2007): Be careful what you wish for. Whether you believe in God, the universe, the law of attraction, or some other deity or way, there is an unflinching truth behind it all. What you think, what you devote your energy to, no matter if it's positive or negative, it will come true, eventually. I have shared several examples of this throughout the book, each of them having manifested themselves because I chose to believe. I can look back now and totally see in every event how my thoughts created the outcome I was looking for. This is huge. Think really carefully about this one—and then practice it, daily.

And the last one—

Believe in Miracles: My dearly departed mother taught me this one—so long ago. Miracles do happen. I am a believer.

Each of these life lessons relates to words I have written in this book. I could have referenced chapter and verse, but I choose to let you, dear reader, equate your own experiences to each one of them, come to your own conclusions, and then—put them all into practice. I know you will.

What would a sign-off be if I didn't address my beautiful grandchildren, Leena, Noelle, Lochlan, Mila, and of course, my newest granddaughter, Sloane Mara, born on January 7th, 2024.

It will do you a lifetime of good to adopt Papa's lessons as your own. They are my eternal gifts to each of you.

Love, peace, and Godspeed . . .

Dana
January 2024

THE END

Acknowledgements

After spending the last several years compiling this history, finally seeing it in print is one of the most cherished things I have ever accomplished. I am eternally grateful to so many bright and knowledgeable people who, over the course of my life, came together to provide their wisdom and influence. Without a doubt, my love of reading, the English language, history, and subsequently storytelling, would not exist without their mentorship.

I will always be grateful for my mother and father's love and patience with me during my formative years. Their quiet guidance and firm convictions were the roadmap I needed to see my world as I did. Mom's command of the English language was evident in everything she did or said. She was my first true mentor. Dad would tell you he only had Grade 8 education, but that did not stop him from being my true hero in life. He was a genius with his hands. There was nothing he could not do when he decided it needed doing. I know I got my creative genes from this man of many talents.

My life would not have been anywhere near as adventurous or interesting if not for my nine siblings. Lorraine, Karen, Greg, Joan, Valerie, Jerome, Rose, Martin, and Noelle, all played a major part in my upbringing and influenced many of the stories written within.

My two incredible children, Stephanie Rose-Anne and Shaun Patrick—I live for you. Even though we are miles apart, we still speak in some fashion weekly. The greatest gift in my life has been these two amazing humans.

There is no greater gift a child can give a parent than to bless them with grandchildren. Without Leena, Noelle, Lochlan, Mila, and Sloane, there would be no incentive to commit my life to print. I am a grateful Papa to these treasures and will forever be blessed for being in their lives. If I am again blessed with more of the same—even though your names are not etched on this page—know you will always have the space needed to fill my heart.

While writing my biography, I often thought of those who had the greatest impact on my character development during my lifetime. The list is exhaustive. So many of you have touched me in some way as to cause me to be the person I am today. Bob and Marg Barnes, Eric and Shirley Flesher, Judy Rintoul, Don Rose, Rod Phillips, Dr. Eric Taylor, Sam Watts, and my parish priests, Father Groom, Father Laforet, and Father Padelt—each of you provided this inquisitive mind with direction and assurance that even though the world was tough to navigate at times, I had a safe learning environment with each of you.

Besides my mother, my Grade 3 teacher, Mrs. Murphy, and my high school English teacher, Mrs. Stellmaker, were the two biggest influences on my creative writing journey. I will forever be grateful to each of them for guiding me through the difficulty and nuances of the English language.

I spent most of my adult life in a very rewarding thirty-five-year career with Sarnia Fire Rescue Service. To the many wonderful colleagues I worked alongside all those years, thank you for always having my back. Two deserve special mention. My first mentor, the first officer in charge of molding this snot-nosed rookie, was Acting Platoon Chief Owen Forsythe. He singlehandedly encouraged and guided me every step of my early years at Sarnia Fire. I am thankful for the energy and passion this fellow East Coaster had for the job, and his ability to pass those traits on to me.

My career would not have taken a monumental turn in my latter years if it hadn't been for Fire Chief Pat Cayen. His friendship and unwavering faith in me gave this reluctant Captain the opportunity for promotion to the rank of Deputy Fire Chief—at a time when I didn't even know I wanted it. Pat, I thank you for your mentorship into that administrative position, and our continued mutual respect and love for each other to this day.

What would a great read be if not for the hard work and dedication of the few people who had the energy to read, reread, and proof the manuscript you just enjoyed. My words would not have flowed off the paper as cleanly if not for my team. The first to get the manuscript were my dear friend Carole Legere, my brother Martin Pitts, and my best friend, Ian Proctor. They took the raw manuscript, and with enthusiasm for the project, combed through the pages, helping me over the first hurdles in the editing process. Thank you again for stepping up when I was in need of a friend. The bulk of the work, however, fell onto the shoulders of the incomparable storyteller from Newfoundland, my friend, Jeanene Walsh. When asked if she would simply read my manuscript and give me some feedback, she said, "Be careful what you wish for." She then proceeded to take the next year to dissect every chapter and verse, and in the end, helped me create a much stronger body of work, one I am extremely proud of. Jeanene, your passion and dedication to your craft, and your ability to translate that to someone else's work, is pure genius. God bless you.

Thank you to FriesenPress—and to each of you individually who worked tirelessly on *Perpetual Motion*. A special shout out to Leah Erenberg, my Publishing Specialist—your dedication shows no bounds.

I would also like to acknowledge several fellow photographers who have given me so much support, both personally and creatively. Their drive to be the best at what they do, and the willingness to share such skills to the world as a community, translates to all aspects of my daily routine. Without their cherished friendship, my retirement years would be pretty damn boring. Wayne Simpson, your quiet strength is what I wish to emulate in this world. Ian Proctor, your undying friendship and your fabulous author image for this book are more than I deserve. Joel Robison, the unrivalled gift of your talents, and your empathy to all mankind, makes every day more bearable. Many thanks to each of you for giving of yourselves and your incredible talents to all of us.

Lastly, a special shout-out to my friend and mentor, Dave Brosha. You taught me the world of photography, and so much more. Thank you for that, and most humbly, thank you for penning such beautiful words of introduction to this book. My storytelling passion exists because of you.

If not for the many fine humans in my world, this book would not exist.

Thank you

Dana

Printed in Canada